Digitizing Race

Electronic Mediations

Katherine Hayles, Mark Poster, and Samuel Weber, series editors

continued on page 240

Digitizing Race

Visual Cultures of the Internet

Lisa Nakamura

Electronic Mediations, Volume 23

University of Minnesota Press
Minneapolis
London

Published by the University of Minnesota Press
111 Third Avenue South, Suite 290
Minneapolis, MN 55401-2520
http://www.upress.umn.edu

Library of Congress Cataloging-in-Publication Data

Nakamura, Lisa.
    Digitizing race : visual cultures of the Internet / Lisa Nakamura.
        p.   cm. — (Electronic mediations ; v. 23)
    Includes bibliographical references and index.
    ISBN: 978-0-8166-4612-8 (hc : alk. paper)
    ISBN-10: 0-8166-4612-0 (hc : alk. paper)
    ISBN: 978-0-8166-4613-5 (pb : alk. paper)
    ISBN-10: 0-8166-4613-9 (pb : alk. paper)
    1. Internet. I. Title.
    TK5105.875.I57N35   2007
    004.67'8—dc22   2007028263

Printed in the United States of America on acid-free paper

The University of Minnesota is an equal-opportunity educator and employer.

12   11   10   09   08   10   9   8   7   6   5   4   3   2   1

Contents

Acknowledgments

I have many people to thank for help in writing this book.

Rena Johnson, Sarah Hamilton, Yu-Ran Kim, Adria Fernandez, David Raschke, Sarah Everson, and especially Lindsey Booth took care of my daughter while I wrote this. They deserve so much thanks for helping me to complete this writing project.

The communication arts department at the University of Wisconsin, Madison, in particular the media and cultural studies area faculty (Michael Curtin, Julie d'Acci, Shanti Kumar, Mary Beltran, and my faculty mentors Michele Hilmes and Susan Cook) deserve much thanks. Julie d'Acci, Kelley Conway, Christine Garlough, and Mary Beltran are righteous chicks and media scholars whom I miss every day. Laurie Beth Clark and Michael Peterson deserve my best thanks of all, for providing the social and intellectual space that validated this book and for building the discipline of visual culture studies at UW Madison. Jill Casid and Preeti Chopra, core faculty members in this research area, also deserve much thanks.

Tamar Brown, Mobina Hashmi, Madhavi Mallapragada, Derek Johnson, Aswin Punathembekar, and Germaine Hallegoua were excellent seminarians and discussants in classes, exams, and defenses, and I learned much from them. Megan Sapnar is the best, most creative, and most supportive teaching assistant and colleague ever.

Erik Gunneson, Kevin French, Matt Rockwell, and Paddy Rourke provided excellent media and technology support at UW Madison.

Leslie Bow, Victor Bascara, Grace Hong, Michael Peterson, Shilpa Davé—
my writing group at UW Madison—read and commented on almost every
word in this book.

Rhacel Parrenas, Ethylene Whitmire, Dana Maya, Cherene Sherrard,
Grace Hong, and Mary Beltran of the UW women of color coffee hour
group provided a congenial space to live, work, and be in the Midwest.

Christina Boufis, Vicky Olsen, Tina Olsen, Susie Wise, and Laura Mann of
the San Francisco Ladies' Reading Group supported this book, and my life.

Espen Aarseth, Matthew Byrnie, Maria Fernandez, Coco Fusco, Phil
Howard, Gus Hosein, Steve Jones, Tom Leeser, Jacques Lezra, Tara McPherson, LeiLani Nishime, David Silver, Jonathan Sterne, and Mark Williams
read and supported this work. They are my ideal reading community.

I am grateful to have been invited to give portions of this book as conference presentations at many venues. This book has been immeasurably
enriched by collaboration with audiences at Teknica Radika (University of
San Diego); the Visual Culture colloquium series at the University of Wisconsin, Madison; the Duke University Asian American Studies Speakers Series;
Harvard University's ColorLines Conference; the Center for the Study of
Communication and Culture at the University of Queensland, St. Lucia cam-
pus; the 2002 media and cultural studies colloquium series in the Communication Arts Department at Madison; the 2002 Visual Culture Colloquium
at Madison; the 2003 art and archaeology graduate symposium at Cornell
University; the 2002 American Studies Association conference; the University of Oslo; the communication department at the University of Illinois, Chicago; the Ford Foundation Symposium on Cyberculture Studies at
the University of Washington, Seattle; the Dartmouth College Cyber-
Disciplinarity Conference; the 2003 Society for Cinema and Media Studies
(in particular, thanks to copanelists Kim Hester-Williams and Tom Foster,
as well as Tom Gunning); and ICA 2004 in New Orleans.

I had excellent reviewers and readers when writing this book: Doug
Armato, director of the University of Minnesota Press, a truly compassion-
ate, insightful, and patient man; Kali Tal; Graham Murphy; Julian Bleecker;
excellent anonymous reviewers at the University of Minnesota Press; Electronic Mediations series editors Mark Poster and Katherine Hayles; Lynn
Spigel and Chris Berry; Stacy Gillis; Phil Howard; and Steve Jones. Copy
editors Nancy Sauro and Bill Henry did an excellent job making the manuscript presentable. Their work is greatly appreciated.

My biggest intellectual debt is as always to Donna Haraway, whose rigor, continued and increasing relevance, and intellectual passion and conscience continue to inspire.

Many thanks to Dyske Suematsu and Trek Kelly for generous permission to reproduce images from their Web sites.

Drs. Teri Woods, Marlin Kriss, Julie Holfez, Lisa Tetrault, and Davi Weisberger deserve thanks for being there when I needed them. Amelie Hastie is still mentoring and rescuing after all these years.

My sister, Judy Nakamura, and brother, David Nakamura, helped me with research; thank you for letting me keep *MultiFacial* on permanent loan and for turning me on to *The Ego Trip's Big Book of Racism*. My father, David Nakamura, and mother, Nancy Nakamura, supported me in all kinds of ways during a very difficult time.

My brilliant husband Christian Sandvig helped me to understand social studies and data analysis, found lost URLs for media duplication, resuscitated dead Web sites, gave career advice, taught me how to use presentation and bibliographic software, kept up high standards in image reproduction, and made me happy. And my beautiful daughter Laura's strong and sometimes snarky spirit is an inspiration to me throughout. I love you both the most!

Introduction

Digital Racial Formations and Networked Images of the Body

A constellation of events in relation to the Internet, digital visual represen-tations of bodies, and racial identity came into alignment in the mid-nineties. First, 1995 was a turning point in the history of the Internet. In 1995 Netscape Navigator, the first widely popular graphical Web browser, had its first public stock offering and initiated popular use of the Internet and, most importantly, heralded its transformation from a primarily textual form to an increasingly and irreversibly graphical one that remediates video and other pictorially representational practices such as photography, cartooning, and digital gam-ing. That process has only accelerated in recent years as the Internet con-verges with nonstatic media forms such as streaming video and television. Much of the earlier research on the Internet discussed it as a vehicle for writing. This primarily textual Internet no longer dominates and in some cases no longer exists: many MOOs, MUDs, and Listservs have gone offline. Much of the research written in the nineties centered on hypertext theory, or on discursive "virtual communities" formed by shared interests that assumed subcultural status for their users. The days in which *Wired* magazine and *Mondo 2000* set the agenda for an elite and largely male digerati have passed; Internet use has definitively crossed the line between hobby or niche prac-tice and has taken its place as part of everyday life. This new way of con-ceptualizing the Internet is reflected in scholarly titles such as *The Internet* in *Everyday Life*, edited by Barry Wellman and Caroline Haythornthwaite, which figures this transition forthrightly. Titles such as Sherry Turkle's influential *Life on the Screen: Identity in the Age of the Internet*, published in 1995, imply not only that the nature of identity has shifted definitively because of the Internet but that that age is still upon us; at this point it is safe to say that we live in a *post*-Internet age. The years since 1995 have seen a shift toward the massification of the Internet as a media and communicative form—earlier questions about its importance in the cultural life of American citizens and its possible relevance as a subject for academic curricula and study have been put to rest in a surprisingly short amount of time. As Steven Shaviro claims: "The Internet and the World Wide Web are no longer places for pioneers to explore and stake their claims; they have been absorbed into the texture of our everyday life. If Barlow's exceptionalism with regard to cyberspace seems dated, this is simply because virtual reality is no longer an exception; today, it is everywhere and everything."[1]

These key years in the development of the Internet as a mainstream practice occurred during a pivotal moment in American politics. The Clinton-Gore administration in the United States heralded an ongoing process dubbed "nineties neoliberalism" by the critical race theorists Michael Omi and Howard Winant. Though Omi and Winant omit any references to the Internet in the updated edition of their seminal work *Racial Formation in the United States: From the 1960s to the 1990s*, this can be accounted for partly by their book's publication date, 1994, a year on the cusp of the Internet's legitimation as a widespread cultural force. It was at this time that pundits debated whether the Internet might be the revolution in communication and human consciousness heralded by its boosters, or whether it might instead prove to be a fad that would, at best, produce an ephemeral technological subculture like that of ham and CB radio enthusiasts. Nonetheless Omi and Winant come to grips with a New Democratic political ideology that had widespread repercussions in the world of Internet policy and its forms of rhetoric. They identify 1992 as the year that marked the beginning of the "emerging hegemony of the racial project of neoliberalism," as Bill Clinton's victorious bid for the presidency was based on a New Democratic platform that "for the first time in almost half a century... made no specific pledge to address racial injustices and inequalities."[2] This universalizing discourse proved extremely popular, as it allowed avoidance of all discussion of race in favor of concerns that were perceived as more "universalist," such as funding to support causes dear to suburban dwellers. The hot button of race, invoked particularly by the Los Angeles riots in 1992, resulted in a "neoliberal project [that] avoids (as far as possible) framing issues or identities racially. . . . To speak of *race* is to enter a terrain where *racism* is hard to avoid. Better to address racism by ignoring race, at least politically." Omi and Winant go so far as to call this agenda a "limited but real adoption of Republican racial politics." This historical moment intersected with the inception of the Internet as a mass technology in the United States. It is in this moment that the neoliberal discourse of color blindness would become linked with the Clinton-Gore administration's identification of the Internet as a privileged aspect of the national political economy. While, as Jon Stratton notes, the 1994 Global Information Infrastructure proposed by Vice President Al Gore at an address in Kyoto depicted the construction of the "information superhighway" backbone as a "humanitarian mission," its core principles as proposed by the International Telecommunication Union were "Private investment. Market-driven competition. Flexible regulatory systems. Non-discriminatory access. And universal service."[3] This emphasis on privacy, competition, lack of regulation, and "nondiscrimination" not only opened the door for the transition from an early-nineties understanding of the Internet as a utopian space for identity play, community building, and gift economies to a more privatized, profit-driven model, one in which the Internet came to function as a "commodity-delivery system for vastly expanded media companies," as Stratton puts it, but it also echoed the language of color blindness or "genteel racism." Vijay Prashad identifies this gentler form of racism as the greatest problem of the twenty-first century—the "color-blind" replaces the color line as the prevailing practice that permits resources to be unevenly allocated based on racial identities.[4] In the philosopher Kelly Oliver's words, "Color blindness is a symptom of racism. Rather than see and acknowledge racial difference, we would rather not see at all. . . . Thus remaining blind to the effects of the sight of race in a racist culture is a symptom of racism."[5] The language of tolerance, or of disavowing racism by simply omitting all language referring to race, functioned to perpetuate digital inequality by both concrete and symbolic means. A visual culture of digital racial formation must take both of these aspects of relatedness to the Internet into account.

The discourse of color blindness is relatively new in American racial politics, and Robert Lee identifies it as a key feature of Cold War liberal ideology. In *Orientals*, he discusses the formation of Asian Americans as a "model minority" after World War II by tracing the ways that the liberal ideology worked to replace biological notions of race, which posited an unassimilable raced body, with the "ethnic" model of race, in which cultural differences replaced racial ones as the salient aspects of identity. Asian Americans were

posed as models of this type of "ethnic" political subject because their low
usage of welfare and political docility, along with their successes in the educational system, made them prime examples of racialized subjects who had
overcome the barrier of color, or race-as-biology, to become model consumers
of commodities as well as creators of economic value: as Lisa Lowe would
put it, they were positioned as both labor and capital. They were also seen
as ideal liberal subjects in that they were figured as not needing the intervention of the state, particularly in reference to education and technology.
"Ethnicity theory met the requirements of liberalism by articulating a doc-
trine of individual competition in a 'colorblind' society or, in Milton Gordon's view, a society in which the state played a neutral role."[6]

Thus the liberal ideology "articulated a vision of the colorblind society
but evaded a critique of the historical category of race altogether." In the
nineties, the Clinton-Gore New Democrats continued to avoid the "wedge
issue of race." The process of deracializing U.S. political discourse in reference to Internet access that began in 1992 only gained momentum with a
crucial change in administration. In 1997, Michael Powell, son of General
Colin Powell and a Clinton-appointed minority commissioner who was later
appointed head of the FCC by George W. Bush, went on record during his
first press conference as saying in reference to the digital divide: "I think
that there is a Mercedes divide. I'd like to have one." This rhetoric depicts
the Internet as anything but a part of a public national infrastructure, like
the "information superhighway" that Gore had posited some years earlier:
Powell's phrasing depicts Internet access as an elective luxury like an expensive foreign car. The Internet had gone from being figured as part of a system
of transportation and education to being a commodity to which American
citizens are certainly not entitled; indeed, in Powell's words, the Internet is
and ought to remain a privilege available to relatively few. Powell is also best
known for deregulating cable Internet services, facilitating media conglom-
eration, and "easing the burden on companies that make voice over Internet telephone technology."[7] When the early Internet's historians wish to
glorify its interactivity, gift economy, and decentralized structure, they tend
to trace its technological and cultural roots to the ethos of the sixties, with
its implicit connections to liberation movements such as the civil rights
movement, the women's movement, and the hippie movement.[8] However,
when we look to the post-2000 graphical popular Internet, this utopian story
of the Internet's beginnings in popular culture can be told with a different
spin, one that instead tracks its continuing discourse of color blindness in
terms of access, user experience, and content that is reflected in the scholar-

ship as well as in nineties neoliberalism's emphasis on "moderate redistribution and cultural universalism."[9] As Anna Everett writes in an eloquent formulation, "The revolution will not be digitized."

A year later, 1996 saw the birth of the interdiscipline of visual culture studies in the United States (also known as "visual studies" in Great Britain), a welcome development that was integrally related to the mainstreaming of the virtual image in aesthetic and popular cultural practice. While visual culture is less interested in communication per se than are other fields, its focus on the production, technology, and reception of the visual image seemed particularly appropriate in relation to the Internet, a form with an increasingly visual bent, a development trajectory measured in months rather than years, a diversifying population of users and producers, a serious and thoroughgoing intervention into American culture and media practices, and a correspondingly crying need for flexible, rigorous, and multimediated forms of analysis. The challenges that the Internet presents to critics and theorists of imaging practices in our contemporary period are serious and myriad: the hybrid form to end all hybrid forms, the Web in particular brings together graphics and textuality, both streaming and still images, synchronous and asynchronous communication, new forms of commerce, amateur and professional production, and community building. Visual culture studies, an interdisciplinary type of theoretical and critical practice with practitioners from all sorts of backgrounds who share a focus on the production of identity in visual forms, seemed particularly well suited to studying an equally hybrid form, the Internet.

My mode of critique in this book is to employ the paradigm of visual culture studies to focus on the ways that users of the Internet collaboratively produce digital images of the body—very particular things for very particular uses—in the context of racial and gender identity formation. While the policy rhetoric around Internet access may have been inflected strongly with the neoliberal discourse of color blindness and nondiscrimination—a paradigm in which failure to overtly discriminate on the basis of race, and the freedom to compete in the "open market" despite an uneven playing field in terms of class, education, and cultural orientation constitutes fairness—the Internet has continued to gain uses and users who unevenly visualize race and gender in online environments. It is crucial that scholarship assess these practices to evaluate the Internet as a popular environment for representations of identity. Visual culture provides a powerful methodology for parsing gender and racial and ethnic identity in these digital signifying practices that became so prominent at the turn of the century. In writing this book, I also wish to posit a corrective model to distressingly abstract critiques of virtual signifying practices by taking material culture into account in my analysis of online digital bodies. It is crucial to examine users in their embodied subject positions, modes of production, especially amateur and low-end do-it-yourself digital cultures, which are usually more readily adopted by newer and less traditionally skilled or trained users, and the paths by which images of the body are appropriated from other offline media. This is far preferable to an ahistorical type of critique that may prove of little use to future scholars, especially because Internet culture changes so rapidly as to render its particular histories irrecoverable in short order. Thus, just as visual culture studies is bringing its concerns regarding globalization, postcolonial imaging practices, identity formation, gender, and different modes of possessing the gaze to bear on new media, it is all the more important to relate this to the Internet's popular cultures.

In 1996, *October*, a well-respected journal among art historians, critical theorists, and cultural studies scholars, sent a questionnaire to a "range of art and architecture historians, film theorists, literary critics, and artists." This questionnaire has since been credited as a seminal text for creation of the interdiscipline of visual culture in the United States, which has been concerned from its inception with avoiding disciplinarity as a possible trap. The questionnaire's four parts delineated crises within, or challenges to, the academic practice of art history and the ways that the newly emerging interdiscipline of visual culture studies might address them. The questions identify a shift from a primarily historical approach to viewing and understanding the arts to an anthropological one, that is to say, one that emphasizes art as a means of culture creation. Most importantly, a few of the questions identify new media-influenced objects and forms of critique in particular as a driving force for this shift. Question three of the document starts out by claiming that some practitioners in the field had come to view the art object as a "disembodied *image*, re-created in the virtual spaces of sign-exchange and phantasmatic projection." Seeing the image as virtual and disembodied rather than material and concrete posed a radical challenge to art history as it had been practiced until 1996. Netscape Navigator, an apparatus created to disseminate virtual and disembodied images on a mass scale, had been widely distributed only a year before, in 1995. Several of the questionnaire's respondents, such as Carol Armstrong, Susan Buck-Morss, Emily Apter, and David Rodowick, all replied in ways that demonstrated their awareness that new media would change traditional art historical ways of both viewing and producing visual images. While some, like Rodowick, expressed excitement at the prospect of creating new methods for critique than had ever before existed in art history, others were clearly frustrated that "visual culture" might go the way of cultural studies, a discipline that Apter dubbed "the academic clearing house," and thus depart definitively from art history proper.[10]

Carol Armstrong's critique of the "increasingly cyberspace model of visual studies" and visual culture's "predilection for the disembodied image" is that it produces the concomitant devaluation of material objects in favor of virtual ones, thus reducing the particularity of physical objects to abstract "texts" that are theoretically equivalent to all other "texts" and foreclosing material culture techniques of scholarship that value "foundational differences between media, kinds of production, or modes of signs, or [the ways that] those differences might matter to either the producer or the consumer of a given object." While earlier art criticism viewed art objects as "particular *things* made for particular historical uses," she views new media-influenced forms of criticism such as visual culture studies as oriented around "exchanges circulating in some great, boundless, and often curiously ahistorical economy of images, subjects, and other representations." This "cyberspace model of visual studies," as Armstrong describes it, would foreclose considerations of the *history* of the digital image. This notion that visual images produced or exhibited via computer screens necessarily have no history, no mode of production, no distinct genres, and in short no material culture of their own is indeed frightening, for without these things, art history and indeed most materially based critique can have nothing to say about digital visual images. However, this notion, which was formed in reaction against the perceived deficiencies of what Susan Buck-Morss identifies as visual culture's main concerns—"the reproduction of the image, the society of the spectacle, envisioning the Other, scopic regimes, the simulacrum, the fetish, the (male) gaze, the machine eye"—assumes that a focus on them precludes considerations of history, materiality, and production. Armstrong emphasizes the importance of paying close attention to particular types of expressive production—"literary or pictorial, painterly, sculptural, photographic, filmic, or what have you"—and expresses fears that the "cyberspace model" might ignore these crucial differences. The reduction of all images to sets of binary code seems to pool them all into an undifferentiated soup of bits and bytes, understandably a nightmare for any type of scholarship.

Thus the formation of visual culture studies in the United States was driven from the beginning by a group of American art historians who realized that interdiscipline was needed to account for the digital and saw the digital as driving other concerns at large with visual media of all kinds, such as "disembodiment" and "cybertheory." This was a significant departure from art history as a critical practice before this time, which had been, as Apter says, concerned with things like "provenance, appraisal, appropriation, [and] authentication." This initial disavowal of the digital by art history is one of the raisons d'être for visual culture; in 1996, scholars trained in visual analysis as art historians conceded that the digital is far too important to be ignored, yet many concluded that its particular histories, intertextualities, modes of materiality and production, technology, and ephemerality either do not exist or do so in such a way that they exceed the range of critique of traditional art history or criticism.

However, as it turns out, many other scholars trained in art history spoke strongly for the relevance and influence of the digital on the field of visual analysis. David Rodowick, a more sanguine contributor to the *October* questionnaire, asserts that the effect of the digital has been to create an "audio-visual culture" in which objects no longer have a material existence as traditionally conceived: "The new media inspire visual studies through an implicit philosophical confrontation. Cinema and the electronic arts are the products of concepts that cannot be recognized by the system of aesthetics, nor should they be." Thus Rodowick posits a shift in the nature of representation itself, begun by cinema and hastened by new media, which renders many of Armstrong's concerns with materiality, history, and production either irrelevant or radically shifted in orientation. Rodowick, along with Nicholas Mirzoeff, Coco Fusco, Lisa Cartright, Marita Sturken, and Stuart Hall, helped to initiate the field of visual culture studies in the academy through their advocacy, which was multidisciplinary in nature (Mirzoeff is an art historian; Sturken and Cartright are media scholars; Fusco is a performance artist, public intellectual, and gender and postcolonial theorist; and Hall is best known as a cultural studies scholar). They have been very successful in this task in a relatively short time, so much so that in 2004 Jonathan Sterne could challenge the perceived hegemony of visual culture approaches to new media by asking "Is Digital Culture Visual Culture?"[11] Since 1996, the date of the questionnaire, visual culture has become a field that has won some disciplinary recognition: it has a well-respected journal, the *Journal of Visual Culture*, which publishes contributions from a wide range of scholars and departments, and schools or programs at several major universities. An examination of the early debates in *October* that initiated the use of visual culture studies in the academy shows us that despite its origins in art history and criticism, visual culture has always been preoccupied with the digital. Lisa Cartright writes that media convergence, an effect of industrial, technological, and economic forces working to deliver content via different devices and modes of viewing, has resulted in a definitive and permanent blurring between genres like film, television, virtual imaging, and writing, and that visual culture is the most appropriate modality of critique equipped to account for this melding of media that had all previously been separate. She asks: "How does the digital, an aspect of late 20th century visual culture which emerged roughly simultaneously with visual studies, figure into the field?"[12]

The first major book-length work that identifies itself with this orientation in an overt way is Andrew Darley's *Visual Digital Culture: Surface Play and Spectacle in New Media Genres*. His critique, which is informed primarily by film history and theory, seeks to understand new media objects through their relationships to earlier types of media simulations, such as rides, amusement parks, and early film forms such as the cinema of attractions. David Bolter and Richard Grusin take a similar tack in *Remediation*, as does Per Persson.[13] The most impressive of these is Lev Manovich, whose brilliant *Language of New Media* is justly credited with creating the first fully articulated theoretical work on the logic of digital media by linking the rigorous affinities between film form and history to the structure and function of computer software and its operations.

However, while Darley, Manovich, and Persson pay close attention to the connections between old and new media forms, reception, and exhibition, none of them writes specifically about the Internet as a platform for digital visual culture. In other words, their critiques neglect the added and determinative element of networking—the facilitation of image production and sharing via linked computers. They write about computer-generated images and simulations as if they were texts and technologies that address the viewer in particular ways, but assume only one viewer; and when interactivity is discussed, it is in reference to the interface itself, rather than with other users. In other words, these critics write about digital visuality as if it were a medium like radio, television, or film, rather than as a mode of communication, like the telephone or the telegraph. This tendency of visual culture to omit considerations of the realm of communication, focusing instead on representations and signification that occur between a visual medium and a viewer, can be traced to its roots in the critical humanities. To use an acronym borrowed from the language of communication scholars, visual-culture-oriented analyses of digital culture concern themselves with HCI (human-computer interaction) rather than CMC (computer-mediated communication). This accounts for the lack of scholarship on digital visual culture that deals with the Internet specifically, despite the Internet's penetration of every media space discussed in their works, such as gaming, film, and art.

New media studies in the United States consists of two branches: humanistic, consisting of literary and media theorists; and empirical or social scientific, consisting of communication, sociology, and information studies scholars. Visual culture studies has the potential to intervene powerfully in the study of new media if it is prepared to discuss the Internet and shared spaces of online communication and identity formation. In addition, communication studies has much to gain from visual culture approaches to the Internet, which would help to parse the complex visual fields that we inhabit and that condition our interactions when we use shared digital networks. However, the discipline of communication studies is no more prepared to analyze the forms of digital images, their meanings, deployments, modes of signification, and techniques for creating identity than art historians were to write about online bulletin board discussions or Internet chat sessions.[14] Discourse analysis of chat tends to elide considerations of the visual field aside from instrumental ones about interface ease of use. While some scholarship on racial and gender difference has been published in the fields of communication studies and digital culture, it tends to center more on reportages of online community building and niche groups creating Web sites for ethnic identity purposes, with little attention paid to a site's look, aesthetics, or specifically visual culture.[15] To sum up, studies of digital visual culture have yet to discuss networking, social spaces, or power relations in terms of race, ethnicity, and gender, but have done a superb job at parsing the history of digitality's address to the eye. Studies from a communications perspective have discussed the dynamics of online interaction quite exhaustively but fail to integrate their findings into readings of what the sites do visually.

This is a serious omission, because the Internet has become an integral part of the visual culture of everyday life for the majority of citizens of the United States. Social and technological practices like Instant Messenger (IM) engender new communicative practices and new visual forms, including but also exceeding the form of electronic writing, and their mutual constitution of these two layers of meaning making conditions the sorts of interactions that can be had on them. CMC occurs within a thriving, complex, ephemeral, and dynamic visual field with its own history, political economy, and engagement with racial and gender politics. Visual culture critique is concerned with tracing the genealogies of media use in new media, identifying specificities of genres or kinds of production and imaging practices, and producing readings of images that gesture toward identity formation in the matrix of power. This is a crucial omission, because young people use IM a great deal. Chapter 1 of this book discusses the visual field of IM and its evolution from text-only forms of chat toward a form that includes user-chosen and user-produced digital images of the body as an integral part of communication, signification, gendering, and racialization. Technological convergence is making all HCI spaces potential spaces for CMC, and vice versa. The continued existence of digital inequality necessitates considerations of identity and power relations—racial formation—along the axes of race, gender, and class. While Manovich's *Language of New Media* stresses the importance of interfaces as vectors of ideology, there has yet to be a visually oriented critique of new media networked communications on the most popular network to date—the Internet—which considers these issues of raced and gendered bodies, both virtual and real.

Visual culture studies was born in response to a crisis in art history: it is an insurgent art criticism that merges at some points with cultural studies but has different foundational texts that are oriented toward constructed social identities and a concern with the visual apparatus. Art history is a long-standing and canonized field in the letters and sciences and had become mired in debates regarding its adherence to traditional modes of analyzing visual objects that resulted in many scholars identifying against it. In theorizing digital racial formation theory, I am proposing a somewhat insurgent response to new media studies, a move that may seem premature considering its recent vintage. However, there are many advantages to correcting the omission in new media studies of gender, race, class, and communication as quickly as possible. Digital racial formation can trace the ways that race is formed online using visual images as part of the currency of communication and dialogue between users. Performing close readings of digital visual images on the Internet and their relation to identity, itself now an effect as well as a cause of digitality, produces a kind of critique that takes account of a visual practice that is quickly displacing television as a media-based activity in the United States.[16]

Several visual culture anthologies have had a hand in shaping the field and its engagement with new media. Three of the most influential—Nicholas Mirzoeff's *Introduction to Visual Culture* and *Visual Culture Reader* (first and second editions), Jessica Evans and Stuart Hall's *Visual Culture: The Reader*, and John Walker and Sarah Chaplin's *Visual Culture: An Introduction*—display varying degrees of engagement with digital culture. Armstrong's fears of ungrounded "cyber critiques" that might be generated by visual culture studies are laid to rest after perusing these volumes, because they take pains to ground themselves in the history of media imaging and technologies, especially Evans and Hall's. While all share a basis in theoretical writings by Althusser, Barthes, Benjamin, Foucault, and Debord, Evans and Hall's anthology, for example, includes a section on photography as an industry, social practice, and imaging convention that takes its material and historical base very seriously. However, this anthology lacks a section or any substantial articles on new media, in contrast to Mirzoeff's and Walker's, which both contain extensive cyberculture sections. Mirzoeff's, which is titled "Virtuality: Virtual Bodies, Virtual Spaces," departs from tradition in that it occurs in the middle of the volume rather than as a terminal section, as it does in Walker's. However, both anthologies make clear the centrality of new media studies to the study of visual culture: indeed, Mirzoeff defines visual culture as the study of "visual technologies . . . any form of apparatus designed either to be looked at or to enhance natural vision, from oil painting to television and the Internet."[17] This centering of the Internet as a visual medium on a par with television and painting is reflected in the second edition of the volume, which increases the number of articles on cyberculture by retitling the section "Global/Digital" and adding a terminal subsection under "The Gaze, the Body and Sexuality" titled "Technobodies/Technofeminism."

While the Mirzoeff and Hall anthologies have sections on racial difference and postcoloniality, indicating the serious degree to which visual culture studies concerns itself with questions of difference and the gaze, only Mirzoeff's combines this with an overt interest in the Internet. Like Armstrong, Hall critiques "cybertheory" along with the branch of literary and textually inflected cultural studies approaches from which it springs and proceeds to position visual culture studies as an antidote to cybertheory's excessive abstraction: he imagines visual culture studies, with its focus on the "specific rhetoric, genres, institutional contexts and uses of visual imagery," as a corrective to "getting lost in the more global identification of cultural trends and their epic narratives of transformations of consciousness in the rubric of postmodern culture."[18] Critics such as Baudrillard, Virilio, Stone, and Shaviro, who posit a wholesale shift in human consciousness as a result of "prosthetic" culture and its attendant discourse of "posthumanism," strike Hall as overly metaphysical and unsubstantiated. This problem was exacerbated by the tendency of much of this kind of scholarship to eschew close readings or detailed specific discussions of particular online practices. In addition, as Tom Foster eloquently details: "The debates about posthumanism demonstrate that there is no fixed meaning either to the understanding of embodiment as plastic and malleable—that is, open to critical intervention—

because socially constructed. In the context of postmodern technocultures and their disembodying tendencies, the materiality of embodiment, consciousness, and human nature can constitute a form of resistance, while at the same time the denaturalization of embodied identities, intended as a historicizing gesture, can change little or nothing" in relation to received hegemonies of gender and race.[19] Foster rightly stresses the "necessity of identifying the racial subtexts that inform the various transformations summed up under the heading of the 'posthuman,'" and his study of cyberpunk narratives works to identify that essential "materiality of embodiment" that underlies and underwrites the possibilities of technologically enabled body and identity transformations (xxiv). Online practices of visualizing bodies have, far from defining users as "posthuman," come to constitute part of the everyday material activity of information seeking and communicating that defines membership in the information society.

Visual culture's engagement with the substance of images holds particular promise and offers critical purchase precisely when brought to bear on digital objects, which do possess distinctive cultures of bodily representation, flow, privacy, identity, and circulation and have created unique communicative and institutional contexts. The purpose of this book is to turn the lens of visual culture studies as grounded in these contexts on a topic that has received little attention from scholars of new media: the popular Internet and its depictions of racialized and gendered bodies.

In earlier work I discussed the ways in which the Internet facilitates identity tourism, creating a new form of digital play and ideological work that helped define an empowered and central self against an exotic and distant Other.[20] However, because the Internet has become an everyday technology for many Americans since that time, the postmillennial Internet has little to gain by identifying itself as an exotic form of travel or access to novel experiences. The adoption of the Internet by many more women and users of color since the nineties has occasioned innumerable acts of technological appropriation, a term Ron Eglash deploys to describe what happens when users with "low social power" modify existing technologies such as the Internet. While in *Cybertypes* I focused on the constraints inherent in primarily textual interfaces that reified racial categories, in this work I locate the Internet as a privileged and extremely rich site for the creation and distribution of hegemonic and counterhegemonic visual images of racialized bodies. In the early nineties the popular Internet was still a nascent media practice, one in which default whiteness and maleness were the result of serious digital divides that resulted in primarily male and white users. Since then, the Internet's user populations have become much more diverse. This has resulted in an explosion of use that has all but eliminated the sense of a default normative identity in all parts of cyberspace; there are many Internet spaces, such as pregnancy bulletin boards, blogs, and livejournals that may now assume a default female user, and others such as petition and dating Web sites that assume users of color.

This book traces that ongoing history since the era of the text-only niche Internet, which was used by a much more exclusive and exclusionary group of users, to its present state as a mass-media form with a popular (but still far from racially balanced) American audience. My readings of digital representations of the body created for deployment on the postgraphical Internet since 2000 attempt to trace a cultural formation in motion, to read it back through its referents in old media and earlier racial formations, in order to write a digital history of the present. We are in a moment of continual and delicate negotiation between the positions of the object and the subject of digital visual culture. To repurpose Omi and Winant's influential theory of racial formation, in this book I wish to posit a theory of *digital racial formation*, which would parse the ways that digital modes of cultural production and reception are complicit with this ongoing process. While scholars from a variety of disciplines have produced valuable work that traces the history of digital racial formation, in many cases predating the Internet and the World Wide Web, and have revealed the ways in which people of color have had extensive involvements with digital technologies, such as music sampling, telecommunications in the context of forms of urban labor like taxi driving, and complex forms of indigenous weaving, these have not been especially visual, and their emphasis on recovering suppressed histories of racialized involvements with technologies has purposely de-emphasized the Internet as a way of reframing the digital divide discourse that persistently envisioned users of color as backward and uninvolved in technology.[21]

Studies of cyberculture have long noted, for good or ill, the identification of a mobile perspective in the context of networked communications with a privileged, omnipotent, yet fragmented gaze. Scholars and critics write about interactivity as if it were a drug, the drug of choice for cultural elites or "networked subjects." "'Choice,' 'presence,' 'movement,' 'possibility' are all terms which could describe the experiential modalities of websurfing," as Tara McPherson writes, and during the Web's relatively short commercial history, they have been integral to the rhetoric of the new networked economy that sells "choice and possibility" as a side effect of digital/analog media convergence.[22] This celebration of fulfilled user volition can be, as she points out, illusory, especially when linked to the enhanced ability to buy things with one click. However, the distinction here seems to be between different varieties of user experience, to paraphrase William James; while there are disagreements about just how empowering digital interactivity may be, there seems little argument about its offering its users more in the way of agency. Indeed, there is a way in which possessing the "volitional mobility" afforded by the Web, in particular, constitutes a particular kind of viewing subject, one who possesses and is empowered by "visual capital."[23] The Internet has created and defined digital visual capital, a commodity that we mark as desirable by conferring on it the status of a language unto itself; we speak now of digital literacy as well as visual and the ordinary sort of literacy. Manovich's *The Language of New Media* presumes that digital media constitute a new logic or typology of meaning. Though he is careful to interrogate this assumption, it is often claimed that interactivity is the salient aspect of this language that distinguishes it from others. Interactivity is envisioned as empowering—the act of clicking and moving one's perspective in the context of the dynamic screen is figured as creating interacting subjects. The myriad ways that interactivity creates a fragmented and decentered subject have been the target of recent critiques; Hall's and Armstrong's are fairly typical. In this book I wish to ground my discussion of the popular Internet and its involvement in the process of digital racial formation by examining the ways that visual capital is created, consumed, and circulated on the Internet. If we are starting to understand what the *subject* of interactivity might look like or be formed, what or who is its *object*?

For there must be one. Parks defines visual capitalism as "a system of social differentiation based on users'/viewers' *relative* access to technologies of global media."[24] This is welcome language in that it stresses *ongoing* processes of differentiation in access, rather than assuming that access to technologies like the Internet are binary; either you "have" or "have not." The problematic that I wish to delineate here has to do with parsing the multiple gradations and degrees of *access* to digital media, and the ways that these shadings are contingent on variables such as class position, race, nationality, and gender. However, it is important to avoid reifying these terms, and to instead stress that they are, in part, constituted by the subject's relation to these very technologies of global media. These questions of identity constitution via digital technologies have tended to get elided in critical discussions of Internet access, or when they are discussed, it is often as inconvenient stumbling blocks that stand in the way of the ultimate goal: universal access. What has yet to be explored are the ways that race and gender permit differential access to digital visual capital, as well as the distinctive means by which people of color and women create and in some sense redefine it. Women and people of color are both subjects and objects of interactivity; they participate in digital racial formation via acts of technological appropriation, yet are subjected to it as well.

In John Berger's influential visual culture primer *Ways of Seeing*, the subject is defined as that which views, and the object as that which submits or is subjected to the gaze: he dubs these two positions that of the "surveyor" and the "surveyed."[25] He is most famously concerned with the gendering operations of the gaze in portraiture and pornography, but his success in creating a critical framework and methodology has much to do with his parsing of power relations in the field of the visual. Digital visual culture presents a challenge to this formulation: while the difference between the viewer and the viewed, the producer/artist and the subject/model, was clear in more traditional art (while reading Berger, it is always clear who he means by "artist," "spectator/owner," and "object" of representation), it is not so clear when discussing networked digital media. New media are produced and consumed differently. In addition, we often get the double layer of performance that comes with the viewer's act of clicking.

So rather than focusing on the idea that women and minorities need to get online, we might ask: How do they use their digital visual capital? In what ways are their gendered and racialized bodies a form of this new type of capital? What sort of laws does this currency operate under? It doesn't change everything, but what does it change? This brings us back to the privileging of interactivity and its traditional linkage with the creation of a newly empowered subject.

According to Lev Manovich's provocative "myth of interactivity," "interactive media ask us to identify with someone else's mental structure." Rather than allowing the user to have an open-ended, seemingly limitless and boundless experience of reading, Manovich stresses the rigidity of hyperlinking as a mode of experiencing information: when "interactive media asks us to click on a highlighted sentence to go to another sentence . . . we are asked to follow pre-programmed, objectively existing associations."[26] According to this interpretation, we are ideologically interpellated into the "new media designer's mental trajectory," just as in Hollywood film we are asked to "lust after and try to emulate the body of the movie star." Manovich's formulation allows us to trace the process of identification that occurs with new media use: he compares it to the viewer's process of identification with the star's body in the realm of film. And just as we have a well-developed theory of cultural capital and viewer identification involving stars, so too must we now view the interface as an object that compels particular sorts of identifications, investments, ideological seductions, and conscious as well as unconscious exercises of power.[27] In addition, just as star bodies provoke the viewer's gaze and must necessarily function as part of what Omi and Winant call a "racial project," so too do new media objects. Interactivity is indeed a myth and will remain so until and unless its participation in the gendered and racialized construction and distribution of embodied perspectives, or particular "mental trajectories" (a far from neutral term), is examined in light of cultural formation theory. New media designers are not yet movie stars, but as interfaces become ubiquitous means of accessing media of all kinds, their work enters the popular sphere and the public culture, and hence a corresponding interest in their modes of instantiating identity—their unavoidable implication in creating "mental trajectories" that we must all follow—must emerge from cultural and media theory. Instead the interface itself becomes a star, and just like other sorts of stars, it works to compel racialized identifications; interfaces are prime loci for digital racial formation.

Part of the attraction of racial formation theory as espoused by Omi and Winant originally, and subsequently by the cultural theorists Lisa Lowe, Paul Gilroy, and George Lipsitz, is its impressive flexibility: it is defined as "the sociohistorical process by which racial categories are created, inhabited, transformed, and destroyed . . . a process of historically situated projects in which human bodies and social structures are represented and organized."[28] The Internet certainly represents and organizes human bodies and social structures in digital games, Web sites, CMC applications such as IM (Instant Messenger) and IRC (Internet Relay Chat) that involve a visual component, as well as in myriad interfaces. The interface serves to organize raced and gendered bodies in categories, boxes, and links that mimic both the mental structure of a normative consciousness and set of associations (often white, often male) and the logic of digital capitalism: to click on a box or link is to acquire it, to choose it, to replace one set of images with another in a friction-free transaction that seems to cost nothing yet generates capital in the form of digitally racialized images and performances. "Racial projects," defined by Omi and Winant as "simultaneously an interpretation, representation, or explanation of racial dynamics, and an effort to reorganize and redistribute resources along particular racial lines," produce race and initiate changes in power relations (125). When users create or choose avatars on the Internet, they are choosing to visually signify online in ways that must result in a new organization and distribution of visual cultural capital.

Racial formation theory has not often been used in reference to new media, however, partly because the frame of reference is so different (and because the early utopian bent to Internet criticism meant that discussions of difference, especially if viewed as "divisive," were avoided). The difference between old and new media lies in the new media's interactivity, as mentioned before, but is also related to the blurred line between producers and consumers. Though utopian claims regarding the Internet's ability to abolish the position of the passive viewer, making everyone a potential publisher or creator of media, are less valid than previously thought (early predictions about everyone's eventually having or even wanting a personal home page have fallen far short of reality, though the popularity of blogs, vlogs, and social networks such as Facebook and MySpace are coming closer to this ideal), it is possible now, since the massification of the Internet in the United States, which is my frame of reference, to view media on the Internet as the product of non–cultural elites.

Since the turn of the century, the continuum of Internet access in the United States has gotten wider and broader—it is best compared to Rich's lesbian continuum and Parks's formulation of varying degrees of visual capital in the sense that everyone has *some* position in relation to it. Rather than a "digital divide" that definitively separates information haves from have-nots, the Internet has occasioned a wide range of access to digital visual capital, conditioned by factors such as skill and experience in using basic Internet functions such as "search" in addition to less-nuanced questions such as whether or not one possesses access at all.[29] While earlier racial formation theory assumed that viewers were subject to media depictions or racial projects that contributed to racialization, and that these projects were ongoing and differential but nonetheless worked in a more or less one-way fashion, new media can look to an increasingly vital digital cultural margin or counterculture for resistance.

AIM buddies, pregnant avatars, and other user-created avatars allow users to participate in racial formation in direct and personal ways and to transmit these to large, potentially global audiences of users. Intersectional critical methods are vital here; digital visual culture critique needs to read both race and gender as part of mutually constitutive formations. For example, in the case of sports gaming, most celebrity avatars are men because of the dominance of men in the commercial sports industry, and many of them are black for the same reason. Yet black men are underrepresented as game designers, and it would be wrongheaded to mistake the plurality of racialized digital bodies in blockbuster games such as Electronic Arts' *Madden Football* to indicate any kind of digital equality in terms of race or gender.

What does an object of interactivity look like? In Jennifer Lopez's music video "If You Had My Love" (1999) the singer portrays herself as the object, not the subject, of the volitional mobility afforded the Web user. Shots of Lopez tracked by surveillance cameras alternate with her image as represented in a Web site: she shares the stage and gaze with the new media design inter-faces in which she is embedded in an extremely overt way. This puts a new spin on the traditional female position as object of the gaze. While the video and its implied Web interface allow the user multiple points of entry into her digital image—streaming, still, live, buffered—Lopez herself is never rep-resented as the user or viewer of this communicative technology, only as the viewed. In this way, the video gestures toward the traditional formulation of the gaze as described by John Berger in relation to traditional portraiture and the tradition of painting and visual representation generally. In other words, Lopez presents herself in this video as an *object of interactivity*, despite her position as the star and the knowing object of the interactive gaze. Exam-ining this video enables a double viewing of interactivity and the star's body, the way that the object of desire (the star) can work with the subject of interactivity—figured misleadingly in this video as the user. In fact, it is really the invisible interface designer whose work conditions the limits and possibilities of interactivity in this case; if we view the media complex that is J. Lo as herself a carefully constructed "racial project," we can see the ways that the range of clickable options and categories available to the pre-sumptive user in this video conditions the sorts of understandings of her raciality that are articulated to us. In this video we are asked to identify not just with the Web designer's way of thinking but with the viewer's way of clicking as well. The conditions of watching this video require us to see from the computer user's perspective; we cannot but shoulder-surf, since the setup only allows us to view the star's body by watching her movements on a Web site, a Web site that we do not control or click through. This is also a decidedly gendered gaze, since we are often put in a position in which we must watch a male watcher watching; we must witness his interactivity as our means to visualize the body of the woman.

In this video we have access to the star's body *through* the viewer's mind. We see her as he sees her, though interface use. This split represents a para-digmatic dichotomy in gender theory: the body is that of the Latina, the woman of color, and the mind is that of a white man. As Donna Haraway writes in her famous "Manifesto for Cyborgs," an essay that Csordas describes as "an anxious celebration of our contemporary transformation into cyborgs,"[30] the "offshore woman" or the woman of color in the integrated circuit of information technology production is framed as an object rather than a subject of interactivity. There is much at stake, however, in observing the ways that members of the Fourth World—women of color, members of linguistic and ethnic minority cultures, the global underclass—negotiate their identities as digital objects and in incremental ways move them toward digital subjecthood. The reason for this is that, as Chela Sandoval stresses quite strongly in *Methodology of the Oppressed*, a work that takes Haraway's notion of the cyborg subject and develops it into a strategy for acquiring power for women of color in the context of a technologized world, "the methodology of the oppressed can now be recognized as the mode of being best suited to life under neocolonizing postmodern and highly technologized conditions in the first world; for to enter a world where any activity is possible in order to ensure survival is to enter a cyberspace of being."[31] In other words, it is precisely because the world inhabited by wired, technologized, privileged subjects requires constantly shifting and contingent work skills, educational preparation, and cultural expertise that the "technologies developed by subjugated populations to negotiate this realm of shifting meanings" can prove indispensable. The Fourth World has always been "just-in-time," having lacked the luxury of guarantees and assurances of care from the state. Indeed, Jennifer Lopez's deployment of shifting visions of ethnicity brokered through Web and television interfaces represents this sort of impressively flexible range of movement through identity positions, one that seeks its niche through the volitional mobility of the interacting viewer.

This music video, Jennifer Lopez's first, was number one for nine weeks in 1999. Lopez's DVD biography on "Feelin' So Good" informs us that "If You Had My Love" was her first number one single, as well as her first video, and that it was certified platinum. The hit topped the Hot 100 for five weeks in 1999, and the single sold 1.2 million copies outside the United States as of 2000. Importantly, the biography describes her as a "multimedia success." In keeping with this notion, it was also digital from the ground up, not just in terms of its production, though much is made of its links with the Web in the "Banned from the Ranch" Web site. (Banned from the Ranch is the name of the production company that programmed the fictional Web interface deployed in the film.) Its subject matter, the way that it compartmentalizes physical space, virtual space, music genre niches, and modes of interaction, is in keeping with the logic of new media as explained in

Manovich's seminal work on the topic: it combines modularity and auto-maticity with the added benefit of simulated liveness. In addition, Jennifer Lopez's rise as star coincides with the Internet's rise as a mainstream visual culture with its own interventions into traditional media cultures. In 1999 we can witness the shift occurring from one mode of influence, old media to new, to another, new media to old.

Like the *Matrix* films, the "If You Had My Love" video visually represents active navigation through data. Clicking on links enables the implied viewer to loop through time: by backtracking, the viewer can instantly restart at the beginning of the video or rewind to watch a favorite bit repeatedly. How-ever, unlike these films and other science fiction films, the video presumes multichanneled viewing in the context of everyday life rather than in an overtly fictional and phantasmatic future. The video opens with a scene of a man sitting at his computer desk in a darkened room of his apartment and typing the words "Jennifer Lopez" into a search field in a Web browser. Her Web site pops up on his screen, and she starts singing and dancing as he watches, alternately typing on the keyboard, which he holds on his lap as he leans back and strokes his own neck and face in an overtly cybersexual gesture. (Early writing on virtual identity by Sandy Stone posited that phone sex was the best metaphor for Internet-enabled telepresence; Lopez's video acknowledges Stone's assertion with a nod to the Internet's most technolog-ically sophisticated, long-standing, and profitable usage: distributing visual images of pornography.)[32] The rest of the video consists of scenes of Jennifer Lopez viewed through her as-yet-fictional Web site as we witness people in a wide selection of networked computing environments watching her: we see a young girl in her bedroom with her computer, a pair of mechanics watching a wall-mounted television with an Internet connection, a rank of call center workers with headphones and computers, and two young Latina women using a laptop in their kitchen. These scenes clearly reference tele-vision/Internet convergence as they depict both public and private televisual screens and solitary and shared instances of screen usage.

But more importantly this is one of the most intimate scenes of com-puter interface usage I can remember seeing; intimate because it is about desire mediated through the computer, men masturbating as they surf the Web to look at sexy images of celebrity female bodies.[33] It is also intimate because it is *close*; as we watch the man keyboarding and mousing, we see Lopez's image respond interactively to it; as he manipulates his joystick, we see a large black ceiling-mounted surveillance camera follow her into one of her "rooms," and computer windows pop up, close, promote, demote, and

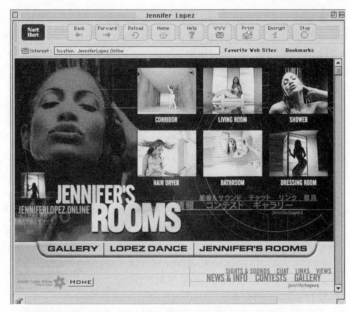

Figure I.1. A fictional graphical interface from "If You Had My Love."

Figure I.2. Musical genres as menu choices in the Netbot graphical interface from "If You Had My Love."

Figure I.3. Male spectatorial desire and Internet use in "If You Had My Love."

layer in response to his typing and clicking. The page on the site titled "Jennifer's Rooms" lists buttons and icons for "Corridor, Living Room, Shower, Hair Dryer, Bathroom, and Dressing Room," thus spatializing the Web site in terms that evoke the star's private home and the space of intimacy. The surveillance cameras and arrangement of the interface as clickable "rooms" enforce webbed voyeurism, evoking the visual culture of liveness through Webcams, and a particular sort of eroticized, privileged view of the star. (Of course, videos have always purported to give a privileged look at a star. The fiction of volitional viewing enacted in this video is a fantasy of networking in the context of interactivity.) Indeed, the video visualizes the interface user's volitional mobility via the cursor, which functions as his proxy in this scene, as it does when we use the World Wide Web generally. We are seeing as he sees: it is an act of witnessing voyeurism. But more importantly we are seeing the mechanics by which he manipulates the view of Lopez as the video's audience watches; the apparatus of the keyboard, mouse, and joystick is foregrounded and in constant use.

The Jennifer Lopez online page features navigation links at the bottom for "Gallery, Lopez Dance, and Jennifer's Rooms." The video as a whole operates as a record of a navigational session within multiple nested interface frames, one of which is called "Internet TV," overtly referencing a greatly anticipated technological convergence that still has yet to arrive and was certainly far from a reality in 1999. The other menus we see at the bottom of the initial interface's splash screen are "sights and sounds, chat, links, views, news & info, contests, gallery," thus displaying the conventional organization and categorization of media types common to conventional Web sites rather than television or video.

This video's mode of production differs quite a bit from those that came before it (but helped to determine those that came after), and this difference is the basis for a fascinating press release by Banned by the Ranch, the production company hired to create the computer interfaces featured in the video. Why did the video's producers feel the need to commission a fictional interface and browser in their attempt to invoke the World Wide Web? The producers address this question quite explicitly on their Web site, explaining that Web-savvy audiences in the nineties require "realistic looking interfaces" to create *televisual* verisimilitude; in other words, in order for the virtual to look realistic, interfaces have to look like they could be "real" as well, and in this case the "real"—Internet Explorer, Netscape, or AOL's proprietary browsers, which were familiar to Internet users at that time—just wouldn't do. This creation of a brand-new interface might also be motivated by some caution regarding copyright law—Apple's "look and feel" lawsuit against Windows had recently brought the notion of the interface as private property into the public eye. In addition, there may also have been concerns regarding conflicts of interest. For example, the films *You've Got Mail* (1998) and *Little Black Book* (2004) feature America Online and Palm personal assistant interfaces prominently; in the first case, corporate partnerships or "synergy" between media companies made this possible, and in the second, conflicting industry interests almost scuttled the project. Problems arose when executives at Sony Pictures Entertainment, one of the companies that was to distribute the film *Little Black Book*, realized that Sony manufactured its own PDA device, the Clié, which competed for market share with Palm. Luckily, the film was greenlighted *after* the Clié went out of production, solving Sony's conflict of interest problem regarding interface use. Giving screen time in a mass-market film to a particular interface has always been seen as an exceedingly valuable form of marketing or product placement, particularly because the logic of the films usually requires that viewers pay close attention to the devices to follow important plot points. The device itself is less the point than is the foregrounding of a particular type of screen within a screen, an interface.

As mentioned before, the interface is itself a star of Lopez's video and is coming to take on starring roles in other types of non-desktop-based digital media, like films, videos, and console games. Creating a fictional interface solves potential problems with industry conflicts as well as contributing toward the sense of an alternative networked world accessible through the desktop computer, giving yet one more means of control to media producers. The deployment and visualization of "fictional software" created for Lopez's video, which was dubbed "NetBot" by Banned from the Ranch and originally developed for the graphics on the hit youth film *American Pie*, envisions software interfaces as key aspects of a televisual image's believability or realness. It is interesting to note that the production of the video preceded that of the star's "real" Web site: Banned by the Ranch's "intention was to make sure the videos' web site would match the real-life Jennifer Lopez web site . . . a site that was yet to be developed" in 1999, a time in which it was clear that the music video was a crucial medium for musicians finding a global market, while the Internet was not. The Lopez site was ultimately designed by Kioken, a high-flying and innovative Web site design business that went bankrupt in 2001.

The "Lopez Dance" screen offers several menu choices: "Jazz, Latin Soul, and House" (we don't see "Jazz" enacted in the diegetic space of the embedded performance, perhaps because this is one of the few popular genres that Lopez is not associated with in any way; it represents a purely speculative and fictional future, one that has a racialized authenticity all its own). Articulating these musical genres highlights the star's diversity, ironic in the case of "If You Had My Love," which, like most of Lopez's other songs, borrows liberally from these genres but doesn't itself recognizably belong to any genre at all except pop, and works as a way to sell and brand otherwise unidentifiable music, very important when half of all music that is listened to is not sold to a listener but rather "shared" among listeners, or stolen. The "Latin Soul" sequence, launched when the male viewer clicks on the link that activates it, depicts Lopez in a short, tight white dress as she performs flamenco-inspired arm gestures and salsa-type moves to techno-salsa music. This musical interlude functions like a cut scene in a video game such as *Grand Theft Auto: Vice City* and *GTA: San Andreas* in that it fragments the narrative and in this case the musical flow. The logic of abrupt movement from one genre of music or media to another reflects the fragmented attention of the viewer, tempted as he is by the array of choices presented by the interface. We are switched from one to another at his pleasure. The pleasure of the interface lies partly in its power to control movement between genres and partly in the way that it introduces musical genres that audiences may not have known even existed. J. Lo's readiness to fill different musical, national, and ethnic niches reflects the logic of the video and of the interface and its audiences; as she shifts from cornrowed hip-hop girl with baggy pants and tight shirts to high-heeled Latina diva to generic pop star with straightened hair and yoga pants, we see the movement as well between identities that characterizes her construction in this video as a digital media object of interactivity. She becomes an object of volitional ethnicity as she is constructed as an object of the user's volitional mobility.

Most importantly, this video walks the viewer through a process of digital racial formation; in a cut scene that functions as the transition to the world "inside" the interface that we see when it is clicked, shards and bits of gray confetti take flight past the viewer's perspective to represent the way data is supposed to look. As this "white noise" resolves itself into a signal, a coherent visual image coalesces from these pieces of data into images of Jennifer Lopez dancing in the nationalized and racialized genre that the user has chosen, and we can see the formation of the colored and gendered body from undifferentiated pixels, at the pleasure of the viewer, and also the formation of the bodies of color, race, language, and nation as playing particular roles, performing particular work, in the context of new media. Like J. Lo, Filipino and Russian Internet "brides" are also clickable, women who can be randomly accessed via the Web. Their performances online are certainly different in kind and quality from that of the site's designer or user: their job is to perform a kind of racialized submission, to the viewer's interactive gaze and to the geopolitics that compel their digitized visual identity performance. In the case of the video, the cursor functions as a visual proxy that in this case stands in for the viewer; it is itself a kind of avatar and in recent times a televisual stylistic convention familiar to us in all sorts of contexts, used in PowerPoint presentations as well as in children's programming, such as *Dora the Explorer*'s use of the computer cursor superimposed on the screen as a point of identification for children. Though Dora's viewers can't control the cursor, they can witness the cursor's movements and implied user control, thus enforcing visual if not functional media convergence between the computer and the television. Sarah Banet Weiser's work on *Dora* emphasizes the ways in which race is marketed as a "cool" way to help children learn language skills, one that hails Latino and other viewers of color in ambivalent, largely apolitical, and "postracial" ways.[34] *Dora the Explorer* depicts the Latina main character as an avatar who guides the child-viewer through the logic of the learning-game interface but does not stand in for the viewer herself: the Latina Dora is an object rather than a subject of interactivity, just as Nickelodeon posits the show's audience as primarily white, middle-class, and able to afford cable, rather than as viewers who "look like" Dora herself.

The visual culture of the female object (rather than subject) of interactivity has yet to be written. The varied audiences depicted watching Jennifer Lopez via streaming video online represent varied subject and object positions and points of gender and ethnic identification: black men and white men from both the working class and the growing ranks of information workers at a call center and from the home office click on her as an object of desire; young girls in suburbia and young Latina women in domestic spaces click on her as an object of identification in a gesture of interactivity that may have something to do with staking out a position as a future subject of interactivity. Surveillance cameras, a technology whose function is to police the division between subject/object relations, are depicted here in the context of the Internet as a means to give instant and interactive access to the star to all groups. The early promise of the Internet to make every user a potential "star" has since contracted to offer seemingly deeper or more intimate user access to stars from "old" media instead. The history of the Web-cammed image, traced by Steven Shaviro from its origins in the Trojan Room Coffee Machine in the computer laboratory at Cambridge University, which went online in 1991, to Jennifer Ringley's Jennicam, which went online in 1996 (and has since gone offline), reveals a progression from an original fascination with the apparatus of webbed vision itself—the "liveness" of the Webcammed image, even in relation to an object as intrinsically unexciting as a pot of coffee—to a particular investment in the naked female body as an object of vision via the Internet.[35]

The thesis of this video is the thesis that describes our media landscape since 1999: convergence has created a condition within which stardom itself has become "multimedia." It is nothing new for stars to excel in multiple media: actors sing, dancers act, singers dance, and many stars have marketed perfumes, clothing, and other commodities successfully. These provide multiple modes of identification with stars. However, the "If You Had My Love" video sells multiple points of entry to the star, multiple ways of seeing and surveilling that are framed as exactly that, exploiting the interface as a visual culture that purveys an ideal and mutable female body of color, perpetually and restlessly shifting "just in time" to meet fickle audience preferences. In this book, I trace how the mediation of digital user and object identity as citizens, women, and commodities on the Internet is regulated and conditioned by the types of interfaces used to classify, frame, and link them.

To argue for the necessary intervention of visual culture studies into Internet studies, one might ask: how does the Internet's visual culture create, withhold, foreclose, distribute, deny, and modulate the creation of visual and digital capital? Visual media are as often as not viewed through the lens (and logic) of the computer-driven interface, making ways of negotiating, navigating, and situating oneself via its landscape of chapter titles, hyperlinks, and menus a necessary aspect of media use. DVDs, satellite and cable television and radio, and DVRs like TiVo and Replay all compel menu trees of choices, choices that, when made, foreclose other choices. The narrowing and piecing-up of the formerly continuous image stream of a film into named and discrete chapters, as in the case of many commercial cinematic DVDs, and the separation of songs into genres like "Electronica," "Boombox," and "R and B/Urban," as in the case of Sirius satellite radio playlists, breaks up what had been a more flow-oriented media experience into digitized separate "streams" (or "channels," as Sirius labels them). This packetizing of media into different categories follows ethnic, linguistic, national, and racialized lines. The "If You Had My Love" video mirrors this logic of the interface and its policing of categories by chopping up and streaming the star's image-body into identifiable ethnic and racialized modes—black, white, and brown.

Jennifer Lopez has been dubbed a multimedia star partly because she appears in several electronic media, but she also has established herself in the world of offline, nonephemeral commodities such as fashion and toiletries. This convergence of separate spheres—"real" versus virtual, abstract versus concrete commodities—mirrors the convergence of media displayed in her video, and also her own converging of differing positions vis-à-vis her own ethnic identity. Her real-life transformation from an "ethnic star," defined primarily by her appearances in "ethnic films" such as Selena and Mi Familia in which her racialized Latina body serves to authenticate the "realness" of the Latino mise-en-scène, to a "global" or unracialized star, as in Out of Sight and The Wedding Planner, is mirrored in the video's modes of identity management via the interface.[36] The interface lets you "have" Jennifer Lopez in a variety of ethnic and racialized modes by clicking on one of many links.[37] It addresses the audience by figuring her kinetic body as plastic, part of a racial project of volitional racialization through interface usage.

The "If You Had My Love" video compels a different sort of media analysis than had been necessary before the massification of networked, interfaced visual communications like the Internet. Earlier modes of reading television and film do not suffice because of the prominence of the interface as more than just a framing device; interfaces function as a viewing apparatus, and in many cases they create the conditions for viewing. Rigorous readings of Internet interfaces in and outside their convergences with photography, film, television, and interfaces from other visual genres such as stand-alone digital games are crucial for understanding how modern race and gender are constructed as categories and (sometimes, sometimes not) choices. The increasingly visual nature of the graphical Internet after 1995 calls for a displacement in our modes of critique from an earlier scholarly focus on textuality to those that examine the Internet's visual culture in a broader way. The extensive nineties literature that celebrated digital textuality's postmodern open-endedness and constructedness by emphasizing the inter-activity offered the user, who became an active user rather than a passive consumer, tended to neglect the specifically visual in favor of developing text-based arguments.[38]

One of my intentions for this book is to broaden the field of Internet studies not only by looking at its visual as well as its textual culture but also by looking at things that are not "on" it—like the Jennifer Lopez video and other media forms that may not be created for distribution via the Internet but make reference to it and share its logic of interfaced interactivity. At any rate, this distinction is eroding at a rapid pace: the Internet's ability to transcode all forms of media means that we would do well to avoid making claims about what is "on" it—while "If You Had My Love" was originally produced and screened on MTV and other music video television stations, it exists as well in digital interactive forms like Lopez's 2000 DVD "Feelin' So Good," as a streaming video file on MTV.com and muchmusic.com, and as a QuickTime movie file that is easily downloaded using free file-sharing software like Kazaa, Acquisition, or Morpheus.

Interfaces inform all media—videos, television, literature—and as this happens we are witnessing the creation of new power differentials in visual capital. Internet scholars define themselves partially as people who are inter-ested in the history and use of digital interfaces in the context of computers, but videos like "If You Had My Love" are hybrid in several ways: for one, they reference a tradition of racialized, gendered relations of looking and seeing that Internet scholars are not accustomed to thinking about outside the context of online communities of color and Web sites about gender. This type of hybrid media object requires a convergent mode of criticism and interpretation—a visual culture of the Internet.

Interfaces are an indispensable part of the media experience of both online and offline visual cultures. They are also inextricably tied to the contemporary racial project of producing volitional racial mobility in the service of new forms of capitalism. Noting their deployment in old mass-media forms like film and television redresses the focus on the remediation of old media forms by new ones that limits Bolter and Grusin's *Remediation*, a standard textbook on new media theory. Bolter and Grusin's method of understanding new media emphasizes tracing its roots in old media to tease out the ways that the new remediates the old. I argue for re-remediation, reading the digital in the nondigital, a method that will become increasingly necessary as media convergence challenges that distinction.

I believe that it is fruitful, if we are looking for examples of the creation of subversive and resistant forms of new media visual capital, to look at smaller-scale, more intimate uses of digital signification by audiences that may be less ambitious or less confident with computer production technology. In chapter 1, I examine the ways that AIM buddies signify ethnic, national, gender, and linguistic identity in the context of Internet youth culture. These personal icons of identity are easily obtained and customized; just a few pixels big, in many cases, they are part of the visual culture of Instant Messenger, an extremely commonly used CMC (computer-mediated communications) technology, and they signify identity in ways that are oral and enacted. This is a necessary intervention because IM is mistakenly perceived as not *having* a visual culture; it seems to be one of the last text-based communication modes on the Internet (people even call the act of sending SMS [short message service] notes on their cell phones "texting.") However, AIM buddies provide a visual frame for what seems to be a purely oral or textual mode. AIM buddies are visual signifying systems that are individually chosen by users and are maximized for appropriation; buddy-sharing sites like buddyicon.info allow amateurs to instantly recirculate their creations among the Internet public at large. AIM buddy creation is a form of vernacular engineering, to use Eglash's term: it is "the reinvention of products and rethinking of knowledge systems, often in ways that embody critique, resistance, and outright revolt."[39] Racialized and gendered AIM buddies often perform complex critiques of the notion of a raceless or neuter digital body. In addition, examining them shows us what is lost when popular Internet cultures are ignored in favor of "artistic" ones that most people will never see. The formation of digital taste cultures that are low-resolution, often full of bathroom humor, and influenced by youth-oriented and transnational visual styles like anime ought to be traced as it develops in its native mode: the Internet. AIM buddies also function as a form of resistance to, and protest against, slick commercial and gaming avatars from licensed media franchises that may not be customizable; the case could easily be made for analyzing AIM buddies as folk art, but my focus instead will be on the ways that they function as sophisticated strategies for users to manage identities that may be multifarious and ambiguous.

In chapter 2, I examine the visual culture of online racial profiling in a Web site called www.alllooksame.com. This site gives users a quiz that asks them to determine whether photographs represent Korean, Japanese, or Chinese people, and then totes up their score. The site is a humorous one that nonetheless refers to a much more sinister practice of racial profiling based on physiognomical photographs and other images that come from anthropology, sociology, criminology, and the other social sciences. Racial profiling has a long and sordid history, especially when viewed within the context of colonial and postcolonial politics, politics that often compelled or allowed governmental functionaries to decide simply by looking whether or not an individual belonged to a specific race. The case of *Plessy v. Ferguson* was a landmark because it stood in opposition to what had been common practice, that is, the visual determination of race on a casual, continual, and extremely subjective basis by "untrained" individuals such as train porters, ticket takers, teachers, and so on. Alllooksame.com playfully asks its viewers to return to a prescientific age in which race is determined by visual means; this constant process of profiling is put to work to call Asian identity into question. The site's interactivity requires the user to participate in the folly of mastering racial "knowledge" by visual means.

In chapter 3, I examine science fiction films' objects of interactivity: what is the visual culture set up by the world of such films that moves into the world of the Internet and its interfaces? In *Gattaca* (1997), *The Matrix* trilogy (1999–2004), and *Minority Report* (2002), the Internet and other networking communications and imaging technologies create a culture of surveillance of the body via databased biometric technologies such as retinal printing, genetic mapping, and other types of body and racial profiling. In *Minority Report* and *The Matrix* I trace the ways that black and white interfaces are defined, and the ways that the Asian American body functions as a liminal space between the two. In my readings of these films, I make a case for the irreplaceable contributions of Internet scholars to methods of film critique—just as a knowledge and grounding of early cinema might be helpful in understanding the culture of animated GIFs (a common feature of

amateur digital signatures and homemade AIM buddies), so too might a critical base in digital interface theory and structure be indispensable to readings
of films that are so mediated by computer interfaces as plot elements, sources
of visual style, and the means of vision itself. Films that use digital interfaces
in such central ways require a method of reading that takes their particular
histories, functionalities, and visual cultures into account. Just as "seeing"
in the context of media consumption today means "seeing through" the apparatus of the interface, so too does the "seeing" of race in these contexts
entail "seeing through" the lens of science as a mode of bodily surveillance
that defines race as a function of biometric measures and databases.

Chapter 4 describes the vibrant visual cultures that pregnant women create when they construct pregnant avatars for their signature files on Internet bulletin boards. While there has been much research about the dearth
of women online and the hostile masculine culture of the early Internet,
there has been little research on women's genres of Internet use in the context of pregnancy and digital production.[40] Women use pregnancy bulletin
boards to become powerful self-signifying subjects of interactivity just as
their status as separate beings and their claims to individual subjecthood
at the turn of the century come into question. As Peggy Phelan eloquently
describes, right-to-life visual rhetoric in the nineties and beyond used technologically enabled medical imaging to reinforce the notion of the fetus's
individuality at the expense of the pregnant woman's.[41] Intersectional critique that would consider how differential access to digital production is
conditioned by race and gender also requires that we pay attention to class,
an issue partly defined in our times by privilege in relation to the Internet
(i.e., high-speed, technically supported access to networked computing both
at home and at work). The avatars that these women produce pose a problem for many upper- and intellectual-class viewers in that they are decidedly déclassé in terms of visual style, as is much of popular digital visual
culture; they are cartoonish, "cutesy," festooned with animated sparkles, flash-
ing animated GIFs, pastel colors, and sentimental stylings taken from older
media franchises like Care Bears, Disney, Hello Kitty, and *Friends*. These
women are not the idealized subjects of interactivity lauded by digital arts
scholars: in some sense, they give the lie to the claim that "as with contemporary art history and visual culture in general, much of the most cutting
edge work on feminism and visual culture in recent years has focused on
new media: the images produced in and through new technologies of representation, often linked to the biotechnology and fertility industries, and
communications fields."[42] Yet while these women's autobiographical digital

signatures are far from "cutting edge" in terms of difficulty of production or conventional aesthetic qualities, they are revolutionary in terms of the power that they take back from institutions that govern and produce particularly powerful types of visual signification, institutions like the very "biotech and fertility industries" that give rise to so many images of women's bodies, digital images that are accorded power and authority.

To possess access to the means of managing personal visual capital is crucial to establishing one's position as a digital subject rather than a digital object in the context of the Internet. In chapter 5, I discuss the consumption and production of the digital divide, and the ways that nonwhite Internet users function as objects and subjects of interactivity. My goals are to understand how power relations work in the digital visual field by looking at subject/object relations in light of access to visual capital, who chooses and is chosen, who sells and is bought, who surfs and is surfed. However, I also aim to challenge binary definitions of the so-called information gap, a term that has lately replaced the older discourse of the "digital divide," or haves and have-nots regarding Internet and digital interactivity, in the interest of enabling a more nuanced look at the modalities of access and ownership of the body and cultural property. Just as infrastructural aspects of urban space such as low freeway overpass ramps worked to differentially screen certain ethnic groups (such as African Americans from Harlem) from New York's Jones Beach while permitting others (such as Italians from Brooklyn, who more frequently owned cars), so too does the Internet work to differentially screen users by race, ethnicity, and language use. Asian Americans are part of, and subject to, a very different digital racial formation than Latinos and African Americans; in recent years, they have claimed a unique mode as objects and subjects of interactivity that exceeds their role as passive objects of representation, as in *The Matrix* films. Chapter 5 describes some of the results of race-based empirical surveys that profile an image of a nationalized Asian American as an Internet "power" user. While taking issue with this somewhat rosy view of Asian American empowerment online based on high Internet adoption figures, the chapter does look to some positive examples of racial-identity-based coalitions that have formed online, partly as a result of this characterization. Relatively large numbers of Asian American users online have led to the formation of vigorous online petition communities that exemplify the notion of a pan-Asian American body politic that protests racism, particularly in the retail sector, as in the case of the Abercrombie and Fitch T-shirt and media racism as it appeared in the *Details* magazine feature "Asian or Gay?"

Studies of older media and "active audiences," such as those by John Fiske, have stressed the ways that audiences resist media images and narratives that are transmitted to them through one-way channels, mass mediated by culture institutions, and filtered through market-driven ideologies that rarely have viewers' best interests at heart. This perspective, which optimistically envisions audiences as more savvy and empowered than had previously been believed, has since been critiqued quite strongly by media critics. Much of Fiske's work establishing this theoretical position was formulated before the popularization of the Internet, much less its increasing adoption by users of color and women. Perhaps an examination of the deployment of the Internet as a racial and gendered visual cultural practice might help us to take a closer look at the ways that cultural resistance to normative gender, racial, and national narratives might be enabled in new digitally interactive spaces. While Jennifer Lopez is probably not the first media figure that comes to mind when pondering the potential of the Internet as a space of resistant digital practice, the uneasy balance between viewer and viewed, ethnically marked and ethnically neutral, producer and produced, commodity and gift, and user and used that we can see in "If You Had My Love" posits a future in which there are no easy answers to the question of identity in the representational world of the Internet. The multilayered visual culture of the Internet is anything but a space of utopian posthumanism where differences between genders, races, and nationalities are leveled out; on the contrary, it is an intensely active, productive space of visual signification where these differences are intensified, modulated, reiterated, and challenged by former objects of interactivity, whose subjectivity is expressed by their negotiations of the shifting terrain of identity, whose seismic adjustments are partly driven by their own participations within it, the result of several major cultural shifts and a digital technology industry that both compels and confounds vision. The last few years have truly seen an explosion in racial and ethnic identity content on the Web: African Americans, Latinos, and Asian Americans are the fastest growing group of Web users, and as Michele Wright notes in 2005: "Four years ago, I could name all the major web sites . . . by and about black communities in North America, the Caribbean, and western Europe; nowadays I simply can't keep up."[43] Earlier studies of race in cyberspace were confounded by a scarcity of concrete examples; the opposite problem obtains today. The popularity of the Internet among a broad spectrum of users arrayed along different axes of identity has certainly not proved to be the magic democracy-enhancing bullet that earlier Internet utopians thought it might be, but it has resulted in a variety of media practices that instantiate race in the visual images that these new subjects of interactivity choose, construct, and consume.

Object and subject are not mutually exclusive roles: it is not possible to definitively decide who is being *interacted* and who is being *interactive* except in specific instances. Individuals can experience more or less interactivity or representational power depending on what they are doing on the Internet; how, where, and how long they are doing it; and whether and how they are represented offline in relation to it. The metaphor of "parsing" might be useful here. Parsing is a term used to describe the ordering or syntactical protocol used by a computer or a programmer when implementing coded instructions in a computer language. The graphical Internet demands a type of interpretive modality that goes beyond the textual, one that replaces the notion of "reading" or even "viewing" with a transcoded model of parsing. The mode and type of iteration, the order and positioning of symbols, and the codes by which it is read determine the way that a new media object interacts with its user. When we look at any example of the Internet's popular culture, we must weigh power differentials in terms of both its overt "content" as well as its user's access to forms of revision, modification, distribution, and interaction to parse the movement of power across the multiple positions available to users of color and women on the Internet. In his work on the network society and the role of the Internet in late capitalism, Manuel Castells has documented the passion for claiming identities that has arisen along with, and has indeed been enabled by, the rise of network technologies. This book parses some of the exceedingly rich and strange visual artifacts unique to the Internet, sites that a newly diverse group of users actively employ to both express and interrogate their racial, gendered, national, and class identities.

1

"Ramadan Is Almoast Here!" The Visual Culture of AIM Buddies, Race, Gender, and Nation on the Internet

"The right to control one's data image—outside of social and entertainment contexts—has yet to be obtained in the current political struggles over citizenship in cyberspace."[1] So wrote David Rodowick in 2001, and it is certainly the case that the Internet has been both the occasion for, and subject of, numerous debates over the extent to which control societies ought to be able to exercise power over citizens through data images. And while Rodowick is correct in asserting that the state has yet to exercise as much control over the use of data images in social and entertainment contexts as it does in others, these are far from unregulated spaces of digital representation. As numerous feminist critiques of female gaming avatars in *Tomb Raider* and *Everquest* have shown, the narrow range of body types available for gameplay certainly deprives female players of the right to control their data images in ways that feel comfortable to them.[2] Digital gaming is a large and highly lucrative and organized form of cultural production, and thus the profit imperative takes the place of the state when it comes to the ways that gaming's visual cultures of bodily data imaging are managed. Rodowick's claim that social and entertainment contexts are *part of* a struggle for "citizenship in cyberspace" is well taken, however, and the notion that these are perhaps fruitful places to look for subversive data images that are more "owned" by their users than those available in commercial, governmental, and corporate spaces is certainly useful. To that end, in this chapter I will examine the use of user-produced buddy icons in Instant Messenger applications on the Internet; these feature visual images of the databody as an instrument used simultaneously for both socializing and entertainment, since in the case of IM, socializing *is* entertainment. I wish to repurpose some of the rightly pessimistic discourse of surveillance surrounding such things as electronic signatures with a more hopeful reading about minoritarian identity creation on IM. In particular, it is possible to find images of national, religious, linguistic, and sexual identities created by users as icons on IM: overtly gay, fundamentalist Muslim or Christian, Armenian, or Asian American visual images are easier to locate there than in other media forms, including other parts of the Internet, and are certainly not often seen in commercial games. The creation and use of these images have particular relevance to questions of freedom, diversity, and racial equality online considering the use of dataveillance technologies to track precisely those groups—fundamentalist Muslims (but not Christians) and immigrants—who are least likely to be fairly or self-represented in American mainstream visual culture. In creating and using these very personal and amateur digital signatures of identity, IM users literally build themselves as subjects of interactivity.

Synchronous or real-time networked textual interaction, from one person to another person, has existed since the early command-line interface days of the Internet. Unix applications like "chat" and "phone" remediated the most familiar person-to-person form of communication known by most people—the telephone—but with little in the way of graphics; clients could regulate the flow of text streaming down a screen so that it didn't appear radically fragmented and thus was more readable, but it really was a text-only environment, with the user's only intervention into it being the size and perhaps style of font displayed. These applications also ran in the background of others and could thus be overlooked by a busy user. Instant Messenger, while it shares these basic qualities with "talk" and "phone," remediates an early application called "write" in that it pops up or supersedes other open windows in graphical user interfaces; it is meant to intrude on the visual field of the user, and though it can be demoted later, its use of alert sounds to signify the arrival of an instant message makes it seem more immediate. Instant Messenger has its roots in ICQ, a text messaging application that became popular in 1996, and occupies a unique position in that it is in many ways a low-bandwidth, anachronistic technology despite its popularity, and one that defies academic prediction. As recently as 2001, new media theorists David Bolter and Richard Grusin and Per Persson seriously questioned text-only Internet interaction's relevance in the coming graphical age. Bolter and Grusin ask: "Can this digital, textual self maintain its claim to authenticity against the claims of the self expressed visually in virtual reality? The MUDs [multiuser domains] and chat rooms of the 1980s and early 1990s were exclusively textual and therefore remediated in the first instance the novel and the letter. Chat rooms may also remediate telephone conversations, but they suffer from the fact that the spoken voice on the telephone has a more obvious claim to immediacy than the typed word. As the transmission of video, animated graphics, and audio over the Internet is improving, these textual applications are threatened." They conclude by citing the now-defunct Palace as an example of a "visual MUD" that "remediates the comic book" and mention that other "visual MUDs may remediate cinema and television more effectively, by offering animated figures or even video images of the participants themselves.... In our visual culture today, it seems unlikely that any textual representation of the self can hold out long against the remediations of a rival, visual technology."[3] One of the central claims of *Remediation*—that one of the most important yardsticks by which to evaluate digital technologies in relation to analog ones is on the basis of their enhanced immediacy—necessarily leads to the notion that online discourse supplemented by visual images is superior in terms of liveness or realness to the "typed word," and thus graphical MUDs must be more appealing than textual MUDs because of their improved immediacy. They claim as well that televisual images made possible by broadband and applications like the Palace, which supported graphics in conjunction with textual interaction, would produce a hybrid form, less book than comic book or graphic novel, which would threaten the survival of text-only chat rooms and MUDs. Their discussion of the Palace dominates the chapter titled "The Virtual Self" because they believe that graphical MUDs are excellent examples of both immediacy and hypermediation not only because they embody both "live" and real-seeming interaction combined with overtly artificial or stylized uses of interfaces and visual conventions, but also because they enable identity swapping across the axis of gender, which is an essential feature of the type of postmodern self that the authors posit as the inevitable product of a networked culture. Per Persson concurs, speculating that cinema-desktop convergence will result in text-only MUDs being inevitably replaced by "'rooms' [that organize online conversations in terms of visual 3-D spaces] and environments like Palace, Active Worlds, or, in more sophisticated cases, VR teleconferencing systems."[4]

Instant Messenger is primarily a textual form in which most of the space and interactivity associated with it consists of typed words, but it also possesses important visual aspects, like emoticons, blinkies, avatars, and buddy icons.[5] These images are often animations rather than scanned photographs, often extremely small, and usually depict set pieces rather than "live" or continuously changing images, and are certainly subsumed to the textual, but their existence supports one claim made by Bolter and Grusin, which is that visual images do enrich real-time textual interactions and are attractive to users. However, predictions that users would prefer more "virtual reality" when it comes to real-time interaction online are disproved by IM's present form, in which images are subsumed to text. Their notion that users might be interested in using imaging technology in the context of online conversation mainly to visually represent themselves to interlocutors, to create "video images of themselves" while chatting online, speaks to a conception of Instant Messenger as being concerned primarily with identity. And certainly, much work has been done on MOOs (multiuser domains object oriented) and MUDs (multiuser domains) that confirms this.[6] Bolter and Grusin are interested in visual MUDs partly because of the ways that they enable identity play across gender, but the authors are less interested in racial formation in this realm of self-representation. Their critique enables a discussion of the ways that the male gaze may be confounded or confirmed online by avatar switching and gender play in the realm of self-authoring, but precludes much discussion of the way that the racialized gaze may contribute to digital racial formation. In fact, a thriving culture of both textual and graphical racialization exists on IM. Some of these engage in both registers to enable racial ventriloquism by literally altering the text that a user writes: helper applications such as Tizzle Talk translate a user's speech into one of seven ethnic and racialized dialects on the fly and accompany it with a matching buddy icon. Tizzle Talk, which can run on top of most popular Instant Messenger programs, lets the user speak in "Ahnold, Ebonics, Jacko, Pig Latin, Redneck, Dubya, Pirate, Jessica, and Engrish." These dialects are all accompanied by small buddy icons representing parodic cartoons of Arnold Schwarzenegger, George W. Bush, Michael Jackson, Jessica Simpson, and William Hung, an Asian American college student with a pronounced accent who acquired notoriety as one of the least musically gifted performers on the popular television show *American Idol*. This application is quite self-consciously automating the process of cross-racial and ethnic mimicry that has always been a part of popular culture's process of racial formation: as Shilpa Davé's work on the use of Indian accents by white voice-over actors in *The Simpsons* shows, the use of "brownvoice" as a form of electronically mediated passing has been a feature of Asian American representation for many years and across media forms.[7] The makers of Tizzle Talk, which is available for free download at www.tizzletalk.com, anticipate that users will find the software offensive, explaining, "We are a diverse bunch. Tizzle Talk originally started as a way to make fun of ourselves," thus deflecting accusations that they are engaging in cross-racial mimicry by whites "against" non-white groups. Though Tizzle Talk has not become a widespread IM helper application, due partly at least to the inconvenience and difficulty of speaking or reading in "Dubya" for extended periods of time, the practice of using graphical buddy icons is widespread, and Tizzle Talk includes these to enhance the sense of racial presence that it parodies.

AIM buddies are tiny bits of screen real estate that operate in several registers. They can work to signify identity in a straightforwardly pragmatic, relatively nonideological way, for when conducting multiple IM conversations, users quickly track who is speaking or "texting" by glancing at their AIM buddy icon. The icons serve as visual flags for shaping the tendency toward distraction that characterizes this type of online activity. Buddies help users with multiple windows open to organize their attention. These icons perform an important cognitive as well as signifying function in the world of IM. However, users do frame their posts with numerous visual objects that are strongly valenced in terms of gender, racial, ethnic, national, and religious identity, the buddy icon being just one among them. If we wish to parse the meanings of this immensely popular application, one that defines the Internet as a communicative tool for vast numbers of its users, we would do well to examine its visual culture. AIM buddies and other user-chosen IM images are the product of a user's desire to create a desktop mise-en-scène that signifies the self, and they are thus part of an ongoing process of digital racialization. They constitute part of a new visual culture, a visual culture imbricated within a peculiarly oral discursive form, the online chat, that brings together cinema, signboard culture, and the graphic novel and works to literally embody desubstantialized and ephemeral virtual speech. AIM buddies run the gamut of cartoon characters, television and movie stars, and figures from fantasy and mythology. It appears that anything from a scanned photograph of Jennifer Aniston to a cell-phone-camera image of the user's cat can be (and almost certainly is) an AIM buddy. These tiny graphical images function as remediations of both older visual media and "sigs," or the automated identifiers appended to the end of e-mail messages from back in the days of text-only Internet. AIM buddies occupy a liminal role between the more traditional graphical avatar and the textual sig familiar to pre-1995 Internet users. Their use as graphical proxies of identity warrants some theorization of its own, yet the visual culture of AIM buddies has yet to be written. This chapter will start that work by discussing the topic in light of racial signification and identity in this area of avatar construction.

In her work on avatars in gaming, Mary Flanagan discusses avatars in terms of film, as synthespians or virtual personalities or celebrities. Because games have immersive diegetic narratives and characters that users may already know from cross-media tie-ins like films and literature, it makes perfect sense to talk about gaming avatars in terms of narrative and character, but it makes less sense to use cinematic language to discuss IM, which lacks scriptedness. AIM buddies are less like synthespians or virtual stars (though many of them may consist of screen shots of stars) and more like avatars in other textual or graphical chats. And unlike synthespians and gaming avatars, images of the digital body that are benefiting so quickly from improved production standards that they verge on photo-realistic representations of the human, so "real" that they have to be virtually "roughed up" to read as digital people, AIM buddies are low-fidelity and will remain so because of screen size constraints. And unlike other avatars used in chats or other synchronous online communication, their quality is far more static and smaller in scale than those in high-bandwidth graphical chats like there.com, which feature three-dimensional high-quality CGI.

It seems particularly appropriate to invoke the notion of iconography in the case of AIM buddies, since they are indeed icons in terms of the way that they function on the computer desktop. AIM buddies are fifty by fifty pixels and consist of either a single still image (usually in JPEG or GIF format) or a series of up to seven images that can be programmed to "play" one after another, at a rate of about one frame per second, to create an image that appears to move. (These images will show up tagged with a "movie" icon if imported into PowerPoint slides.) The images are usually fairly low quality, consisting of around 75 dpi, and even multipart animated buddy icons are very small, around 8 KB or so. Animated buddy icons can be arranged in a series of sequences that are themed but not meant to convey a sense of movement or temporality, as in the case of animated GIFs that consist of different but essentially unrelated head shots of the same star, such as Angel from the cult television show *Buffy the Vampire Slayer,* or they can consist of slightly altered versions of the same image, thus simulating movement in the same way that early flip-card books did. In many cases, they are hybrid forms that do both: examples I look at in this chapter reserve the first three frames for a short "movie" or animated sequence that depicts an avatar's body, and the last two or three for photographs, slogans, and signs such as national flags and other sorts of imagery. I will also focus on the communicative aspects of these icons as well as their formal ones. They address the eye in a particular way, but they are also objects that exist on the margins of the popular and heavily used networked communicative space of IM that involves a complex of different types of icons, fonts, windows, and other visual frames for what is essentially a textual event, that is, the creation of written messages, themselves written in a colloquial English of such recent vintage that it is unintelligible to most readers over the age of twenty. This English, composed of abbreviations, symbols, and numbers from the QWERTY keyboard, and emoticons, is a hybrid language designed to facilitate person-to-person computer-based communication as quickly as possible, in real time. Thus AIM buddies are tools of person-to-person communication in a way that other avatars, such as gaming avatars from nonnetworked games, are not.[8]

In the first case, an homage to a star like a *Buffy* buddy icon works like a photo album that one flips through; the viewer is presented with a selection of photographs of the star in different poses that remediates a traditional slide show in which still images are shown in a particular order, or a "shrine" of photographs that a teenage girl might build as a display in her room. Though the order in which these are shown may signify something, we cannot properly call them moving or cinematic images. In the second, we can see an attempt to remediate cinema by creating extremely low-bandwidth animations that test the limits of legibility; at fifty pixels square (approximately one-quarter inch at low resolution) and about one frame per second, far below the twenty-four frames per second required to simulate movement on a more traditional cinematic screen, they are a form that requires elegance of expression and enforces strict limits on what sorts of images can be displayed.

As I have already noted, this is an anachronistic technology. AIM buddies belie the technologically determinist argument that "better" image quality, smoothly streaming video images, higher image resolutions, and photo-realism or near photo-realism are always more valued and preferred by the user. Instead, AIM buddies have more in common with a signifying practice from the early days of the Internet, the "sig" (or digital signature, a form of digital racial formation that I will focus on in more detail in chapter 4). Like ASCII art, images constructed with QWERTY characters that were often deployed in conjunction with early pregraphical Internet sigs, AIM buddies are extremely compact and designed to load onto users' systems quickly.[9] Because there are relatively few pixels available to create them, since they need to coexist with the IM window, they often have the grainy, chunky, pixelated, or "tiled" quality of earlier graphical forms in digital environments. In addition, their function is more akin to that of the sig, which is to signify identity in a static way. However, while early sigs were appended to e-mail messages, which are an asynchronous electronic textual form and are themselves made up of written words, AIM buddy icons are designed to accompany a form of Internet writing that is more dynamic, in real time, and fluid in nature—a form of writing that is in constant motion. Instant Messenger is a writing practice that is live, and this form is reflected in AIM buddies that also move; this is particularly true for animated GIFs.

Tiny, low-bandwidth icons that are customizable by the user are characteristic features of many popular commercial operating systems and Web portals. Apple's Operating System X requires a user to choose an image of an animal, an abstract pattern, a logo (such as Apple's own), or a nature-based picture such as a flower or a leaf to identify himself or herself as a user distinguishable from other users in their multiuser mode, as does Windows XP. These desktop images are, like many screen saver and desktop patterns, tasteful, bland, and corporate. They are decorative and are never expressive of identity categories like race or ethnicity (this is not as true for gender: kitten and flower icons are most likely intended to appeal to female users). Indeed, the ubiquitous green rolling hills and cerulean blue clouds that are the default desktop image for Windows XP are meant to invoke a space outside the office or the computer: they present a soothing image of nature. Their neutrality in terms of user identity works by invoking nature, a conspicuously missing and correspondingly overvalued part of digital culture, and also by interpellating users into a community of consumers unified by the twin priorities of shared aesthetic "good taste" and an equally strong devotion to the notion of user choice. Thus, while the visual styles of these icons are quite homogeneous, the emphasis lies on the user's customization of everyday digital space with the icon that appeals to him or her personally, thus communicating identity in a narrow, depoliticized, ostensibly nonideological way.

Buddyicon.info, Badass buddies, and "The Doll Palace: Where Cartoon Dolls Live" are Web sites that all offer a variety of AIM buddy icons for downloading. Their mode of organization creates distinct types or genres of buddy: nationality is one category, listed along with gender, but not race. This dodging of race as a category or an overt subject of discussion or reference is characteristic of Web sites of this kind: several years ago in *Cybertypes*

I described the ways in which race is routed around in menu-driven interfaces, a point to which I will return in more detail later in this chapter. Buddy icons from noncorporate, volunteer-run sites are far from neutral, and these sites frame their icons as overtly marginal, in conscious opposition to more conventional icons: they flag themselves as "badass" in terms of the subversiveness of their content. Considering their close ties to digital youth culture production, they are best viewed as contested spaces: like everything else on the Internet, they are possible sites of resistance, but certainly not necessarily so. The drive to signify identity on the Internet continues as one of their most robust features.

AIM buddies are liminal objects in several ways. They occupy the space separating still image from cinematic sequence, icon from avatar, between personal signature and mass-produced image, between photo-realistic representation and cartoon representation, between orality/textuality and visuality. AIM buddy icons function somewhat like avatars in digital games in that they are meant to reflect the self; however, because they are often static, they are not keyed as closely to the user's movements through an interface.[10] In addition, while Bob Rehak stresses the role of the avatar as a means of resolving the split engendered by the mirror stage, he posits this in the context of a game/player relationship that doesn't include other players; the game itself functions as the mirror. His analysis takes no account of games as a social or communicative medium. Because IMers almost always know each other, unlike chat room users, buddy icons are deployed among a community of people likely to share the same cultural referents (*Elf* is the most popular AIM buddy at MSN as of April 2005.) These images have a structurally global circulation but in fact circulate in a limited way. They also have a small tag that lets you know the number of downloads: thousands are typical. Buddies that depict beer drinking, vomiting, drug use, sexual acts, passing gas, and other acts dear to the hearts of adolescent boys are the mainstay of sites like badassbuddies.com.

While many of them are quotidian, tacky, embarrassing, in poor taste, and inexpertly produced, it is essential that new media theory develop a method for analyzing taste in our inquiries into digital culture. The Internet is the largest participatory mass medium in use today, and as its user base continues to grow, we can expect it to resemble reality television rather than PBS, but with fewer controls, more interactivity, and even more sensitivity to trends and youth culture. Youths envision AIM buddy icons as they do other accessories of popular culture, such as cell phone ringtones, digital photographic images, cell phone and backpack charms, T-shirts, key chains, and car modifications—in other words, as ephemeral, often replaced or swapped-out modules of signification that convey a sense of identity, style, and community in everyday life, particularly for girls. And like them, the language of AIM buddies has much to do with popular televisual media, licensed characters such as Hello Kitty and Powerpuff Girls, and musical trends. Yet on the other hand, AIM buddies differ from these in that they are part of a graphical real-time communicative practice that occurs on the computer desktop, the same space most commonly associated with the Internet and computing. David Silver's study of teen girls' use of the Internet represents them as a group of users who are more resistant to the commercialization of the online sphere than had been thought, and notes that the online activities most popular with girls, e-mail, IM, surfing for fun, and visiting entertainment Web sites, have more to do with communication than with consumption: "Female teens approach and use the Internet as a communication tool rather than as a consumer medium. It appears to us that although American female teens are eager to use and explore various activities on the Internet, e-commerce is not one of the major ones."[11] He also defines IM as a "girl dominated activity" along with using e-mail and obtaining dieting and fitness information, and he documents unsuccessful attempts by new media industries to commodify IM, perhaps as a response to having failed to do so before it reached its current height of popularity with youth. In any event, the commercial stakes as well as the theoretical ones for articulating IM with identities in formation, in particular female and racialized diasporic and other marginal types of identities, are undeniably high. Herbert Gans's writings on the formation of popular culture preferences and practices shed some light on this issue. Given that the Internet is used with particular intensity by youth, it makes sense to look to networked new media for representative examples of diasporic taste cultures. Gans defines popular culture as the raw material for "*taste cultures*, because each contains shared or common aesthetic values and standards of taste. *Aesthetic* is used broadly, referring not only to standards of beauty and taste but also to a variety of other emotional and intellectual values that people express or satisfy when they choose content from a taste culture."[12] IM is a communication practice that possesses a mixed and chaotic taste culture partly because it has resisted formal modes of commodification until now, and part of its potential lies in its ability to be repurposed or tweaked in ways that convey identity differently from received digital networked images.

Identity is a category that has long been perceived as central and important in cultural studies. Stuart Hall describes the development of the concept of identity into the central term that it is today in his provocative article "Who Needs 'Identity'?" and explains that we do: "identity" is a term that persists in critical discourse despite anti-essentialist challenges to its usefulness because it permits analysis of the ways that discourse *creates* subjects. Identity is a concept that proves particularly useful in the case of signifying forms that, like new media and IM in particular, engage in the active rearticulation of self and discourse. "It seems to be in the attempt to rearticulate the relationship between subjects and discursive practices that the question of identity recurs—or rather, if one prefers to stress the process of subjectification to discursive practices, and the politics of exclusion which all subjectification appears to entail, the question of *identification*."[13] These subjects are created partly by a process of identification and disidentification: in this, Hall agrees with Judith Butler, among others, who asserts that "all identities operate through exclusion." When we speak of diasporic and female populations, questions of identity and culture become especially layered, complex, and important. While in earlier work I have stressed the ways that Internet users in the mid-1990s employed online discourse to create cross-racial conversational performances or identity tourism, the racialization of IM has worked much differently since the massification of the Internet as a popular form.

The figure of the performative self is central to the scholarship on online discourse and has been part of the argument establishing the Internet as a postmodern communicative space: as Hall writes, "the endlessly performative self has been advanced in a celebratory variant of postmodernism."[14] Indeed, the Internet seems made to argue postmodernism's case, as online anonymity makes it necessary for identity to be signified in active rather than more passive ways. However, as the Internet's user base changes, and changes in software make it a more enriched graphical space that enables youth in particular to express their taste cultures, which are often imported from other media, the "profiles" and avatars they create to literally embody themselves in disembodied spaces become less about performing a cross-gender or cross-racial alternative or "passing" self to deploy in public communities and more about expressing diasporic, ambivalent, *intersectional* selves to use within closed communities.[15]

What is the visual culture of nation, race, gender, and age on the Internet? In what ways do we see immigrants, girls, youths, and people of color using the medium to express themselves as subjects of interactivity in the face of their persistent objectification by digital imaging practices such as computer gaming, videos, advertising, and commercial Web sites? Justine

Cassell and Henry Jenkins's seminal *From Barbie to Mortal Kombat* addresses this question in relation to gender and age with a collection of scholarly articles in addition to a group of interviews with producers of girls' games, thus acknowledging the importance of intervening into the generally sexist genre of computer gaming, which tends to be dominated by first-person shooters and scantily clad, Barbie-shaped images of women. One issue not taken up quite as directly, but perhaps by implication, in their argument is that of racial representation: this is a problem most clearly and obviously demonstrated in the popularity of mainstream blockbuster games, such as the *Grand Theft Auto* series, let alone in "fringe" games like *Vampire: Bloodlines* and *Ethnic Cleansing*. All these games figure ethnic and racial minorities as victims of screen-mediated violence initiated by the player, who is exhorted to do things such as "Kill the Haitians!" in *Grand Theft Auto: Vice City*. (This line of dialogue was later removed from the game after Haitian Americans protested strongly against it.)

Clearly, gaming is a tremendously important aspect of digital visual culture.[16] In this chapter, I will get at a different but related aspect of this field by examining the comparatively less glamorous visual culture of Instant Messenger. IM is a particularly important use of the Internet for youth and women, and its users, in particular the young female users who make up much of its participant base, are engaging in significant and complex forms of digital subject formation in creating, sharing, and deploying buddy icons. Though AIM buddies are deployed by more people than will ever use more rarefied parts of the Internet or will ever view digital art, they are a dramatically underexamined, though ubiquitous, feature of online life for many users. These icons are sites of robust identity creation in which we can already see girls actively scripting and circulating images of the body, of nation, and of race and language use. This pattern of use contrasts with the state of things in digital game development, which, despite the interviewees in Cassell and Jenkins's 1998 book, has not markedly improved in terms of creating content that will appeal to girls or, most importantly, in involving girls and women in the most important aspects of game development. Purple Moon, a girls' game company headed by Brenda Laurel, a pioneer in the field of gender and computing, went out of business since she was interviewed for the collection, and the other women's companies that were profiled have failed to produce any popular girls' games. This is a sobering fact, yet one can find girls creating digital images of themselves to deploy in social spaces on the Internet if one is willing to shift focus from digital media forms that require relatively heavy capitalization and distribution mechanisms, such as computer game production, to those that are free, ubiquitous, and native to the Internet, such as Instant Messenger, a form of computer-mediated communication that dominates young people's use of the Internet. Since users usually already know the identities of their interlocutors, these avatars serve a radically different function than that served by avatars in early online social environments like MUDs and MOOs and in other multiplayer digital games. Rather than embodying a user who has no other body in play, thus functioning as part of a culture of identity deception decried by earlier Internet users, instead these avatars work as *supplementary* imaging practices: they are part of a visual culture in which identity is added to, rather than replaced by, images of race, gender, and nation. To initiate a session, users of IM must already know the screen names of those they converse with, and message senders are likely to be ignored if they are not already known by, and on the buddy lists of, the message recipients. Thus Instant Messenger is a communicative practice with an avatar culture that needs to be discussed quite differently from earlier ones, like MOOing and chatting, since it is part of a social network that is founded on prior offline relationships. AIM buddy avatars do not stand alone to signify a disembodied self; instead they represent choices made by the user who wishes to build an online identity that is warranted by a preexisting offline relationship. Much Internet utopianism, especially that which used metaphors from travel and tourism to promote the notion of diversity, assumed a public-access structure for real-time textual interaction in which users might encounter strangers, "random" interlocutors, and thus widen their circle of friends or social contacts beyond what their physical worlds and offline neighborhoods offered them. Thus would "diversity" be served. The heady early days of the Internet both mocked and celebrated the idea that an African American youth might find herself talking to a Scandinavian grandfather encountered in a chat room. This representation of the Internet as a social leveler and bringer-together of disparate races, cultures, and backgrounds was always problematic—digital inequality made it much more likely that one might encounter a Scandinavian man than an African American of any gender in the nineties—and has become even more unlikely today, in an age in which parents' injunctions not to talk to strangers have become incorporated into the ways that parents now often monitor their children's buddy lists as part of familial caretaking. And while some television advertising has continued to invoke the notion of the "global village" in relation to what the Internet offers, such ads have become the exception rather than the rule. The 2004 eBay commercial titled "Clocks," a notable exception, depicts racial and ethnic diversity in the context of online commerce. While earlier advertisements stressed the idea of cultural and ethnic diversity for its own sake, "Clocks" envisions access to global marketplaces as an asset to users who wish to buy commodities at the lowest possible price.[17]

It is all the more important that we pay attention to girls' labor on the Internet, since there is a covert identity politics regarding race, class, and gender at work in much of the scholarly discourse regarding digital production and its implications for media that acknowledges their marginal position in light of digital media, despite a narrowing digital divide in terms of use. In short, girls are envisioned as avid users but not producers, as consumers but not creators. In "Quentin Tarantino's Star Wars? Digital Cinema, Media Convergence, and Participatory Culture," Henry Jenkins describes the potential of digital cinema to empower DIY-oriented fans to produce their own media. He proposes that the creation, distribution, and exhibition of fan-produced media on the Internet—a complex that he classifies as participatory media—is the antidote to a serious problem with media's current political economy. This is the problem of media consolidation, or increasingly few companies controlling media production.

Jenkins's argument that audiences of the digital age demand and deserve the right to participate in the formation of media texts to put in dialogue with those that they see around them, thus resulting in productive forms of "textual poaching," puts much faith in the notion that this is a desirable outcome because it will result in "better," or at least more diverse and democratic, art. In the epigram to the article, Jenkins cites Francis Ford Coppola's ringing endorsement of digital camcorders and the way that this technology will enable "a little fat girl in Ohio" to use her dad's equipment to become the "new Mozart" of digital filmmaking. Digital production is thus envisioned as empowering potential Mozarts who might formerly have been kept out of the realm of media creation by the Hollywood cultural gatekeepers who police the production, distribution, and exhibition of film. The celebration of the digital as an inherently democratic medium is nothing new: discourses of liberatory interactivity have been around since the early days of text-only Internet and hypertext theory, which posited that readers could choose their own endings to digital narratives and thus exercise their postmodern subjectivities and literalize the notion of readerly resistance to authorial intention by becoming coauthors of a work. In *Web Theory*, Robert Burnett and P. David Marshall term this the "cultural production thesis" and define this blurring of the line between audience and author as a key feature of the World Wide Web.

As Jenkins goes on to describe fan-produced films such as *Alien5* and *Alien 5(2)*, which were made using some *Alien, Mork and Mindy,* and *Planet of the Apes* action figures filmed against a backdrop of a television screen running a copy of the *Alien* video game, all filmed and edited in-camera with digital equipment, one cannot but marvel at the ingenuity and creativity displayed. Indeed, the logic of new media relies on the notion that compositing of digital media ripped from other sources constitutes a legitimate means of artistic creation, perhaps the only kind that is possible in a postanalog environment. The *Alien 5* films were created by male teenage prodigies, devoted *Alien* fans who initially conceived of the film as a way to fulfill the requirements for a school project and later distributed the film via the Web.[18] Thus Coppola's and Jenkins's idea that digital image production, distribution, and exhibition redistribute power in a radical way across formerly impassable barriers of gender, region, body type, and age seems amply proven by this and other examples. However, the two identity positions that are pointedly omitted here are race and class. How much differently might Coppola's claim read if he inserted them into the list of objectionable attributes—obesity, femininity, provinciality—that go into the formulation of a hypothetical "little fat girl in Ohio" as a possible "new Mozart"? If this statement was formulated to read "fat little black girl" or "fat little Asian girl," it would read as racist, and what's more, it would acknowledge an unpleasant fact; the cultural gatekeepers keep out not only the young, the female, and the obese but also the poor (defined as people whose fathers don't own digital video cameras, in this case) and people of color. Coppola's claim is a variation of the now-iconic cartoon from the *New Yorker* published on July 5, 1993, during the early days of the Internet's massification, which depicts a dog using a computer and the caption "On the Internet nobody knows you're a dog!" In the years since that cartoon's publication, scholarly concerns regarding new media and power relations have shifted. The Internet's supposed anonymity and status as a race-free space has been challenged, and in addition, there has come into being a new emphasis on the Internet's promise as a place of radical production or intervention rather than as merely a space of anonymous consumption. Indeed, Jenkins seems to value the Internet precisely because it allows disenfranchised members of society to make themselves visible as cultural producers of media. Both formulations assume that former voiceless beings, such as dogs and young, unattractive females, can be given voices via the Internet: that they can become subjects rather than objects of interactivity.

The craze for self-representation on the Internet mirrors in some sense the mania for photographic portraits that characterized nineteenth-century America: hordes of middle-class people wishing to use the new technology to create images of themselves and their families clogged daguerreotype parlors and were parodied in newspaper illustrations. Much of the popularity of early photography was premised on the idea that it enabled a do-it-yourself culture in the realm of the image; a popular 1839 picture by Maurisset titled "La Daguerreotypemanie" depicts people waiting eagerly in line to purchase photographic equipment while artists hang themselves in the margin, indicating that the new technology had rendered them jobless and suicidal. In addition, professional photographers themselves were depicted as marginal, thus putting the emphasis on the user as cultural producer, as well as on the form of self-portraiture as a means of asserting class identity and agency. When we look at the case of AIM (AOL Instant Messenger) buddy icons, we can see an instance of popular digital culture in which the desire to intervene in existing media franchises—many AIM buddies are screen shots from current Hollywood films and cartoons—is bent toward the service of self-representation or self-portraiture. In addition, their circulation and production has a multiply distributed quality: they are available for free download from a multitude of Web sites, and they possess even more ephemerality than other new media products: BuddyIcon.info organizes its icons by popularity, and this changes often. Britney Spears buddies give way to Jessica Simpson buddies, and many users change their buddy icons frequently, as they do their cellular phone ringtones, to keep up with these trends from older media. AIM buddies reflect a particular moment in our collective digital history in which mainstream youth culture is beginning to present a challenge to the corporate and hacker/engineer/hippie countercultures that preceded it. IM users participate in established media franchises and popular iconographies in all kinds of ways, and it is the networked form of the technology that enables this. In this chapter I examine a set of AIM buddy icons downloaded from a popular Web site that depict racial, gender, national, and linguistic identities from the perspective of adolescent girls. The visual culture of Instant Messenger allows us to see active and creative digital production by precisely that group of users who are least enfranchised, even within academic discussions of digital disenfranchisement, and to parse the ways that they employ aspects of icon creation such as animations, juxtapositions of idealized female body images and national and religious slogans, and how they otherwise manage the limited digital space of the buddy icon to articulate complex statements of often-reviled identities.

Professionally created buddy icons are available through the software companies that create Instant Messenger applications and make them available as freeware, such as MSN, Yahoo!, and AOL, but there are also numerous "amateur" Web sites run by individuals who collect them and make them available for free download. Thus AIM buddies are definitely a part of the gift economy of the Web; sites such as buddyicon.info and badassbuddies .com invite users to both download and "donate" buddies that they have created themselves, and these same sites have links to avatar-building software as part of their package. Budding Mozarts in the field of AIM buddy production are thus invited to hone, display, and share their cultural products, and in so doing, if Jenkins's premise is correct, to theoretically circumvent the "cultural gatekeepers" such as Microsoft, AOL, and Yahoo! that govern the visual culture of IM. The peculiar and extremely specific technical requirements of buddy icon production are demanding, and I wish to focus on actual rather than theoretical fifteen-year-old girls who create minifilms in AIM buddy icons that express nuanced and layered representations of nationality, ethnicity, race, and gender. In contrast to Coppola's notion of a hypothetical and valorized marginal and deracinated digital social subject who uses media technology to create great "art"—a universalizing definition of aesthetic value that remains unchallenged in this formulation—we see in the case of ethnic AIM buddy production and use a genuinely new digital expressive form that, while not "artistic" by conventional standards, creates raced and gendered bodies with a distinctive and innovative visual culture and mode of circulation and deployment. Ethnic AIM buddies are sites of digital racial formation and part of a racial project of carving out an imagistic computer-mediated communication (CMC) practice for youth of color online. It is their deviation from unproblematic notions of artistic value carried over from older media—the Mozart paradigm, which invokes traditional classical music—that accounts for their peculiarities of form and, I would argue, innovative use of cinematic and iconographic convention.

The buddyicon.info Web site offers thousands of AIM buddy icons (28,838 by my most recent count), as well as "away" icons and "blinkies," and many of these feature animated GIFs. Most of them appear to have been made by amateurs, and the site organizes them into different categories such as "animals, animated, buddies, cars, cartoon, celebrity, college, dollz, drinking, funny, holidays, jobs, logos, love, men, movies, music, nationality, other, personal requests, religion, sports, tv, videogames, website, women, and wrestling." The "requests" icon page features icons made by users at the specific request of other users, thereby exhibiting the value given in this site to participatory media creation and the generosity with which users with graphical "skillz" employ them at the request of strangers whose only link with them is participation in IM as a media and communicative practice. Indeed, this volunteering of help at image creation is itself a way of suturing together media, communication, and identity: by creating a "gay pride" icon for use by the community, a user can help make literally visible identities that may not come through in the medium of IM writing. The fact that users wish so strongly to signify their identities in this medium attests to the ways that racial, gender, sexual, national, and other identities (such as sports and university affiliations) are willingly brought into play in a medium where the majority of users already know each other—as mentioned before, IMers rarely IM with users who are not already on their buddy lists—yet are not physically copresent.

The site's complicated relation to identity is signaled on the splash page that I accessed on April 26, 2005, which listed two "featured" icons, one of which displayed a rainbow and the words "gay pride" and the other one, titled "homophobe," that contained a mininarrative told in a cinematic language consisting of ten GIF images or slides that are programmed to cycle one after another. Each image contains the word "homophobe" in large letters at the bottom of the box and depicts a cartoon character approaching a closed door, uttering the words "Richard?" and "ya there?" in two cartoon bubbles. The next few frames depict him confronting another character clad in a rainbow shirt who emerges from the "closet" to say, "I'm gay, Tim." The last two frames of the animation represent a puff of smoke as "Tim" disappears. This icon, accompanied on the site by a description that reads "fear the gay," has been downloaded 148 times in comparison to 246 for "gay pride." Both were posted on the same day, March 12, 2003, and the fact that they appear together signifies the heterodox nature of the site's principle of icon organization. There is no implication that one ideological stance regarding homosexuality is favored over another; instead, the download statistics are provided to speak more or less for themselves.

The "dollz" category is the largest, containing over twelve thousand icons. In contrast to the state of gendered production in digital gaming, which is still dominated by men and male avatars, these are mostly female and appear to have been made by girls, since most of the nicknames of those who claim authorship of them are female. Most of these depict curvy cartoon female figures, many of whom "wink," and whose images depict entire bodies represented in pieces: the first slide consists of a head, the second a midriff (often bare, and conventionally buxom), and the third a pair of legs. Of course, this is a practical technological move that enables a relatively large image to be conveyed in a space that is only fifty by fifty pixels large. These slides are then followed by three to seven more that contain a textual message, such as "gettin' dirty" or "I'm going crazy, I need to be your lady." (This last one contains the lyrics to a popular song; as the creator writes in the "description" box, "I love this song!") Importantly, despite the gift economy of the Web site, users are careful to signify the source of the image: one poster writes of her icon, titled "I Love Mike," "for anyone who loves a Mike *I didn\\\\\\\'t make this, got it from another site and changed some stuff*."

At first glance, it may seem that there must be more of a sense of ownership or consonance with self achieved when a user makes an avatar for herself as opposed to downloading one made by another. Filiciak agrees with this idea: "Obviously, it is easier to identify ourselves with something that is partly created by us than with pictures imposed on us by somebody else."[19] If we follow this line of thinking, then, it would seem that the more "original" an avatar is, the better an indicator it must be of a user's individual identity and subjectivity. If this is true, then amateur-produced buddy icons from buddyicon.info downloaded by users who do not modify them further might not necessarily be more effective at communicating "unique" identities than Yahoo!'s or Microsoft's corporate sites; they would simply offer a wider range of identity categories, but these would still be keyed to received notions of identity and might in fact serve to reify and stereotype users even more than had been the case before. However, users' modifications of existing avatar or doll templates or the insertion of a single extra slide in a premade animated GIF on buddyicon.info attest to the flexibility that allows buddies to be at least "partly created by us" or collaboratively created even though the modifications might be minimal. The notion that even small alterations to a new media object might legitimately be counted as original production is part of new media theory and indeed one of the key aspects by which new media are distinguished from old media. Lev Manovich writes that the logic of new media defines the principle of selection as a subset of the act of production, thus calling into question the idea of "original creation." This is meant not as a downgrading or criticism of the principle of selection but as a modification of the notion of authorship. He claims that just as some Web page creators put up sites that are simply links to other sites, so too does the logic of new media production create "a new type of authorship" in which "the user does not add new objects to a corpus, but only selects a subset." It is the "logic of the advanced industrial and post-industrial societies, where almost every practical act involves choosing from some menu, catalog, or database," that gives rise to "the logic of identity in these societies—choosing values from a number of predetermined menus."[20] This line of thinking is the logical consequence of a postmodernist notion of diffused, compromised, or even dead authorship that can be traced back to Foucault and Barthes.[21] A meaningful definition of self-authorship in the case of AIM buddies resides in another basic principle differentiating new media from old, according to Manovich: modularity. "Media elements, be they images, sounds, shapes, or behaviors, are represented as collections of discrete samples (pixels, polygons, voxels, characters, scripts). These elements are assembled into larger-scale objects but continue to maintain their separate identities. The objects themselves can be combined into even larger objects—again, without losing their independence."[22] The stress in this passage on the independence and singularity of new media objects foregrounds the ways that "discreteness" is also part of the language of new media: digital compositing works to create an illusory sense of seamlessness where none properly exists. AIM buddies, on the other hand, do not strive for or attain seamlessness; they are a form whose overt modularity and independent parts betray their origins in amateur experiments in modular self-authorship and visual representation. This formulation is also useful because it can be read in reference to the process of diasporic and gender identity creation, particularly under the sign of new media: just as the assemblage of digital "objects" continually references the independence of their parts, so too do the signs of identity in late capitalism consist of recombinations of aspects rendered discrete by categories of racialization, gender, and nationality. Because AIM buddies are put together from already-existing body parts, clothes, fonts, borders, decorations, and other graphical "pieces," they are hybrid images that sometimes radically violate the principles of aesthetic and media continuity. Some of this radical fragmentation is accounted for by the purpose of these buddies: unlike corporate desktop images, these images overtly highlight extremely varied political positionalities, geographic locations, religions, and sometimes-occluded nationalities not covered in the conventional IM query requesting age, sex, and location: "A/S/L?"

Buddyicon.info offers twenty-seven alphabetized separate categories for buddy icons and away messages. Some of these reference other media forms, like "celebrity" and "tv," but others, like "women," "nationality," and "religion," directly confront identity (as is typical on sites of this kind, there is no category on this site for "race"). Armenian ("Armo Thug"), Salvadoran ("reppin' that Salvi life"), Polska, Irish, Serbian ("Serbian Pride"), Boricuan, Asian ("AZN pride"), Macedonian, Turk, Ukrainian, Latvian, and Arab buddies all appear under the category of "nationality," but so do "Anarchy," "Capricorn," "3 Nails + 1 Cross = 4given," and "Muslim." And though there are separate categories for "women" and "dollz," most of the buddies that depict human forms feature girls. (Under "religion" there is an icon depicting a white male wearing a baseball cap; this is so exceptional as to be noted in the description: "Description: i love Godalot of guys say there is not anofe guy icons so here a guy icon saying i love God.") Rather than interpreting this use of the "nationality" category as a sign of an inaccurate understanding of what nation, race, religion, and astrology mean, the particular mode in which these categories overlap indicates a multidimensional conception of what "nationality" means. Since users decide where to post their own buddies on this site, this mode of categorization reveals intersectional thinking along the lines of race, politics, language use, religion, ethnic identity, and references to nationally defining historical events such as September 11. Many of the buddies that indicated American identity overtly referenced 9/11: one reads "God Bless America" and depicts a still photographic image of the World Trade Center towers; its caption reads "a little tribute to the heroes of 9/11." This buddy's purpose is thus stated as a memorial to fallen national heroes: the modest modifier "little" in reference to the icon as a "tribute" figures AIM buddies as sites of memory. This buddy works less to represent an absent body, as an avatar does, and more to mark a national political identity, displayed in the same spirit here in the space of Instant Messenger as other types of public/personal iconography worn in offline public spheres, such as bumper stickers, pins, and T-shirts.

In a neoliberal gesture that informs the "color blindness" of these categories of categorization, the site's designers omitted a "race" category, yet users have managed to work race, such as "AZN," or Asian, into the discourse of nation because they have pressing reasons to do so. Pan-Asian identity relies on a notion of race or at least a partially shared geopolitics and orientation to American racial politics that challenges the idea of separate and conflicting Asian nations, with different and competing interests, priorities, and degrees of political power. On the other hand, the "nation" category does have the effect of including whiteness, a category that would generally be omitted from the "race" category even if it were offered. While it fails to challenge the idea of whiteness as a normative social identity on

IM, it does work to question the idea that whiteness has no relation to ethnicity or geographic location. Latvians, Irish, Italians, Poles, and other nationalities appear in the same category as Puerto Ricans, Salvadorans, and "Asians," a term that might normally appear under "race" if such a category existed. On the other hand, there were few African American or diasporic African buddies to be found in any category. There was also strikingly little diversity under the "religion" category: all the buddies in it represented Christian identities except for one, titled "Taoist ying yang."

The "Muslim," "usachick," and "nails n cross" buddy icons appear in the "nationality" category. They work to create intersectional identities in terms of race, religion, nation, gender, and politics. They are all built using the same "doll" template, a slender yet buxom cartoon avatar with easily replaceable hair colors, styles, clothing, and poseable limbs. The three buddy icons are all composed in the same way: all are animated GIFs consisting of four to seven separate images that play in sequence. "Muslim" depicts a blue-eyed, pink-chador-wearing avatar whose clothing, composed of a formfitting, long-sleeved, high-necked pink sweater emblazoned with the designer brand DKNY in large white letters on the chest and a long but formfitting blue flared skirt, conveys an ambivalent combination of "traditional" Islamic modesty and Western teen fashion. The veil is open in the front to reveal a conventionally pretty face—the same face shared by the dolls in "usachick" and "nails n cross"—with medium tan skin, a sidelong gaze, and a smile. As this animation plays, the first three slides, which depict a veiled face, a torso, and a lower body, are succeeded by three other images, which do not depict this female digital body but rather the religious and geographic images that define the ways we are to read it. Slide four consists of a pink field on which is written, in darker pink letters, "Ramadan is almoast here!" and it is followed by slides five and six, which represent first a digital image of a dark field with a gold crescent moon and star—the sign of Islam—and conclude with a scanned photograph of Mecca. When this last slide is reached, the program loops to the first slide and continues to play this six-slide sequence during an IM session until it is disabled. Thus the female body is depicted from top to bottom, sutured to a religious exhortation having to do with observing Muslim ritual and holidays, followed by the images of particular national identities and religious sites. The effect of this is to situate the viewer's observation of this religiously "observant" female teenage body— revealed yet virtuously covered up, modest yet winking, veiled yet exposed— within a narrative that reminds the viewer that we are to see it (and by extension the user) framed by the context of Islam. The author of "Muslim" is

Slide 1

Slide 2

Slide 3

Slide 4

Slide 5

Slide 6

Figure 1.1. "Ramadan is almoast here!" animated GIF AIM buddy icon. Source: buddyicon.info.

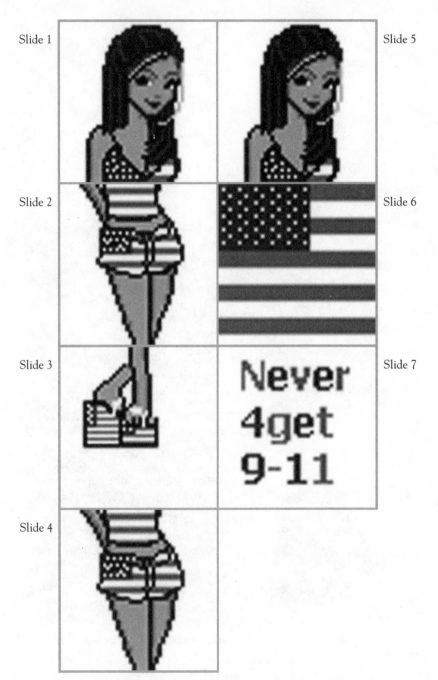

Figure 1.2. Animated GIF AIM buddy icon "usachick." Source: buddyicon.info.

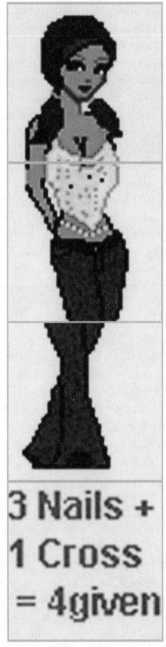

Figure 1.3. Animated GIF AIM buddy icon "nails n cross." Source: buddyicon.info.

a user who claims to be a fifteen-year-old girl from Detroit, a city with a large Arab American population, who chooses the nickname "shishkabob." The creation of this complex AIM buddy attests to the way that this signifying space is used by young women of color who wish to signify an unpopular religious subject position and also attempt to stay within the confines of convention regarding sexualized digital female bodies in the space of IM. This buddy was downloaded 470 times since it was posted in October 2003, attesting to the need to convey this sort of complex identity among other young female users as well.

The construction of a Muslim American girl as religiously traditional yet "hip" in her DKNY sweater and stylish but modest skirt can productively be contrasted to "usachick," subtitled "9/11," contributed by a different user, an icon that is constructed on almost exactly the same formal lines: it consists of a multiple slide depiction of a female avatar body divided into equal parts, followed by a slogan and an image. However, the seven slides of "usachick" are used slightly differently: the first three slides depict the same "doll" base as used by "Muslim," but the female figure is wearing an American-flag-patterned bra top with exposed midriff, very short shorts exposing bare legs, and platform thong sandals, all featuring the Stars and Stripes. Slides one, two, and three divide up the female body as in "Muslim," but slides four and five then repeat slides two and one in reverse order, thus showing the female body from top to bottom, then bottom to top. Slides six and seven depict first an American flag, then the slogan "never 4get 9-11." The use of numbers in this slogan remediates the unique abbreviated language of IM, which often substitutes numbers for letters in the interest of saving space and making typing faster and places it in the context of another numerically inspired abbreviation—9/11—that has a political and national valence that is here attached to the figure of the "American girl," a figure depicted as practicing her own sort of observances of national identity.

My third example, "nails n cross," has only four slides and depicts the same avatar used in "usachick," only with larger and more exposed breasts and darker skin, and its first three slides show the figure wearing a green top that exposes her midriff, low-slung boot-cut blue jeans, and the slogan "3 Nails + 1 Cross = 4given." Thus the animation of the female body shown from top to bottom is sutured to a virtual signboard that uses the same hybrid alphanumerical discourse as "usachick," which then loops back to the image of another, less modest than "Muslim," but equally observant religious body— that of the American Christian girl. Her clothing does not signify her identity in the same way; rather, it signifies the notion that the "uniform" of

American Christianity has less to do with ethnicity and its attendant signs, like the chador and a lack of exposed skin, and more to do with normative teenage fashions for American girls. This is the default fashion ensemble of American girls: rather than the abbreviated starred and striped top and shorts of "usachick," the Christian girl keeps her legs covered, albeit with formfitting jeans, and does not wear her religion on her virtual body. The burden of representing religion in this buddy rests solely on the signboard that follows it.

Theorists of new media have made much of the notion of cinema as the dominant language of culture and of the computer desktop as a cinematic space: "screen culture" is posited as the hegemonic cultural interface. IM is itself an anomaly, one that has eluded commodification by new media industries precisely because it seemed such an unpromising and graphically non-immersive user practice; its unexpected popularity demonstrates that digital print culture possesses durable attractions. AIM buddies suture together print culture and cinematic screen culture in two ways. First, within the form of the icons themselves, they create cinematic sequences that strikingly remediate the form of early film in that they alternate moving images of the body with explanatory textual titles or signboards that interpret the body's meaning and identity for the viewer. Like the cinema of attractions, which worked less to tell a complex narrative than to demonstrate the powers of the medium itself to simulate "real" experiences, these animated GIFs work like minimovies that have one purpose: to signify identities. Second, they work in conjunction with the practice of real-time text interaction, riding "on top" of the IM application and supplying a graphical component to online writing that expresses cinematic intersectional identities, but using narrative and spatial techniques unique to the form, techniques that were constructed by users themselves specifically to illustrate identities that exceed narration by either purely graphical-cinematic or textual means.

Per Persson describes the transition from early to modern cinema as occurring between 1905 and 1915 and explains the ways in which the drive for cultural legitimation directed the movement of the film form toward longer, more narratively complex structures that remediated theater and literature, as opposed to the earlier cinema of attractions, which remediated vaudeville and other lower-class entertainments. Several theorists have noted the way that new media remediate these earlier media forms: the similarity between digital games and the cinema of attractions, both of which attempt to reproduce an experience rather than tell a conventional story with a beginning, middle, and end, as Persson also follows this line.[23] Unlike other scholars, however, Persson is especially interested in the ways that digital space, in particular the computer desktop, remediates early cinema in terms of its conventions regarding the use of backdrops, the rudimentary use of montage, and the visual disposition of human figures. Animated GIFs are like film in that they are a "push" medium, and like early film, they are silent. Also, like the early cinema of attractions, IM lacks cultural legitimacy. The popular sense of IM as a "time waster" positions it close to the perceived social function of early cinema, which before 1905 had not yet acquired the respectability accorded to narrative forms like literature and theater. Like the animated GIFs I discuss earlier, early films negotiate screen space in ways that promote a sense of spatial discontinuity and a flat, artificial looking backdrop. In an increasingly rich and photo-realistic digital landscape, one in which even desktop images provide an astonishing sense of depth and richness, IM buddies remain flat and one-dimensional. As in Muybridge's early films, IM buddy backdrops are usually a single color. Also, IM and early cinema share a mode of exhibition: both are exhibited in relatively private screen-viewing situations. As Persson notes, white-screen projection of early films was adopted after the peep show; and as Manovich notes, personal computer screens are private, rather than public, viewing devices. The sense of gazing into a private screen is shared by IM users, particularly when they are using laptop computers. In addition, the sense that the viewer is witnessing something voyeuristically or has a privileged view—in other words, is not being overtly performed for—is missing in both forms. There is little or no sense of witnessing a "private" body on AIM buddy screens. This is particularly true in the case of the female avatars in the animated GIFs I have discussed, which like early vaudeville and cinematic actors address the user in face-to-face situations and "gesture and gaze at the user."[24] Persson compares this early form of acting with the way digital assistants like Microsoft's "Clippy" perform cinematically in the context of desktop computing.

The most striking formal similarity, however, and one with ideological implications, has to do with the way that shots or slides are sequenced and meant to signify in relation to each other. Persson explains that early cinema did not create or assume spatial continuity between separate shots. "Whereas viewers of today make spatial inferences between different shots, early cinema and its audience did not conceive of relations between shots in spatial terms."[25] Thus two contiguous shot sequences were not assumed to inhabit the same physical space. One of the most vivid examples he supplies is the way that Dr. Jekyll and Mr. Hyde (1912) presents a long shot of Hyde trashing his office and follows it with a close-up insert of a hand holding a bottle of poison, depicted against a flat black backdrop that is at odds with the shot that came before it. The conceptualization of space as discontinuous that we can see in early film describes perfectly the cinematic logic that structures animated GIF buddies like "Muslim," "usachick," and "nails n cross," which promiscuously mix photographic and cartoon images of cities, signboards and slogans, avatar bodies, and flags. Far from occupying the same space, these minifilms exploit the discontinuity of these images to produce a complex intersectional identity in a highly compressed form that runs ad infinitum or loops in the context of IM.

Thus, when analyzing these icons, one can identify two forms of movement in play. The movement of the avatar itself—the means by which it can be made to appear to wink, for example—is accomplished by sequencing two images together that depict a identical face with open and then closed eyes, simulating a change in facial expression. This kind of movement requires minimal intervention by the producer. This is basically the same means by which all animated video sequences are created. The other and more innovative one, one that is specific to, and characteristic of, this genre, directs or simulates the movement of the viewer's gaze by depicting a whole body revealed in pieces, thus creating the sense of looking down an entire body. The slow frame-per-second rate of these animated GIFs produces a slow, deliberate quality in the user's gaze that draws attention to the use of slides to represent a whole body. This slow fps rate remediates Eadweard Muybridge's card sequences that one could flip to simulate motion; however, AIM buddies' low-bandwidth animated sequences are cartoonish and far from photo-realistic.[26] Unlike Muybridge's "films," which worked with high-quality photographs to create an illusion of movement, the effect is more like an animated cartoon or minifilm, which, like a peep show loop, repeats itself inexhaustibly. The difference between Muybridge's cinematic technologies and animated GIFs in the context of AIM, however, is that high-res and low-res digital cinematic forms coexist on the Internet rather than replacing each other. It is quite possible and likely for an IM user to engage in an IM session using an animated GIF while viewing a movie on streaming video in another window on the same screen. One technological innovation does not replace another, in this case, but rather occupies different forms and communicative spaces, thus affording "ordinary" users the opportunity to create digital signatures without needing to own expensive software or advanced graphical skills.

Animated AIM buddy GIFs loop, or "play" until they are turned off. In this way they resemble early filmic peep shows, in particular pornographic ones, and like them, their subject is a female body that is optimized for viewing. The visual culture of these buddies governs the gaze to take in tiny images of curvy "dollz," digibodies that are flirtatiously revealed to the user as a series of slides that unveil the body's parts in sequence. This breaking up or partitioning of the female body into pieces to be put on separate slides invokes a way of looking that constructs the female digital body as a fetish.[27] As Mary Flanagan writes: "The role of fetishism, particularly the fetishization of the woman, in digital media is of great interest to any critical understandings of this new landscape, for digibodies are created from discrete elements and are positioned within a command and control paradigm of desire. Thus what is proposed here is that the means of this particular kind of 3D artifact production allows the body to be thought of as segmented and zoned. This breaking up of the female body into discrete elements, i.e. the creation of the image of woman as series of objects, is in terms of fetishistic scopophilia, focusing on the object or body part used for sexual enjoyment."[28] As does Manovich, Flanagan stresses the modular independence of the individual digital parts that make up digibodies and all new media objects, but unlike him, she identifies a "command and control paradigm of desire" that expresses an overdetermined female body that works as a site of visual pleasure in Western culture. Thus "independence" on the level of the image's structure and function results in a dynamic in which independence in political and representational terms is withheld from women themselves. Animated GIF AIM buddies of women's bodies or "dollz" employ this scopophilic mode of envisioning, virtually panning down the female body to represent it in parts, mimicking the surveying gaze of a spectator who "checks out" female bodies in the world. The sequence of images representing a face, a curvaceous torso, and a pair of feet repeat to imitate a stereotypically masculine gaze. As Roland Barthes writes in his dissection of the dynamics of looking embodied in striptease: "There will therefore be in striptease a whole series of coverings placed upon the body in proportion as she pretends to strip it bare."[29] In the case of the "Muslim" buddy icon in particular, the form of the animated GIF and its pan down the virtual female body accomplish a kind of virtual striptease, an unveiling of the veiled body in the very act of asserting its own religious difference. The insertion of messages, slogans, flags, and other nonbodily signs alternates with this visual trail down the female avatar body, valencing it in political, religious, and national terms that assert key differences between these bodies despite their shared means of digital exhibition. Thus the position of the viewer is inherently a fetishistic one, one in which AIM buddy female bodies are both fetishes and fetishized. They are specifically fetishes of difference, signs of identities that are embattled and particular: there are thousands of buddies in use and under construction because there is an unappeasable demand. This compulsion to repeat when it comes to buddy creation and the compulsion to view them looping endlessly in a short repetitive sequence reflects the desire to signify identities that vary, even infinitesimally, from each other in terms of race, nationality, religion, and language use.

The blazon is described thus by Barthes: "The spitefulness of language: once reassembled, in order to utter itself, the total body must revert to the dust of words, to the listing of details, to a monotonous inventory of parts, to crumbling; language undoes the body, returns it to the fetish. This return is coded under the term blazon. . . . Similarly with the striptease: an action, denudation, is predicated on the succession of its attributes (legs, arms, bosom, etc.). . . . As a genre, the blazon expresses the belief that a complete inventory can produce a total body."[30] In this passage from his monumental work of structuralist literary analysis, S/Z, Barthes describes the blazon as a mode of representation that systematically lists body parts in a "monotonous" fashion. "Muslim," "usachick," and "nails n cross" represent a female body cut into three discrete pieces, head, torso, and legs, so as to fit a sufficiently detailed "total" body into a small space; but this method, which may have originated as a technological fix for dealing with a space shortage, results in a mode of viewing that fetishizes the female body, creating a virtual "inventory" of its parts, a term that predates the notion of the digital database but is homologous with it. Though, as Manovich notes, all films are basically databases of images, this portioning of the body into parts is relatively uncommon in early cinema, which tended to depict the human form in its entirety. As Persson notes, it was considered "bad composition" to represent a body with its feet outside the frame.[31] Viewing the stately yet sprightly march of an animated GIF that cycles through its seven cards in an unchangeable cadence reminds one of the deliberateness of this mode of vision, one that offers no surprises and plenty of repetition and depends on a conventionalized succession of images to create something impossible: a "total" body. This interest in reproducing "total" bodies informs the current fetish with digitally photo-realistic bodies.

The collection, production, and deployment of these tiny modular female bodies evokes at least one aspect of the practice of collecting of miniatures: that is, fetishism. In On Longing, Susan Stewart anatomizes the ways in which the impulse to collect miniatures and in particular to create a specific form of the miniature, the tableau, satisfies psychic needs: "There are two major features of the tableau: first, the drawing together of significant, even if contradictory, elements, and then the complete filling out of 'point of view'; and second, the simultaneous particularization and generalization of the moment."[32] Just as in AIM buddy icons, which are digital tableaux, tableau arrangements stress both the individuality of the user and the creation of identities that are irremediably particular along *with* the shared and generalized nature of these identities: though the AIM buddy icon depicting a fashionably dressed observant Muslim girl in pink intercut with a flag, an image of Mecca, and "Ramadan is almoast here!" may seem extremely eccentric, other users share enough identification with it to have downloaded it hundreds of times. In addition, the transposition of these graphical elements and textual signs in a digital motion sequence certainly draws together "significant, even if contradictory elements"; indeed, that may be its main purpose.

Barthes's revolutionary idea that any cultural product or practice, such as cheese advertisements or professional wrestling, can be read using the same sort of formal analysis that one would use to read classical French novelists such as Balzac, the author of *Sarrasine*, opened the door for the discipline of cultural studies to gain legitimacy. Semiotics seemed particularly well suited for studying popular culture and emergent expressive forms that were not yet covered under existing disciplines of academic theory. The Internet produces new media practices constantly, and there is still a lack of consensus over where and how they ought to be studied in the academy.[33] Nonetheless, despite cultural studies' open-mindedness regarding "proper" objects of study, there is already a canon of fetishized new media objects for academics, and AIM buddies do not belong to it. This may have something to do with the "tackiness" of amateur-produced AIM buddy icon images; along the axis of taste, cheese and wrestling are like Shakespeare compared to the AIM buddies I have discussed. The new media canon, as exemplified by work such as Manovich's, Darley's, and Galloway's, privileges interfaces, virtual reality applications, and digital art, games, and Web sites. The lower tier is reserved for youth-oriented ephemeral activities, like chats and IM, which may account for the dearth of critical research on these visual digital practices. While there has been published research on IM by social scientists mainly regarding discourse analysis, there has been little by cultural theorists. AIM buddies are everything that new media, as described and idealized by formalists such as Manovich, is not or is not supposed to be: while the ideal form of new media as described in much of the scholarship has value because it is interactive, synchronous, fully featured, immersive, possessed of spatial depth, adventuresome in terms of content and form, and richly textured, AIM buddies are low fidelity, fairly uninteractive, often tasteless, and poorly produced simulations. This may account, at least partly, for their neglect by scholars; in a field that privileges the "virtual" for its ability to create convincing simulations and postmodern identity experiences, AIM buddies are on the low end of virtuality *and* virtuosity. However, perhaps for these very reasons, they are locations of overt and controversial identity formation by large numbers of IM users from minority groups who may not engage in any other graphical production practices online, which makes them an important aspect of analysis for scholars who study online community. These users are quite likely to be relative newcomers to the Internet, as young people are one of the fastest-growing groups of Internet users, as are people of color. Thus it is especially important that their creation of a visual culture in a networked communication form that is assumed not to have one—Instant Messenger—be examined carefully and considered in light of its ability to express identities that are resistant to normativity and presented alternatively to commercially produced images of the networked body. It is the confluence of textual and visual discourses that makes IM and its AIM buddies distinctive: while the conversation in IM rambles on in its distinctively disjointed, abbreviated, and free-associative way, the AIM buddy remains fixed in place, either marching through its predetermined frames, which simulate repetitive iconic movement, or standing still. The cinematic space of the animated AIM buddy anatomizes the use of gesture in the construction of gendered identities: winks, wiggles, and smiles direct the viewer to a performance of femininity that is far from resistant to gender norms. The containment of this digital image of identity creates a subject of interactivity who remains fixed within a small space, a space that cannot expand and is permanently supplementary to the performance of "live" conversation. On the other hand, the wild variety of buddies created and used by people who fit in "other" categories attests to a thriving, as yet relatively uncommodified visual culture of digital body representation. The ability to swap out slides in animated GIFs of female identity such as "Muslim," "usachick," and "nails n cross" creates a type of volitional ethnicity that can work as part of a new economy of digital visual capital, with several users figuratively sharing a common body but modifying it with references to Islam, Christianity, 9/11, or brand preferences that cause it to parse differently.

2

Alllooksame? Mediating
Visual Cultures of Race on the Web

During World War II, Navajo "codetalkers" transmitted and received radio messages in a code based on the Navajo language. This unique form of speech, a hybrid between a "natural" language and an artificial one, was a code unbreakable by eavesdropping Japanese troops. Thus human code succeeded where machine code could not; while other forms of encryption could be broken, legend has it that the Navajo language was so inscrutable, so "irregular," that no enemy operator could understand it. Unlike the Enigma code used by the Nazis during World War II, which was generated by a machine that performed mechanical encryption, the Navajo code was never broken. This notion of human language as the ultimate form of secure encoding, one that transcends anything that thinking or computing machines can produce precisely because of its idiosyncrasy and irregularity, figures "alien" languages such as Navajo as human rather than nonhuman. While binary code is distinguished by its transcodability and relatively easy modularity across shared digital protocols such as TCP/IP, creating a common language of machines, human discourse in its ethnic and national diversity is unaccountable, irregular, and untranslatable, and it retains its particularity. In this paradigm, ethnicity and language literally make the difference; they make humans unlike other humans as well as unlike machines.

Windtalkers (2002), an otherwise undistinguished film directed by the Hong Kong filmmaker John Woo, dramatizes the dilemma that faced Navajo communications specialists in the U.S. Army. Many of these soldiers had

been the victims of missionary schools committed to beating native language use out of students as part of the mission to civilize their savage ways
and hasten the process of assimilation to the U.S. nation-state. The ongoing process of American colonization of native populations is referenced as
ironic in the context of this war in particular, with its enhanced need for
secure encrypted communications. As the Navajo codetalker Ben Yazzie
(Adam Beach) relates his story of being chained to a radiator for two days
in a church basement as punishment for speaking Navajo during a Catholic
service, marine Joe Enders (Nicholas Cage), the soldier assigned to guard
him, dryly remarks that the army has changed its tune: "They sure are letting
you speak it now." The tension between national and linguistic identity is
clearly outlined in this exchange: Yazzie the Navajo is an unassimilable and
objectionable presence in the context of a United States at peace, at best irrelevant and at worst a threat to a white national identity, but crucial to national security when at war. This does not, however, make him a valuable or
empowered subject even within a military context: part of the tension in the
movie lies in the fact that Enders cannot get too attached to Yazzie, for it is
his responsibility to kill him rather than let him be captured and tortured,
thus letting the Nazis penetrate the secret of the Navajo code. The integrity
of the code itself is far more important than the man: while it is Yazzie's identity as a unique and scarce ethnic subject—a Navajo—that creates his value
for the military, he himself is envisioned as merely a carrier for this crucial
linguistic code; while the code itself is the signal, he is the noise, a necessary
but devalued adjunct to "information," a commodity infinitely more valuable
than bodies in the context of this war.

There is another axis of tension, though, which runs along the line that
separates race from ethnicity and language: in the film's climactic battle
scene, the Americans are pinned down and taking heavy fire from their
own troops because their radio unit has been hit and they are unable to
communicate correct bombing coordinates. As the doomed soldiers lie in a
foxhole, Yazzie notices a dead Japanese soldier and remarks, "I look just like
a Jap." This echoes an earlier moment in the film when he had been beaten
while taking a bath by a racist anti-Indian American soldier who "mistook"
him for a Japanese while he was out of uniform. Consequently, in the heat
of battle, Yazzie decides to put on a dead Japanese soldier's uniform so as to
get behind enemy lines to access the radio. This scheme succeeds, we are to
believe, because Yazzie is one of "us" but reads like one of "them," or rather,
he cannot be profiled accurately by either Americans or Japanese in terms
of language, nationality, or racialization. He literally cannot be understood,

either when speaking in code—eavesdropping Japanese radio operators intercept his speech and say, "It sounds like English, but like someone talking underwater"—or when spotted on the battlefield, for the Japanese do mistake him for one of them, we are to believe, because Enders teaches him a single word of Japanese, the word for "prisoner." This moment of racial and phenotypic misrecognition is exploited in the logic of the film to highlight yet another way in which a nationally useful Navajo difference—language— can be exploited in another vein; the phenotypic similarity shared by dark-haired, dark-skinned Asians and Navajos enables and indeed inevitably produces cross-racial passing. Unique linguistic codes like Navajo are commodified as a valuable kind of difference in the context of a war between nations, while the racialized bodies that produce that difference function as a liability in the film's logic, or only as an asset insofar as they permit temporary cross-racial mimicry.

The case of Navajo codetalkers demonstrated quite graphically how humans could stand in for computers and indeed do a more efficient, faster, better job. As Yazzie notes in an effort to justify his usefulness to an initially skeptical Enders, "I can do in two and a half minutes what it used to take hours to do." While the use of mechanical encryption devices like the German Enigma machine required a trained operator, an up-to-date codebook, and plenty of time to perform accurate decoding and recoding operations, a Navajo codetalker with a radio could produce live, on-the-fly, secure encrypted communication, a necessity for soldiers and tacticians in battle. The use of Navajo codetalkers as part of a secure real-time communication network anticipated the sorts of tasks that computers would be employed to perform in the age of the Internet.

This narrative has particular resonance when it is factored in with a parallel one, the story of the Enigma encryption device. Alan Turing, who is often credited as one of the founding fathers of computer science, was instrumental in breaking the Nazis' Enigma code. His work at Bletchley Park, an English mansion converted to the war effort and staffed with mathematicians, cryptographers, engineers, and linguists, resulted in the construction of one of the earliest computers and started his pioneering work on artificial intelligence. He also devised the Turing Test, which has proved immensely intellectually generative to theorists of technology, identity, and intelligent systems. This test posited that if a computer could produce messages through a computer console that could convince a user that the computer was a human, it could be considered sentient. Though the test has not yet been passed by any software program, it is still performed today at universities (such as the University of California, Riverside; UC San Diego; and MIT).[1] Turing's test assumed that it is not possession of a physical biological body, but the quality of possessing the ability to deceive humans into believing that the computer is producing thought, that defines intelligence. This notion of the body as merely a container for information—worthless "meat" or noise to the mind's signal—resonates strongly with the narrative of the Navajo codetalkers, whose inconveniently raced bodies were tolerated in exchange for the unique and valuable knowledge that arose from that very inconvenience. It is precisely because Navajos, once citizens of a fully autonomous sovereign nation located in the United States of America, had become scarce even within its bounds as a result of a national policy of racial, cultural, and, in particular, linguistic genocide that their code possessed value. The lack of a written language, the crushing poverty that prevented travel outside national borders, the disenfranchisement of the Navajo within the U.S. school system, and the cultural devaluation of their spoken language all contributed to making their language work as a code. It went from being worse than worthless to becoming national security information worth killing for to protect; indeed, the existence of Navajo codetalkers and their service in decisive battles in the Pacific theater, such as Saipan and Iwo Jima, was classified information and remained a secret until 1965.[2] Racist anti-Indian U.S. laws and policies partially contributed to the Navajo language's status as being "off the map" of known languages: despite Hitler's deployment of thirty anthropologists to study the language when he learned of the code, his attempts were unsuccessful. Turing, who died by suicide, also understood the tension between a socially worthless or abject body and the valuable code or knowledge that it could contain. He underwent "oestrogen therapy" in an unsuccessful effort to cure his homosexuality. Despite his value to the war effort, he was nonetheless persecuted for his sexual difference. Like the codetalkers, Turing as well can be seen as ultimately an *object* of interactivity, rather than a *subject*; his disempowered status as a social subject despite his importance to the military industrial complex constitutes an early paradigmatic example of an intolerably and ultimately disposable queer body that is tolerated provisionally because of its ability to produce machine code. The dream of a secure communication network that could work in real time that was temporarily realized by Navajo codetalkers was partly fulfilled by Turing's early work in machine cryptography, which has since led to secure digital information systems.

The visual culture of racial, gender, and sexual passing also ties these two stories together. If the computer that passes the Turing Test constitutes a potentially posthuman consciousness, Navajo codetalkers and indeed Turing himself occupied the other end of the spectrum, possessing abject and reviled bodies that could not be assimilated into modern society, even ultimately in moments of national emergency. Turing's position in the closet uncannily echoes the notion of an artificial intelligence judged by its ability to pass as human purely by its effects on humans; computer-generated speech was unique partly because it did not need to involve the presence of a body, and the test necessarily had to be performed blind, with the human subject unable to see his or her interlocutor. Ben Yazzie's passing narrative conflates the notion that all dark-haired, dark-skinned peoples look alike enough that they cannot tell each other apart, even in the context of a war between opposing nations. The notion that a Japanese soldier would not be able to tell a Navajo from another Japanese after hearing him speak his native tongue, even in the heat of battle, participates in the conception of race as transcending any individual, national, or cultural differences. This model is clearly faulty—wars have successfully been waged between phenotypically similar nations and groups without an excessive number of misrecognitions resulting in mistaken casualties. The foregrounding of this type of passing narrative demonstrates the ways that race (as opposed to culture) becomes reified, a process actively initiated and supported by the state. As Jon Cruz writes: "It cannot be denied that race in the United States is a state-constructed and state-sanctioned mode of institutional materiality anchored in the fine print of juridical-legal language and shored up by apparatuses of what Weber called *legitimate force*."[3] Unlike ethnicity, an aspect of identity that in the case of Navajo codetalkers could be considered a benefit or commodity, race operates differently: it is a code that evokes a specific type of regulating response from the state that serves to make race "real." The reification of race as a social and quasi-empirical category by the state "hinge[s] on highly institutionalized and formalized juridical-legal racial codifications that operated as state law (which is precisely why 'race' and 'ethnicity' should not be conflated as interchangeable terms, a tendency quite common in the social sciences)."[4]

As Michael Omi notes, one strategic response to the reification of race by many of its subjects, for example, newly anointed "Asian Americans," a racialized term that Omi asserts did not come into existence until after the civil rights movement, has been to employ the notion of panethnicity as a way to gain political power by enabling them to form a larger political constituency.[5] The purposeful elision of significant and often divisive cultural, linguistic, and ethnic differences between groups such as Japanese, Chinese, Filipinos, Vietnamese, and Koreans enforced by U.S. policies caused race to signify far more than ethnicity. This led to coalition building around the idea of a shared racial or "panethnic" identity that could temporarily or provisionally trump ethnicity or nationality. This created a paradox, in which panethnic "racial pride" came to possess a political valence that promised potential resistance to racism yet also tended to assume the notion of race as "real," as both a visual and subvisual or genetic code shared among people who were otherwise quite different. The emphasis on racial or visible phenotypic difference as the primary defining quality of all nonwhite people has always been an especially salient aspect of America's wars with Asian nations and resulted in what was called in Vietnam the "mere gook rule," by which any dead Vietnamese was counted as a dead enemy. As Lee describes, this rule obtained as well in the world of race relations in the United States during times of economic, rather than military, wars with Asian nations: the 1987 murder of Vincent Chin, a Chinese American who was mistaken for a Japanese and killed by two white autoworkers in Detroit, exemplified the ways that even during times of peace "the mere gook rule overrode ethnicity."[6] This elision of cultural differences between different groups from Asia produces misrecognitions that often anger Asian Americans; one of these manifestations is the cliché "they all look the same."

The Web site alllooksame.com uses the Internet as a Turing Test to see if users can tell different "types" of Asians apart. It does this by asking users to look at photographic portraits of people's faces. The site requires the user to guess whether photographs of Asian faces are Chinese, Japanese, or Korean, and then calculates the user's score to see if he or she can accurately tell the difference, which the majority of users cannot do. Thus the site works to deconstruct the idea of race as code, as well as the notion that this code operates visually. It emphasizes the ways in which the *visual* has always had primacy in our understandings of race; the mistaken-identity problem or the mere-gook rule that killed Vincent Chin was an example of the way that racialization occurs on the fly and on the ground. Chin was misread because the dynamic of Asian American racialization relies on a lexicon of visual appearances, to the exclusion of other aspects of identity such as those signified by the oral or linguistic. In recent times, the Internet is becoming a site of increasingly visual rather than textual reading; the shift toward graphics and away from text-only environments online occasions the need for a new method of interpretation and analysis that will account for the role of visualization in the process of racialization. The Internet is an outstanding example of a racialized medium, in Omi's sense: he explains that he and his frequent coauthor Howard Winant "employ the term racialization to signify the extension of racial meaning to a previously racially unclassified relationship, social practice, or group."[7] The Internet is certainly an infrastructure and a medium that seemed to many to be race free or color blind but is in fact imbued with racial politics as a result of the digital inequalities evident in its demographics, its political economy, and its content. It has also become an increasingly active purveyor of images of race as well as narratives about them. The Internet's turn away from text and toward graphics, away from the literary and toward the visual, is supported by users' preference for images as well as the infrastructural improvements that accommodated them and was anticipated in William Gibson's seminal cyberpunk text *Neuromancer*. In this novel, Gibson imagines a fully networked society inhabited by both natural humans and artificial intelligences who can acquire citizenship within nation-states despite lacking physical bodies but who are heavily regulated by the Turing Police. This society has become post-textual; the protagonist and hacker Case employs voice recognition and streaming audio as well as tactile inputs to interact with his computer. In this future, a hacker relies on postliterate interfaces, using hardware that resembles a game controller rather than a conventional computer keyboard and navigating through an imagistic dataspace made up of images and icons rather than words.[8] Gibson anticipated a cyberspace that would look and feel much more like a digital game than like reading and writing. This explains why characters from the uneducated lower classes such as Case are able to gain proficiency in it; Gibson's vision of the cybernetic sublime assumes first a transcendental state of spiritual fusion with the machine enabled by willing disembodiment, but also a primarily postliterate graphical computing environment much at odds with conventional notions of literacy, education, and the cultural and ethnic specificity that goes with them. Cyberpunk posthumanism is based partly on the loss of individual print cultures and their codes and their replacement by global imagistic and machine codes. An artificial intelligence that Case interacts with remarks sadly that humans have lost the ability to read: in answer to Case's question "Can you read my mind?" the AI reminds him: "Minds aren't *read*. See, you've still got the paradigms print gave you, and you're barely print-literate. I can *access* your memory, but that's not the same as your mind."[9] Print culture is envisioned as part of the technological nostalgia that characterizes cyberpunk: Gibson gestures toward a return to preliterate times in parts of the world that are victims of digital inequality when he describes letter-writers on a Turkish street with their voiceprinters: "A few letter-writers had taken refuge in doorways, their old voiceprinters wrapped in sheets of clear plastic, evidence that the written word still enjoyed a certain prestige here. It was a sluggish country."[10] A high valuation of the written word is linked here to cultural "sluggishness" or backwardness; power lies instead in mastery of what Gibson would identify in a later novel as visual "pattern recognition," particularly in the realm of the digital or corporately branded image, rather than in literacy.[11]

Much of the Internet's traffic consists of streaming video and audio and images of all kinds rather than text alone. This has resulted in media convergence, a topic in which there has been intense academic and journalistic interest, but also in an environment in which there has been significantly less interest. In this graphical environment, literacy matters far less than it did, and linguistic codes partially replace visual and graphical ones. Looking has become as important as reading: icons constitute a language of the interface that, while still culturally specific, alters the cultural and educational requirements for Internet and computer use. The Internet's increasing visuality may potentially represent great promise in terms of overcoming its current state of geopolitical digital inequality. However, there is a different but related outcome that produces a great deal of anxiety among postcolonial theorists; that is, by giving nonliterate users access, it may transmit cultural values that are destructive to local ones, a matter of much concern to media theorists such as Ziaddin Sardar, Faye Ginsburg, Ien Ang, Eric Michaels, and others. As Michaels notes in his study of the Walpiri aborigines: "I was able to observe the rapid adoption of electronic media by people who rejected print. This provides us with the intriguing but perhaps no longer so unusual situation of a people's moving rapidly from 'oral' to electronic society, but bypassing print literacy." The preliterate Walpiri had been pressured into literacy by missionaries who wished them to read the Bible, and the Walpiri had compelling reasons for resisting it. They were, however, quite amenable to electronic media such as "Hollywood iconography" and become avid television watchers and producers. Thus they proceeded directly from oral culture to electronic culture, bypassing print culture altogether. As Michaels notes, their case is an example of an increasingly common challenge to the notion of "unilineal media evolution," the orderly progression from orality to "literacy, print, film, and now electronics."[12]

Neuromancer asks us to envision an even more radical violation of this progression by depicting a future in which users on the cultural periphery move directly from oral culture to networked digital culture, bypassing television and film altogether. While there has been a fair amount of scholarship on the impact and meaning of television adoption in preliterate societies, there has been relatively little on Internet adoption, though the popularity and spread of cybercafés and gaming parlors on the global scene certainly signal the massification of the medium among wider numbers of users. New media collectives such as Sarai in New Delhi work to facilitate the adoption and deployment of digital media among some of India's poorest users, many of whom are preliterate. This exploitation of the Internet's increasingly visual and graphical nature works to empower users of color in a way that is useful to oppose the reification of race through visual means online. In this chapter I begin by analyzing the Web site alllooksame.com to parse the ways that race is ultimately deconstructed as a visually meaningful term. My position is that rather than resulting in successful racial profiling, the site provides more occasions for racial misrecognitions, thus exposing the active process of the reification of race. I end the chapter with an assessment of postcolonial theoretical stances regarding Internet adoption across ethnic and national borders. Clearly there is much at stake in this debate: the Internet is feared by many postcolonial media and technology critics partly because they see it as an obstacle to the preservation of rare or endangered languages.[13] The dominance of majority languages like English and Japanese could potentially contribute to the eradication of rarer languages like Navajo, languages with possible use value beyond their use as codes during a war.

Web sites such as Dyske Suematsu's alllooksame.com effectively employ interactivity and the spectacle of race online in ways that offer distinctive forms of resistance to racial and visual categories. Alllooksame.com critiques vision itself as a way of understanding race, culture, and the body both online and off. There is a tendency in new media criticism to valorize ethnic identity Web sites that have an overtly progressive political stance as being more culturally "authentic" (and thus less corrupted by the West) than others.[14] I chose to examine alllooksame.com because it is a space produced by an Asian designer for an Asian and Asian American audience that debates national and ethnic identities rather than simply affirming them. In addition, alllooksame.com is a comedic site and thus part of a dramatically under-examined genre that gets little critical attention even from Net critics.[15] Alllooksame.com is a weird, weird site. Interacting with it produces a mixture of guilt and fascination and a lingering feeling of discomfort. In short, it is uncanny. The initial screen features the familiar iconography of a Scantron exam form with its ranks of numbered oval blanks, along with a "welcome" narrative that reads:

Figure 2.1. Alllooksame.com home page.

Chinese. Japanese. Korean. What's the difference? Some say it's easy to see. Others think it's difficult—maybe even impossible. Who can really tell? That's what we want to find out. For this first test, we'll show you a series of 18 pictures of CJKs. Select which country you think each is from. When you're finished we'll tell you your score and how you stacked up to others. Future tests will include landscapes, names, architecture, and more. And if you're wondering whether or not to take offense, remember: alllooksame is not a statement. It's a question.

After the user completes a short registration form, she is routed to the "test," which consists of digital photographs of young men and women. The form requires the user to click one of three boxes to move ahead in the site: one must guess whether the photograph is of a Chinese, Japanese, or Korean person. After the user does this for all eighteen images, the site calculates the score; the average score is seven. Users are given the corrected version of their test so they can guess which ones they got "wrong," and are told that they are "OK" if they get a score higher than average.

Suematsu writes that he designed the site "ultimately as a joke" and that he "didn't mean this site to be some sort of political arena." Despite this, as he writes in an essay to the user, "Some people felt that this site would pro-mote racism, or that the site itself is racist. Others felt quite the opposite. I was very surprised to receive many emails with encouraging words from Chinese, Korean, and Japanese people. In some ways, I was expecting to upset many of these people." The wide range of responses to the site demon-strates the ways that this particular kind of interactivity, one that puts the user in the position of a racial profiler of sorts, functions as a nexus for Asians and Asian Americans to actively consider race as an act of seeing. The site's bulletin board encourages active conversation about the meaning of the test and most importantly constitutes a valuable and unique opportu-nity to study the Asian American new media user. As Elizabeth Bird writes in her perceptive study of media audience ethnography in *The Audience in Everyday Life*, ethnicity and gender produce significant differentials in the qualitative research process that must be thought through more carefully. In her study of Native Americans and their media use, she noticed that group interviews worked well in gathering information because they used a "com-municative style . . . more collaborative and less competitive than Anglos," but she discovered that this was only the case among single-sex groups, since Native American females tended to defer to older males in group settings.[16] Bird encourages a careful interrogation of what she calls the "ethnographic encounter" in a broad sense, taking note not only of the ethnographer's own identity and its relation to the type of interaction she is likely to have with informants, but also whether the presence or absence of the researcher might foreclose or enable particular kinds of conversations. Asian Americans tend not to be especially forthcoming about themselves in non-anonymous or interview situations for several reasons: if they are undocumented immi-grants, they may not wish to call attention to themselves, and many Asian cultures tend to frown on individuals speaking about personal matters or opinions in public settings. For these reasons, Asian Americans may post to the Internet in cases in which they might not confide in an interviewer. In addition, people who have noticeable foreign accents may be mocked or devalued as "FOB" (Fresh off the Boat) in settings that require spoken lan-guage, and the use of imperfect or nonstandard written English may also be a source of embarrassment to survey takers. It matters what type of Web site

Figure 2.2. A test question screen from alllooksame.com.

is being examined as well when we are evaluating Asian American participation in new media discussion boards; a board like alllooksame.com, which
is produced by a Japanese immigrant and whose overt content is about Asian
American identity, creates a discursive space that is particularly hospitable
to honesty and openness. Many of the posters to Suematsu's Web site used
"broken" or nonstandard English in their posts, a factor that may have encouraged others who write in similar styles to post when they might not
have otherwise done so. Thus the medium of this Internet bulletin board
and others like it may be an especially valuable way to gain insight into the
reception of new media by Asians and Asian Americans.

Users of the alllooksame.com bulletin boards commiserate with each
other about their low scores; and importantly, the low scores that most users
get confirm that seeing is *not* believing—the "truth" about race is not a visual
truth, yet it is one that is persistently envisioned that way. Alllooksame.com
is an apparatus that deconstructs the visual culture of race. The confusion this
entails—users seem to be radically divided as to what the site signifies—
provides a unique intervention into the ways that the visual participates in
taxonomies of race. The most challenging aspect of this, an aspect that is
specifically enabled by the site's interactivity, is that the user is forced to confront her inadequacy in the face of visual "evidence" of race. The low scores
that most users get seem to surprise them: in the extremely extensive discussion area of the site where users post their comments, many note that before
using the site, they thought they could tell the difference, but their low
scores convinced them otherwise.[17] On September 12, 2002, "Annette"
posted a particularly thoughtful set of questions to the discussion board:

What does Japanese mean? Does it mean ethnic Koreans, who speak
Japanese and no Korean, who are third generation Japanese born? Or is it
my friend who is half Japaneese, half Korean who grew up in Puerto Rico??
Well maybe it is the children of a Japaneese and his Korean Bride.

What does Korean mean? Is is people from south western Korea who
decended from Chinese in those areas whose names are not Kim and Lee but
Chang and Moon??? Or does it mean Koreans who are 1/2 Chinese or
Japanese? Nah. . maybe Korean means the child of a Fillipina (or Chinese or
Indonesian for that matter) mail order bride (passing as Korean) and her
Korean husband. Then again, they could be those in Uzbekistan forcefully
moved there by the Russians 50 years ago, or those in eastern China. What
about the Mongolians or Manchurians who came across the border to North
Korea. . Korean??

And just what does Chineese mean? Those Koreans born of Chinese
Decent? Or those who have been in Peenang Malasia for over 100 years,
who have mixed with the Indians or Malays at some point?? Or does it mean
one of the hundreds of recent Chineese labourers to S. Korea. WHAT IS MY
POINT YOU ASK? Well/ . . . None of these groups are "pure" (ie no mixture or
outside influence), nor are they homogeneous. Even among the Koreans
who are considered the most homogeneous most inbred in Asia, there has
been some mixture. . that's whay ie may be difficult to tell. . . but then. . Is
it infact important to tell??????? The world is changing. I for one can't wait
for the day when there are so many new groups and categories on the census
that they will have to drop the race/ethnicity category.[18]

Anthropologists have long agreed about the uselessness of the "race/
ethnicity" category as a census term. In the face of empirical evidence of
the failure of vision as a means of identifying race, "Annette" redirects the
conversation in such a way that the categories themselves are deconstructed.
Her comment that race and ethnicity will eventually become uncategoriz-
able, and thus unavailable to empirical analysis, takes the site to its logical
conclusion.

Alllooksame.com is an immensely popular Web site: in a post dated August
2004, Suematsu claims that over 1.3 million people took the test since its
inception, in August 2001. Alllooksame.com is a very popular Web site with
Asian Americans. As a result of the site's success, in March 2002, Suematsu
was invited to address the Asian American Students Association at Harvard
University on the topic of "Asian American community." In his speech,
which he reprints on alllooksame.com, he claims to have no interest in producing an "Asian American community," asserts that he is not a member of
any such thing because he was born in Japan, and goes on to question the
importance or relevance of Asian American studies as a discipline and Asian
Americanness as a meaningful identity based on anything other than shared

racial oppression, the existence of which he professes to doubt. It seems that the default whiteness of Web content is so pervasive that Harvard students were inclined to think that any visual representations of Asian Americans online constituted an act of community building. But by calling into question what "Asian" is, at least in visual terms, Suematsu is interrogating the basis on which racial taxonomies like "Asian" are built, and in so doing is producing a community of a different kind.

By uniting Asian users in the act of deconstructing and questioning their own visual notions of race, alllooksame.com produces a community based on a shared act of interactive self-reflexivity. By discovering that Asian identity is in the "eye of the beholder," as the site asserts, identity is detached from biological bodies and reassigned to the realm of the cultural, political, and geographic. Even more to the point, the act of severing the visual as a way of knowing from racial identity addresses a sore point within the Asian American community: that is, racism *between* Asians.[19] In "Indonesia on the Mind: Diaspora, the Internet, and the Struggle for Hybridity," the media theorist Ien Ang argues that "the dominant discourse of the passions of diasporic identity are being globalized in a dramatic fashion by cyberspace," and her studies of Huaren, or diasporic Chinese, Web sites reveal the extent to which they contributed to intra-Asian prejudice and essentialism.[20] Ang found that "the immediacy of the Internet promoted a readiness to buy into highly emotive evocations of victimization which worked to disregard the historical complexity and specificity of the situation within Indonesia, in favour of a reductionist discourse of pan-ethnic solidarity cemented by an abstract, dehistoricized, and absolutist sense of 'Chineseness.'"[21] The site served as a vector for appeals to an "authentic" and essentialized Chinese identity. In this sense, it promoted "ethnic absolutist identity politics." In contrast to this case, alllooksame.com is a site where racial visual essentialism can be critiqued in an active, participatory way with its own built-in apparatus: the test.

Alllooksame.com remediates several cultural institutions allied with race construction to comment on race as a mistaken notion, one that is more easily gotten wrong than right. The site's iconography invokes the Scantron exam, a distinctive feature of Western higher education's obsession with the empirical, as well as the pictorial convention of the mug shot and the lineup, both connected visually with the judicial and legal system. The confluence of the academy and the police gestures toward the participation of both within the system that maintains racial codes. The site also shows that racial codes come from the user as well as the interface or content of the site itself. The site exposes the user's participation in this construction; it shows how individual acts of viewing and "typing" or clicking create race just as surely as do large institutions such as schools, medical establishments, and the law. Of course, individual acts are inflected by these institutions; when this is acknowledged, they come less to seem like personal "choices" and more like part of a complex or dynamic by which race occurs and is instantiated in everyday acts of seeing.

Perhaps the most salient example of an institution that regulates racial visual codes and taxonomies has yet gone unmentioned, and that is anthropology. This field's long association with racial typing is referenced by Robert Lee in "The Cold War Origins of the Model Minority Myth." In it, he writes that after Pearl Harbor, "for the first time, being able to tell one Asian group apart from another seemed important to white Americans. Two weeks after the Japanese attack on Pearl Harbor brought the United States into the War, *Life* magazine ran a two-page pictorial entitled 'How to Tell Japs from Chinese.'"[22] The article provided pictures of representative Japanese and Chinese faces along with commentary that interpreted the visual images in terms of their differences from each other. Some of these markers are described as follows: Chinese are described as having a "parchment yellow complexion, more frequent epicanthic fold, higher bridge, never has rosy cheeks, lighter facial bones, longer narrower face and scant beard," while the Japanese face "betrays aboriginal antecedents, has an earthy yellow complexion, less frequent epicanthic fold, flatter nose, sometimes rosy cheeks, heavy beard, broader shorter face and massive cheek and jawbone." In so doing, Lee writes, "*Life* reassured its audience that cultural difference could also be identified visually,"[23] in short, that the "truth" about race, particularly regarding "Orientals," lies within the systematic and scientific study of the face.[24] This visual culture of racial typing endorsed by anthropological method and convention persisted in the presentation of the images themselves: "To lend an air of precision, scientific objectivity, and authority to the photos and the accompanying text, *Life*'s editors festooned the pictures with handwritten captions and arrows simulating anthropological field notes."[25]

Alllooksame.com remediates this older anthropological discourse of phenotypic categorization.[26] In addition, the site's destabilization of Asian identity based on visual essentialism works to expose the user to her own participation in creating these categories. However, the key difference between this site and the *Life* images lies in its audience and its intention. While the *Life* images are designed to educate a white audience that had never considered or cared about the visual differences between Chinese and Japanese people, the alllooksame.com ones are at least as much for Asian and Asian American users who care very much about the differences and may need a reverse kind of education. That is to say, while whites can't tell the difference and don't care, many Asian Americans believe that they can. A young Asian American woman in Victoria Nam's collection *Yell-Oh Girls!* asserts that "contrary to what *haole* America thinks, we don't all look alike, and we can tell a Japanese from a Chinese from a Korean from a Filipina from an Indian."[27] Race is figured as a visual code that only certain users can break. This sense of essential and visual difference between Asian groups is long-standing, and despite the panethnic tendencies of recent Asian American immigrants, who are much more likely to identify with Asianness as a race rather than a culture, "for traditional native Asian groups, intra-Asian coupling was miscegenation."[28] For members of these groups, the site achieves both an Asian American identity as a cultural formation and the kind of "subjectless" position advocated by Kandice Chuh, for the site represents "Asian/American" interactive new media content produced by and for consumption by Asian Americans, yet at the same time it questions that identity by fostering debate and conflict around questions of race and ethnicity. Ultimately, as Suematsu writes, "Alllooksame is not a statement. It's a question." Alllooksame.com actively works to destabilize notions of Asian identity and nationality in compelling ways that are rendered particularly personal by the user's participation in the site. It is exemplary of a current movement in Asian American critical theory away from essentialist notions of Asian American identity toward a greater recognition of both hybridity and toward an imperative to "appreciate fully intra-Asian American difference."[29]

Chuh constructs a persuasive argument for the "impossibility of understanding 'Asian American' as an unproblematic designation, as a stable term of reference and politics that transcends context."[30] She posits that Asian American studies would gain critical purchase and relevance if it were to become a "subjectless" discipline, that is to say, one that is defined not by the identity or cultural authenticity of its objects of study but rather by its distinctive method and critical concerns. If defining the term "Asian American" is too fraught with internal incoherence to prove useful, and in fact might be doing more harm than good in its insistence on eliding differences between Asian Americans, Chuh is correct in claiming that Asian American studies would do best to find other ways to perform its critique. The critical study of Asian American new media provides a key opportunity for an intervention into a still-developing media practice. Even more importantly, it centers on the possibility for hybrid and de-essentialized Asian identities that address contemporary narratives about power, difference, perception, and the visual. Indeed, the distinctive culture of Asian America online creates a new representational landscape for issues of identity because it offers a degree of participation and interactivity lacking in more static media. Interactive media like the Web can question identity while building discursive community in ways that other static media cannot.

Likewise, the study of Asian American critical theory offers a great deal to scholars in new media studies and cyberculture studies. First, failing to examine Asian American online culture results in a misreading of the Internet's demographics and representational landscape. Just as large a percentage of English-speaking Asian Americans use the Internet as do whites, according to the Pew Internet and American Life study "Asian Americans and the Internet: The Young and the Connected."[31] More importantly, however, the study of Asian American online practices throws a much-needed wrench in the overly simplistic rhetoric of the digital divide. As the 2001 anthology *Technicolor: Race, Technology, and Everyday Life* shows, people of color have long been instrumental in the innovative use and creation of high technologies in a multitude of ways, and their erasure from the discourse of the digital tends to perpetuate very real power imbalances in the world. And just as importantly, this figuration of cyberculture as white by default tends to demonize people of color as unsophisticated, uneducated, and stuck in a pretechnological past.[32]

In addition, the rhetoric of the digital divide tends to look only at the color of cyberspace's users. To formulate a critical practice that takes account of the nuances of participation online in terms of identity, power, and race, it is vital to know as well the specific conditions under which new media are produced as well as consumed, circulated, and exchanged. Interactivity goes both ways as well; Web sites create users who can interact with them, just as texts create their readers. Alllooksame.com's challenging use of interactivity encourages the creation of a user who is forced to question and eventually discard some essential notions of what it means to be or look Asian. Alllooksame.com has proved influential enough in the Asian American community that it has encouraged spin-offs such as "Am I a Hapa: Biraciality Test." This test contains eighteen photographs of Asian American biracial people and is formatted in a similar way. Its header reads:

> If you think the person is 1/2 Asian then please mark YES, if not, then please mark NO. WARNING! This test is made deliberately to fool you. It proves that you can't always tell if someone is half-Asian. Good luck! This test was inspired by www.alllooksame.com, which is far superior to this site. I

suck at HTML :(If any of these pictures is of you, and you disapprove of its use, then please e-mail me and I will remove it. I found all of these pictures online.[33]

Recent years have seen a welcome increase in the amount of scholarly writing about Internet adoption in the context of non-Western cultures and languages. Rishab Aiyer Ghosh's anthology *Code: Collaborative Ownership and the Digital Economy* does not focus on the Internet per se but is exemplary in the way that it improves on earlier formulations of the "digital divide" as a problem to be "fixed" by giving everyone access to technology. Instead of using the language of cultural development or uplift in the context of digital media, *Code* examines the negotiations that ensue when cultural objects that have never been conceived of as property become so as a result of fast networks of cross-cultural transmission. As Faye Ginsburg notes in her study of video, film, and television diffusion in the context of indigenous and minority populations, the question that "haunts much of the research and debate on the topic of cross-cultural spread of media" is "whether minority or dominated subjects can assimilate media to their own cultural and political concerns or are inevitably compromised by its presence."[34] The range and tone of responses to cyberspace reflect a deep split in the ways that this new communication technology is viewed by non-Western cultures and races. Ziauddin Sardar sees the Internet as a tool of imperialism, and in "Alt.civilizations.faq: Cyberspace as the Darker Side of the West" he asserts that it is simply the newest example on a continuum of imperializing practices perpetrated by the West in its ongoing domination of other cultures.[35] He regards cyberspace as a medium that can only transmit imperialistic ideologies; its background in military research and high cost of access make it intrinsically a Western technology with no potential for resistance by people of color. In short, he sees the Internet as a medium that is inherently flawed by its association with modernity, tropes of colonialism, and hypercapitalism.

His critique is similar in many ways to Chinua Achebe's famous essay "Racism in Conrad's *Heart of Darkness*." There is no turning back from the way that Achebe single-handedly politicized Conrad's novel; the Norton Critical Edition of *Heart of Darkness* includes Achebe's essay because it has become part of the discursive field of postcolonial criticism, as well as being a virtuoso reading of Conrad's text. Achebe demonstrates that Conrad's novel depicts African natives as irredeemably Other, as the West's dark side. Sardar says that cyberspace accomplishes the same thing. Eric Michaels, in his study of the Walpiri, dubs this "culturecide." However, Michaels makes the point that Western media are not the threat to the Walpiri; rather, the "newly constructed, media-simulated Aboriginality, delivered as content by AUSSAT satellite to the remote communities, can succeed at subverting their traditions in a way that no other invasion has. It is not, then, through the dumping of European content to these locations but through the transmission of a powerful competing Aboriginal image, appropriated from the bush, purchased at the expense of local media, and filtered through the grid of a manufactured history that culturecide could readily be accomplished."[36] His claim has far-reaching consequences, for it posits that a compromised type of aboriginal new media production might prove more destructive to native culture than any outside influence. The appropriation and transmission of a false, manufactured, inauthentic type of nativism through cyberspace, potentially a more global medium than even television, has the potential for immense harm.

On the other hand, many new media collectives in traditionally "media-poor" countries who lack widespread access to the Internet strongly assert the usefulness of Internet and computer use in the context of non-Western culture. New Media Centre Sarai in Delhi is trying to make software for people who are nonliterate as a means to wrest the medium away from cultural elites.[37] Even more importantly, this move away from textual literacy produces expressive forms that are more in line with the culture's distinctive media landscape, thus reducing the dangers of imperializing incursions from the West. Jeebesh Bagchi, a Sarai member and a Raqs Media Collective artist, claims that "India is a song and visual sign board culture" and asks, "What kind of dialogue with this strange and eclectic world do we want to create, not based on domination or populism?"[38] Envisioning and using the Internet in visual rather than primarily textual ways can be a radically empowering move for nonliterate groups.

Seen in this light, the Internet has tremendous potential for challenging colonial regimes of power, particularly those that privilege access to the written word. Sarai asserts that the Internet need not be a manifestation of the West's darker side but can be retooled as an empowering device for non-Western users. Sarai's emphasis on reaching nonliterate users acknowledges the power dynamics associated with literacy. Before there was a digital divide, questions of power had always worked themselves out in the written-word divide. New electronic mediations that will successfully reach the "people" may do so by detouring around the written word, a particularly appropriate tactic in visual cultures such as India's. As Bagchi explains: "So far in India popular culture has been defined by film. There is a tradition in India to interpret society through film." As the Internet becomes richer in moving images, it may have more to offer users whose cultural vernacular encompasses video and signboards, visual cultures of movement and signification, rather than text.

Shuddhabrata Sengupta, a filmmaker and media practitioner who is also a member of the Raqs Media Collective and a founder of the Sarai New Media Centre in Delhi, articulates some of the complexities of cultural negotiation regarding new media forms in the postcolonial context. In his discussion of the practicalities of using Hindi as an Internet language, he weighs on the one hand the imperatives of "cultural authenticity"—that is, retaining the Hindi character set despite its incompatibilities with existing hardware—against the loss suffered by having to translate Hindi to the Roman character set, which cannot accommodate Hindi without expensive equipment that makes the translation cost-prohibitive in a country where any network connection is already a precious commodity. Sengupta's solution is that Indians must give up the typographical "purity" of Hindi to enter the digital commons. Questions of the postcolonial politics of translation and language are foremost in Sengupta's argument. He writes that though "the sense of inauthenticity accompanying this stance may produce some discomfort, it at least brings with it a means of entering the digital commons on reasonably fair terms. Once there, we are free to forage for new meanings and new identities." The discourse of "purity" is here weighed against the appeal of the "digital commons" and found wanting. The desire for cultural purity implies a drive to keep unproblematic notions of race, identity, gender, and other subject positions untainted by cultural hybridity in any form, from either new media or old. Sengupta is willing to trade a "pure" Internet Hindi for the opportunity to use new media to forge "new meanings and new identities," which will necessarily be hybrid in nature.

Thus, despite their many ideological differences, both Sardar and the Sarai founders seem to agree that the Internet will produce "impure" or "inauthentic" expressive forms. Where they differ is in the question of whether this is a trade worth making and whether it is pragmatic to resist it.

Of course, these are not the only two "postcolonial" positions vis-à-vis the Internet; postcolonial theory is far too complex to produce only two modes of interpretation on this or any subject. To sum it up, however, critics like Sardar are concerned primarily with preserving cultural authenticity and see the medium of cyberspace itself as a vector for Western ideologies,

regardless of its content. Bagchi and Sengupta are concerned with providing access to the Internet to people traditionally left out of the global communications loop and are interested in doing so in ways that are image
based rather than text based. They acknowledge that changing existing
Indian linguistic forms to make them computer-friendly may produce an
"inauthentic" medium, one that has suffered a loss of identity at the hands
of the West. However, their emphasis on creating a visual Internet for nonliterate users seems designed to remedy that particular representational violence, in a sense. I will return to this crucial issue later.

It is difficult to see a middle ground between these two positions. What
is quite striking about them, however, is how extremely closely they match
up to much older foundational debates in postcolonial theory regarding literary and linguistic imperialism that have been circulating for the last few
decades, since the legitimization of postcolonial critique as an academic
discipline. Indeed, to use computer talk, in a sense postcolonial theory itself
has been ported from literary studies, where it has a strong presence, to other
areas, the Internet being the most recent of these. In any event, the similarity of the two debates may prove instructive regarding questions of the Internet, cultural authenticity, and race, in both global and American contexts.

Examinations of the ways that language and literary forms produce
power, identity, and "race" as a cultural construct have always been central
to postcolonial theory. The works of Ngugi wa Thiongo, Gloria Anzaldúa,
Chinua Achebe, Ama Ata Aidoo, Salman Rushdie, Homi Bhabha, and
Edward Said all privilege the language and the literary as a field of discourse
within which the battle over cultural hegemony has been waged. The specific
literary techniques and tropes that have produced the "native" in Western
literature and the attendant issue of the place that Western languages such
as English ought to have in non-Western institutions have been debated for
some time now. And just as Sardar and Bagchi/Sengupta split over the issue
of the Internet, so too do postcolonial literary critics part ways over the
appropriateness of Western literary forms and languages in the postcolonial
context.

Of course, there is a range of positions over this issue, but the writings of
Ngugi wa Thiongo and Salman Rushdie typify two opposed ones that align
fairly neatly with the poles of thought represented by Sardar and Bagchi/
Sengupta. Ngugi's project as a writer and activist is to reclaim indigenous
language use as a central aspect of the project of cultural independence. His
much-publicized decision to write only in Kikuyu after having produced a
large body of well-respected literary works in English arises from his politi-

cal conviction that language is the "collective memory bank of a people" and that imperial languages such as English participate in the "captivation" of colonized peoples, especially when they are used by non-Western novelists as a part of their literary production and work to define a cultural elite that is then Western.[39] He asserts that "when [nations] meet as oppressor and oppressed, as for instance under imperialism, then their languages cannot experience a genuinely democratic encounter. The oppressor nation uses language as a means of enriching itself in the oppressed language."[40] For him, language is ineluctably a "carrier of national cultures," and he holds the line against the attractions of hybridity.[41] For Ngugi, African literature *must* be written in African languages. He and Sardar share a commitment to cultural authenticity and a wariness of Western media forms that is based in a deep awareness of the historical abuses of the past (and the present).[42]

Salman Rushdie occupies the other side of this debate. He asserts that "English has become an Indian language" and that "the true Indian literature of the first postcolonial half century has been made in the language the British left behind."[43] Rushdie describes Indian literature written in English (which he terms "Indo-Anglian" literature) in language that evokes commercial discourse about the Internet: he calls English "the most powerful medium of communication in the world" and lauds Anglophone literature as "a means of holding a conversation with [it]."[44] He acknowledges the role of high technologies in this imperative, saying that "the new Silicon Valley–style boom in computer technology which is transforming the economies of Bangalore and Madras has made English in those cities an even more important language than before." Hence the economic benefits to using Western media forms are presented as a strong reason that Indians should embrace English; Rushdie's position, however, is based on a much more radical notion, which is that India has "colonized" English, rather than the other way around. He anticipates critics such as Ngugi, writing that "for some Indian critics, English-language Indian writing will never be more than a postcolonial anomaly—the bastard child of Empire, sired on India by the departing British." Its continuing use of the old colonial tongue is seen as a fatal flaw that renders it forever inauthentic. Again, this painful sensitivity about the possible loss of cultural purity that characterizes Sarai's stance is weighed against the benefits of entering a "conversation with the world," and the "world" wins. While Sarai acknowledges the possible losses to Hindi identity that Internet adoption may bring about, Rushdie is strikingly unambivalent about the superiority of English as a literary language, especially in the hands of diasporic writers, but also aware of accusations

that such literature is "deracinated" and "Westernized."[45] And all throughout
his discussion in the *New Yorker* article titled "Damme, This Is the Oriental
Scene for You!" in which he formulates this position, he makes no mention
of race whatsoever.[46]

The rift between the two camps in postcolonial literary theory maps well
onto the impasse between thinkers in postcolonial Internet theory. On the
one hand, some fear miscegenation between media and worry that uneven
encounters between "pure" non-Western cultural forms and "tainted" electronic media must necessarily result in a muddled, deracinated mediascape.
Others seem to welcome the opportunity that multimedia may give them to
produce new cultural forms which are hybrid, multicultural, and by implication multiracial. This is not to say that cultural authenticists are condemning racial muddling or mixing along with media muddling, or saying
that one is the effect of the other, but rather that the rhetoric of purity and
the discourse of "deracination" must evoke earlier discourses of "biological"
purity and racial authenticity. Why are these colonial fears of racial and cultural miscegenation resurfacing in discussions of the Internet and new media?

In a sense this set of concerns is moot, for the Internet is penetrating cultures, markets, ethnic groups, and genders at a tremendous clip in total
defiance of what the critics think. However, the debates within postcolonial
theory over language adoption can prove useful in parsing out the ways that
new media can seek to avoid a seeming deadlock between contradictory
positions. The fact is that there are few, perhaps no, media forms that are
"purely" authentic, just as there are few that are homogeneously and uniformly hybrid. Media forms are bumpy, layered, and pitted with the imprint
of contact with other cultures; none avoid the mark of imperialist power
relations. And the Internet is no different. What the Internet does offer,
however, is a range of imagistic and interactive practices that produce a distinctively different mediascape from the world of the static literary text. The
potential of the Internet to transform visual cultures like India's or at least
to engage with them in ways that literary texts cannot must be examined if
we wish to avoid repeating the same arguments regarding cultural purity
versus cultural hybridity. This is a Hobson's choice that would better be
avoided for a number of reasons, not the least of which being that it fails to
account for people who are not textually literate in any language, thus per-
petuating the analog class and education divide.[47] Postcolonial debates that
pose the stern and noble (but ultimately doomed) cultural authenticists like
Ngugi against the freewheeling postmodern hybridity of Salman Rushdie

both start from the assumption that the Internet is purely Western because it is dominated by American content and interfaces. However, sites like alllooksame.com and others like it demonstrate the ways that the Web can produce sites that express concerns that are unique to particular cultures and can perform what Faye Ginsburg calls "cultural activism": the aboriginal use of "a range of media in order to 'talk back' to structures of power that have erased or distorted their interests and realities."[48] The anthropologist and visual culture scholar Christopher Pinney argues that though photography was originally a Western introduction to African culture, it has become so "firmly inserted into everyday practice" in Western Africa and has given rise to so many innovative uses of form and composition that serve the unique and particular cultural needs of the Yoruba that it is "best seen as the confluence of overlapping visual regimes rather than the province of one."[49] Indeed, as the Internet drives the convergence of visual regimes that had previously been separated in space and time, regimes of governmentality, classification, the law, and the interface overlap to form a hybrid experience of media. Ginsburg is quite correct to locate the primary debate regarding postcolonial media around the use of television, video, and film, since these are the media most enthusiastically taken up by non-Western cultures, as Michaels notes. As the Internet becomes a televisual form that encompasses straight-to-QuickTime filmmaking, such as the professionally produced boutique shorts featured on bmwfilms.com, projects that involve globally successful stars such as the director John Woo and the actor Clive Owen, we can see the interpellation of the Internet into the existing aesthetic values and star system of traditional Hollywood film narrative. Yet on the other hand, as Henry Jenkins notes, the Internet has encouraged the production and distribution of all sorts of DIY and fan-produced videos that give a voice to those left out of the film production system as it stands.[50] These examples of "indigenous media" (if we can conceive of fans as constituting an oppressed and marginalized minority group of sorts) in the context of the United States bypass the traditional distribution systems for video and film and are thus a particularly promising vector for minority and indigenous people in particular. Though Jenkins is far more interested in the Internet's ability to enfranchise fans rather than oppressed ethnic groups and people of color, his point that this type of user-driven production represents a return to oral cultures, in which narratives were produced collaboratively in dialogue with audiences, has particular relevance to the postcolonial context. If, indeed, it is an important goal to preserve the spirit of indigenous cultural media, the Internet's ability to approximate preliterate narrative forms while also permitting access to a transcoded signboard or film culture may make it the most appropriate medium to achieve these goals.

However, as has been noted in the past, the rush to bridge the digital divide participates in a dangerously paternalistic discourse of uplift and cultural imperialism that is compounded by the medium's intense attractiveness on both the cultural and economic levels; it is a medium that is conceived of as being inherently educational in a way that television has never been. The Internet differs from television, video, and film in the sense that it has been accorded the cachet formerly given to literacy; its early associations with research, education, and the written word, coupled with its increasing convergence with moving-image forms, give it a positive cultural valence that is hard to match. Eric Michaels notes that the popular perception of television as a vast wasteland of mind-corrupting, contentless content extends to both domestic and international contexts. The Western bias toward literacy and against television and video, a way of thinking that sells "literacy as a prosocial, prodevelopment medium" and denigrates television and video as "antisocial and repressive,"[51] springs partly from Neil Postman's influential critique of television as a means by which we amuse ourselves to death. In alllooksame.com, Asian Americans create networked spaces for questioning identity that pinpoint the lines of fracture between race, nationality, and ethnicity. If pattern recognition, or visual literacy regarding the digitally mediated visual image, is indeed our new post-Internet paradigm of knowledge and cognition, then the obligation to shake up old patterns of identity fulfilled by allllooksame.com constitutes a welcome and important intervention into race's cultures, visual and otherwise.

3

The Social Optics of Race and Networked Interfaces in *The Matrix* Trilogy and *Minority Report*

Computer interfaces and their theatricalized use have become increasingly common in contemporary film and television. As I note in the introduction to this book, as well as in other chapters, the massification of the Internet as an everyday technology for many people has resulted in the creation and exhibition of innumerable telegenic fictional and "real" interfaces as a ubiquitous feature in genres like science fiction, action/thriller, and military films, and they are increasingly common in mainstream film genres like romances, such as in *You've Got Mail* and *Something's Got to Give*, music videos, and dramas set in contemporary times. These scenes allow insight into both the characters that use them and the ways in which information, surveillance, and visualization function in the realm of the film and in society at large. The proper relationship to the interface is codified quite clearly: competency or mastery is defined by the level of immediacy the user experiences in relation to it. Eugene Thacker defines immediacy as follows: it "involves the use of new media to the extent that the media themselves—the 'window'—disappear, bringing forth a kind of direct experience where technology is transparent and unnoticed by the subject."[1] This is an eloquent formulation of entitlement regarding the new media interface. Internet users all engage with interfaces over which they have more or less control, experience more or less comfort or alienation, more or less immediacy, more or less ability to create or produce, more or less investment in the interface's content and forms of representation. *The Matrix* trilogy and the 2002 film *Minority Report* racialize digital information access and production by depicting scenes of white and male users experiencing "direct" or immediate relations with computer interfaces, while users of color are relegated to the background, depicted with truncated and relatively distant, highly technologically mediated relationships to their hardware and software. These users are visible reminders of the necessity of human objects to support and underwrite others' sublime experience of "transparent" and direct interactions with digital technology; they supply the marginal blackness in the *Matrix* films and *Minority Report* against which whiteness stands in sharp relief. And in both films, Asians and Asian Americans function as the material base for technologies of digitized vision and surveillance.

These films, along with the extremely successful Apple iPod advertising campaign that began in 2004 depicting dancing silhouetted bodies, create a visual culture that reflects highly codified conditions of labor, race, and the body under informational capitalism. Several theorists have noted that the move toward informationalism and its political economy, networked consciousness, and new cultural categories for classifying sorts of people and things has resulted in a reconfiguration of concepts of race. Patricia Williams writes: "It is with caution that we must notice that with the advent of a variety of new technologies, we presumed free agents are not less but increasingly defined as body-centered. We live more, not less, in relation to our body parts, the dispossession or employment of ourselves constrained by a complicated pattern of self-alienation."[2] Her thinking is invoked specifically by "the legal precedents and rhetoric around women's reproduction, eugenics, and organ transplants," all developments enabled by information technologies, and she ultimately posits that technology has made the body even less "ours" than it was in the past. Rather than freeing us from the body, as cyberpunk narratives of idealized disembodiment foresaw, informational technologies have turned the body into property in a particular way—gene lines, organs, stem cells, and other bodily products have a market value based on their informational transcodability across or between races, which constitutes their use value. Donna Haraway as well sees a return to "self-alienation" and dispossession of the body as a result of technoscience but not in its previous early modern forms. In her discussion of "SimEve," the digital composite of a woman created as a representative of "the future face of America," Haraway remarks: "We are abruptly returned to the category of databases and the marriage of genomics and informatics in the artificial life worlds that reconstitute what it means to be human. Here, the category so ethereally and technically reconfigured is race."[3] It is only in the abstract world of cyber-space that this ideal visual racial synthesis can occur; in our world, we instead fight bitter battles over stem cell use, transgenics, and racial profiling on the level of the gene. Haraway concurs with Williams that information and communications technologies are both a product and a symptom of an ideology that centers the body in a new way, a way that legitimates racial categories as real and useful under the sign of science. In her "20th Century Biological U.S. Kinship Categories" chart, Haraway writes that from the 1940s to the 1970s, "race is an illusory object constructed by bad science," but from 1975 to the 1990s, "race reemerges in medical discourse on organ transplants and drug testing."[4] It is difficult if not impossible for the poor, socially disenfranchised, and raced individual to own one's own body in the best of times, but the terms have changed since the seventies; in a dataveillant society based in informational or late capitalism, ownership or at least partial control over one's digital or databody is essential. In other chapters of this book, I discuss the ways that users of color and women create their own raced and gendered visual avatars or digital signatures as part of a technique of databody production and ownership. In this chapter, I discuss the ways that the struggle over control of racialized databodies in four post-millennial science fiction films—*The Matrix* trilogy and *Minority Report*—encode race as property. The racio-visual logic of race in these and other science fiction films that depict interface use sets up distinct roles for particular races, and distinct ways of conceptualizing the racialized body as informational property for use in dataveillant state apparatuses. As might be expected, white users enjoy a privileged visual relationship with digital networked interfaces, either eschewing the use of the interface altogether or interacting with it sans keyboard, mouse, and other hardware devices and instead using gestural computing. In contrast, black users are depicted as witnesses and support staff to these feats of interface use. Moreover, efforts to hack biometric codes set in place as regulatory devices by the dataveillant state can be seen in the racialized traffic in organs for transplantation in *Minority Report*, reenacting the power dynamics that already obtain between the First World and the Fourth World.

The visual culture of computing has long excluded non-Asian people of color, in particular Latinos and African Americans; one of the features of the postmillennial visual field is that this is no longer the case. *The Matrix* trilogy in particular seems to break new ground in depicting black men in relation to computers, both as their operators and as members of the resistance against their monstrous multiplication in human life. I would argue that the second and third films in the trilogy are especially invested in addressing whiteness as a racial formation with its own visual culture and machine aesthetics, its own mode of appearing and embodiment in the visual field of new media and cinema. While studies of race in cyberspace as still relatively rare, studies of whiteness in cyberspace are vanishingly so.[5] The Matrix trilogy proposes that whiteness is an object, which, like new media itself, reproduces and spreads virally. These films embody the essential paradox of whiteness, as Richard Dyer describes it, for in them is demonstrated both the ways in which "the equation of being white with being human secures a position of power"[6] and the way that "being nothing, having no life, is a condition of whiteness. The purity of whiteness may simply be the absence of being."[7] Hence, when we look at the sinister agents in the film, all of whom are white males without exception, we can see how they embody both privilege and death, a radical lack of identity and humanity coupled with infinite power and mobility, seeming transparency linked to oppressive types of control. The paradox of whiteness is the very paradox of new media. Computer use is also a privileged site for looking at the ways that black and white identities are constructed in relation to new media in this trilogy. Indeed, the trilogy has been credited with an incredible amount of intellectual heft and import generally; as Patricia Pisters writes, "There is probably no other contemporary film that better serves as a kind of Rorschach test for contemporary theory than The Matrix."[8] What does the trilogy tell us about racial identity in light of interface culture and networked hegemonies?

In this chapter I investigate the nature of African American mojo in the trilogy, in particular in The Matrix: Reloaded, and discuss the ways in which African Americans' authenticity as racialized subjects is put to work in the films. This authenticity is made to represent a kind of antidote or solution to the problem of machine cultures that specialize in reproducing white masculine privilege. The problem with computers and their interfaces—that is to say, the problem posed by the Matrix itself—lies in their hegemonic relation to the subject. The domination and subjugation of the subject by machine culture—here represented as whiteness in the form of white men, its "agents"—is shown to the viewer of Reloaded to have its roots in the interface's creator, or "architect." The Architect, who is represented in this film as an older white man with a white beard, is called an "old white prick" by Neo to further underscore the alliance between race, age, and power in the integrated circuit.[9]

A key sequence of chapter 10 of the DVD edition of The Matrix Reloaded intercuts images of Link (the Nebuchadnezzar's pilot and operator, here de-

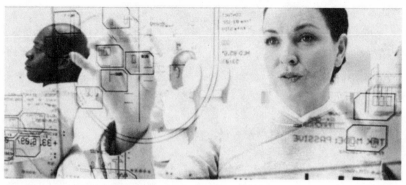

Figure 3.1. White interfaces in *The Matrix: Reloaded*.

picted guiding the ship into port) with images of the Zion gate operator, a white woman. As the two converse, two competing image sets of interface design are put into conversation as well.

These images literally contrast "black" and "white" interface culture— while the Zion gate operator's clothing, monitor, and face are all white, transparent, and futuristically modern in the classic visual style of science fiction from *2001: A Space Odyssey* (1968) to *Space: 1999* (1975–77) and onward, Link and the *Nebuchadnezzar* are part of the Afro-futuristic visual culture that the trilogy has exploited so effectively throughout.[10] Link wears dreadlocks and a grubby, semi-unraveled sweater; his ship is dark and shadowy; and his black padded analog-style headset resembles equipment you might see in the past rather than in the future. The Zion gate operator wears blindingly white and tailored clothes, occupies a spotlessly clean space, wears her hair in a tight bun, and is herself smooth and pale. Most importantly, she has a radically different relation to the computer and its interface than does Link. While he types commands on an antiquated keyboard, she is jacked in differently. Her body is linked to the computer through a more direct means: gesture. While it has been a familiar trope for cyberpunk narratives to deploy pastiches of historical and sartorial styles to depict an unevenly developed and dystopic technological future, this scene superimposes the two contrastingly racialized visual styles of the interface to invoke the crucial difference in this film: that between white culture and black culture. Indeed, as Roger Ebert writes, "The population of Zion [and the film] is largely black," and "a majority of the characters were played by African Americans." This is extremely unusual for science fiction narrative, in which people of color are largely absent as main characters. Ebert addresses this anomaly as follows: "It has become commonplace for science fiction epics to

Figure 3.2. Black interfaces in *The Matrix: Reloaded.*

feature one or two African American stars but we've come a long way since Billy Dee Williams in *The Return of the Jedi.* The films abound with African Americans not for their box office appeal—because the Matrix is *the* star of the movie—and not because they are good actors (which they are) but because to the white teenagers who are their primary audience for this movie, African Americans embody a cool, a cachet, an authenticity. Morpheus is the power center of the movie, and Neo's role is essentially to study under him and absorb his mojo."[11]

When we oppose the multicultural "earth tone natural fiber fashions"[12] of the Zionites with the minimalistic, ultramodern interfaces and styles of generic computer culture, as depicted in the white interface image, we can see why these two competing visual fields are intercut with each other: the mojo effected by both the trilogy's black characters and its forging of a new Afro-futurist cinematic mise-en-scène is posed as a solution to the problem of fractious machines, machines that we know are machines because they are identical to each other, infinitely replicable, and spread in a viral fashion. So too do we know that they are inhuman because they are represented by white men, the "agents," most notably Agent Smith, who embody the uniformity of white male culture and equate it to machine culture. This is how the films portray their strong critique of information society, post-Internet, as well as how they pose their solution to this problem—while machine culture is viral, oppressive, and assimilative, Afro-futurist mojo and black identity are generally depicted as singular, "natural," and, as Ebert puts it, unassimilable and "authentic." Blackness retains its identity in the face of technological change, white power and privilege, and racism.

The agents are depicted as the agents of white male privilege, and their radical lack of authenticity is apparent in the scenes in which they are replicated infinitely into identical copies of themselves. This is most apparent in the fight scenes between Agent Smith and Neo in *Reloaded* and *Revolutions*. These fight scenes, the most elaborate and extended of which has been termed the "burly brawl" by the filmmakers, were noted mainly for their dazzling, if monotonous, special effects. They reappear in *Revolutions*, which is no wonder, since some of the film's visual effects took two years to render. It is only sensible that such time-intensive special effects would be recycled. However, their significance goes beyond economies of scale. For these scenes, effects coordinator John Gaeta created photo-realistic digital copies of Hugo Weaving, who plays Agent Smith, and manipulated them rather than grafting footage of the actor into the frame from nondigital sources. At the time, this raised provocative questions among filmmakers, such as whether this technique might replace "real" actors.[13] Do images of characters rendered via a computer interface—that is, images of humans that are digital from the ground up—threaten the notion of authenticity, singularity, and identity that the film itself wants to depict as ultimately victorious in the face of the infinite replication of images and ideologies that our machines produce?

It is notable that Agent Smith replicates via penetration, then multiplication. Whiteness thus spreads in a manner that exemplifies a much-favored paradigm of e-business in the nineties: viral marketing. Steven Shaviro defines it as follows: "The message propagates itself by massive self-replication as it passes from person to person in the manner of an epidemic contagion."[14] Here Agent Smith's literal self-replication mimics the movement of information from user to user on the Internet. And the connection with whiteness is made even clearer in Dyer's formulation: "White power nonetheless reproduces itself regardless of intention, power differences, and goodwill, and overwhelmingly because it is not seen as whiteness, but as normal."[15] The reflexivity of whiteness—its ability to reproduce itself infinitely—is depicted here as essentially viral in nature. Agent Smith's mode of reproduction echoes one that Lev Manovich identifies as one of the "popularly held notions about the difference between old and new media," which is the idea that "in contrast to analog media where each successive copy loses quality, digitally encoded media can be copied endlessly without degradation."[16] This brings to mind Agent Smith's speech to Morpheus near the end of *The Matrix*, in which he describes humanity as a "disease" that spreads without check, like a virus.

In addition, this network of invasive whiteness produced by the multiple Agent Smiths evokes the homosociality of modern computer networks. There are no female agents—this sets up a queering dynamic in which information

Figure 3.3. Multiple Agent Smiths confront Neo in the "burly brawl" scene of *The Matrix: Reloaded*.

is passed on exclusively via male-to-male penetration, replication, and appropriation.[17] Women are literally out of the loop. And while Smith and other agents routinely penetrate other white men, such as truckers, bums, and other policemen, and morph them into agents, they are unable to do so with Neo and Morpheus; indeed, no people of color undergo this virtual colonization of identity. Neo, played by Keanu Reeves, is not included as white for two reasons: first, the actor has self-identified as multiracial; and second, the character he plays loudly disavows whiteness in a key scene of *Reloaded*, during which Neo has a long dialogue with the Architect. In this interminably long, pretentious, and confusing scene, Neo calls the Architect, the program responsible for creating the Matrix, an "old white prick." In this eloquent outburst, Neo encapsulates the problem that the trilogy set out to solve. In the logic of this scene, the way to survive the future intact, as a nonreplicable subject with a unique identity and authenticity, is to resist "old white pricks," to resist becoming them, in the case of Neo, who is definitely not old, though debatably white, either by penetration by the agents or by media replication. Indeed, the use of "white" as a racial epithet, a kind of post-millennial hate speech when used by Neo in reference to the Architect, functions as a casting off of whiteness as a racial or ethnic identity, a move that racially differentiates Neo from identification with the agents. The antique television screens behind the architect represent a particular kind of horror mediated by an older communication technology with a different interface but similar problematics. Neo's horror at seeing himself reproduced so promiscuously is like the horror engendered by the horde of Agent Smiths populating the burly brawl—which is the "real" one? If new media are characterized by the creation of copies without originals—that is to say,

Baudrillard's model of the simulation, "the generation by models of a real without origin or reality: a hyperreal"[18]—then what happens to the notion of personal identity in the age of new media? And how can the domination of both old (television) and new (computer interface) media by old white pricks be resisted? Certainly Neo's handsome but, as the oracle in *The Matrix* points out, not too bright countenance holds no answers to this question.

Both Link and Tank (the operator from *The Matrix*) wear dreadlocks. Cornel West, who makes a cameo appearance as a council member in *Reloaded* and *Revolutions*, wears his trademark short Afro hairstyle. West's inclusion in the films merits more discussion; as perhaps the most visible African American public intellectual of recent years, West is an academic superstar, whose migrations from Princeton to Harvard and back constitute front-page news. He is an icon of black visibility in an area other than sport, music, or crime. In addition, in his writing West strongly critiques what he has called "racial reasoning." West wants to "replace racial reasoning with moral reasoning, to understand the black freedom struggle not as an affair of skin pigmentation and racial phenotype but rather as a matter of ethical principles and wise politics."[19] He critiques racial essentialism by claiming that "all people with black skin and African phenotype are subject to white supremacist abuse.... In short, blackness is a political and ethical construct. Appeals to black authenticity ignore this fact."[20] This emphasis on blackness as a "construct" uncannily echoes the films' concerns with authenticity, and West's solution to the problem—that is, to envision the "black freedom struggle" as being about principles and politics that transcend phenotype and skin color—meshes well with the depiction of a racially mixed Zion in the *Matrix* films. Yet West is careful to make clear that blackness, while it may fail to possess biological facticity, is a dangerous role to perform in the world. The idea that blackness is a "construct" does not make being black in a racist society any less difficult. So while the film trilogy attempts to co-opt black "mojo" or style as a construct that all can share in the name of generic "freedom struggles," in this case against oppressive whiteness, West's presence in the film reminds us that this particular "racial reasoning" has a longer history and a larger context to contend with.

In a trilogy that spares no expense to create distinctive visual effects, why this insistence on black style? I posit that blackness is represented as the source of human agency in this techno-future (which is, of course, our present, as Annette Kuhn writes in *Alien Zone:* science fiction is always about working out social problems of the present using forms that can articulate what realistic narrative cannot).[21] There are inhuman agents and Architects, who are always white pricks; mentors, oracles, and operators, who are always black; and benign software programs like Seraph, the Keymaster, and the displaced information-worker South Indian family depicted in *Revolutions*, who are often Asian. This very particular deployment of racialized identity marks race itself as an essential quality of being "real," or being human, with whiteness occupying the null zone all too often claimed by whites in the "real world," who envision and often represent themselves as having no race and no culture. The trilogy takes whiteness's claim to universality, normativity, and control and attempts to turn it on its head; Morpheus's comment to Agent Smith in the first film that "you all look alike to me" repurposes earlier anti–African American racist discourse to apply to it to whites, but on different grounds: since whiteness represents the soullessness and seeming transparency of modern interface culture,[22] the multiple Agent Smiths, all literally rather than seemingly identical, represent the vanishing point of personal identity and subjectivity. In this film, it is whites who all look alike.

The interface culture that is represented to us as an alternative to whiteness prizes visual qualities (and values) such as thickness, opacity, texture, solidity, depth, and idiosyncrasy over cleanness, uniformity, sharp edges, and neutral colors. The contrast between *The Matrix*'s opening credit sequence (which persists throughout all three films of the trilogy) and the white interface depicted in the Zion gate operator scene embodies this visual distinction—while the white interface seems to stylistically hail an imagined future, *The Matrix* credits, with their old-fashioned scrolling green-on-black graphics, undoubtedly reference an imagined past. And it is by dipping into images of the past, which include images of blackness, that *The Matrix* creates a counterdiscourse to cyberutopianism, one that comes at an especially opportune time as we exit the millennium with the knowledge that the Internet has failed to live up to its much hyped potential to liberate users from their bodies, from racism, and from inequalities of all kinds.

The strong critiques of white masculinity in *Reloaded* and *Revolutions* are lessened through the films' poor critical reception. While it would be overly reductive to say that *Reloaded* and *Revolutions* are bad films with their hearts in the right place, some critics assert that such a reading might not be too far off the mark when it comes to race and gender. As Ebert writes in his review of *Revolutions*: "*Reloaded* was notable for the number of key characters who are black; this time, what we notice is how many strong women there are. Two women operate a bazooka team, Niobe flies the ship, the women have muscles, they kick ass, and this isn't your grandmother's Second Sex anymore." I would add as well that the two women—Zee and Charra—operating the bazooka team are black and Latina, and the heroic pilot, Niobe, is black; the future of Zion, it seems, has a great deal to do with women of color acquiring key roles, a compelling prediction in light of Donna Haraway's writings on cyborg subjectivity and the role of women of color, or the "offshore woman," as a worker in the information economy. As Haraway writes in "A Cyborg Manifesto": "Earlier I have suggested that 'women of colour' might be understood as a cyborg identity, a potent subjectivity synthesized from fusions of outsider identities and in the complex political-historical layerings of her 'biomythography.'"[23] Yet as Haraway is careful to note, terrible inequities still exist between "offshore women" and their more privileged First World counterparts; while Niobe, Zee, and Charra are all heroic women who do important work in the film, the kind of work they do is fairly low on the food chain of the "integrated circuit," for "'women of colour' are the preferred labour force for the science-based industries, the real women for whom the world-wide sexual market, labour market, and politics of reproduction kaleidoscope into daily life."[24] In other words, like the Korean prostitutes and electronic assembly workers of whom Haraway writes, they are denied the subjectivity and agency that comes with the only form of truly valorized labor (other than fighting) in the trilogy—that is, computer programming. They are objects, not subjects, of interactivity.

There are no women-of-color hackers; their function is to lend mojo and authenticity to a war movie in which the war is being waged on two fronts: that of the abstract world of code and interface—Neo's world—and Zion, the concrete world of embodied sociality. Hence the film's critique is weakened by its continued separation of the two worlds and its coding of this separation along racial and gendered lines. "Key roles" for blacks and women do not necessarily add up to a progressive message.

Coco Fusco's show "Only Skin Deep: Changing Visions of the American Self" at the International Photography Center demonstrates that they never did. In her introductory essay to the show's catalog notes, also titled "Only Skin Deep," Fusco writes that "the premise of this exhibition, however, is that rather than recording the existence of race, photography produced race as a visualizable fact."[25] Her eloquent formulation pins down the ways that photography is part of a complex of related social formations, racism and new media among them. New media also produce race as a visualizable fact. Marginal black figures visible in the visual culture of computer interfaces can be seen in great detail in both The Matrix: Reloaded and Minority Report. Neither of these films has been read as being particularly "about" race, but Fusco notes in "Only Skin Deep" that "race" is often read in relation to the photographic image only when people of color or overt acts of racism are depicted. This way of looking is far too narrow and has the effect of blocking off discussions of race that might prove uncomfortable to viewers because they might address such issues as the unquestioned centrality and normativity of whiteness. What is the relation between digital imaging, interface fetishes, and the function of blackness in popular film narratives about computing? What is the means of production of the digital image? The scene of production of the digital photograph is not the camera, necessarily, but the desktop. Final Cut Pro, Photoshop, Morph 2000, and other tools of the digital image artists' trade run in the context of another set of frames, that of the interface.

Studies of the interface have long occupied a privileged position in new media criticism. Lev Manovich's *The Language of New Media* devotes several chapters to it, and books like Steven Johnson's *Interface Culture* posit the interface as the paradigmatic aspect of computer culture that can be taken to represent all of new media. These studies concern themselves with the matter of new media form as divorced from content or politics. However, there is a racial politics that obtains in popular images of interface usage. But what is the presence of blackness doing in these images? I argue that it anchors this uncanny visual setup in which the interface has become an object of racialized anxiety, a fetish.

In Sander Gilman's groundbreaking article "Black Bodies, White Bodies," he "attempts to plumb the conventions (and thus the ideologies) which exist at a specific historical moment in both the aesthetic and the scientific spheres."[26] He reads the "aesthetic" (as embodied by paintings by Manet and Picasso) and the medical together as a set of "overlapping and entwined systems of conventions." I would like to add the digital to this list. In our "specific historical moment," we are surrounded by ubiquitous images of interfaces. The most privileged of these are interfaces that we use to control operating systems and manipulate images—ATM usage and pumping gas at electronic pumps are uses of interfaces as well but do not have the element of production and open interactivity associated with these privileged interfaces. Interfaces are seductive: interface designers call a successful interface "transparent" when it is easy to use, intuitive, and immersive, and when it provides its intended user with a sense of "fit." The metaphor of transparency is literalized in scenes depicting interface usage in *Minority Report*.

As previously discussed, *The Matrix: Reloaded* depicts a racialized division of labor in which white users interface with computers either with gestural computing or in even more direct ways, by being "the One" who needs only to think a command for it to be done. Neo, the former "Mr. Anderson," embodies the power user, the person whose interactions with digital interfaces are supremely transparent and intuitive. Similarly, *Minority Report* depicts its own scenes of computing privilege, as John Anderton, played by Tom Cruise, uses gestural computing in some of the most beautiful and memorable scenes in this extremely stylized film.

The film's images of a transparent interface, controlled by gestures of the hands rather than a keyboard, are modeled after an MIT Media Lab experiment. The interfaces are literally transparent: we can see through them; we are on the other side of the looking glass, occupying the point of view of the computer itself, were this a traditional setup. As Anderton "scrubs" and manipulates the image, we hear classical music, which reinforces the idea of the interface user as a conductor, a master of digital production. The connection between these two masterful male hackers from two different techno-thrillers is confirmed by the similarity of the protagonists' names: *Minority Report's* John Anderton and *The Matrix's* Thomas Anderson (aka Neo). Both are troped as users with mystical privileges and uncannily close relations to computing machines. The fantasy of fusion with, or total control of, the machine carries dangers along with it, as it is a desire that when fulfilled results in either a queered whiteness, as in Agent Smith's example, or a decadent and ethically problematic position of detached privilege, as in the case of the Architect. Only Anderson/Neo's liminal whiteness through association with blackness and Asianness saves him from these fates; and, as I discuss later, Anderton's disenfranchisement by the dataveillant state works as well to envision his body as nonwhite. At this point, however, I wish to discuss the presence of the black figure in the midst of all this modernist transparency.

Figure 3.4. Transparent interfaces in *Minority Report*.

Figure 3.5. Marginal blackness in *Minority Report*.

Gilman writes that "the figure of the black servant in European art is ubiquitous," and that its function is to "sexualize the society in which he or she is found."[27] Gilman focuses on the visual culture of black female bodies in this aesthetic tradition. Black male servants of the interface perform work in the visual culture of filmic interfaces in the *Matrix* films and in *Minority Report*. They are loyal servants of white interface users and, most importantly, visual anchors of darkness that symbolically emplace white interface users in real reality versus virtual reality. In these images of interface usage from *Reloaded* and *Minority Report*, we can see the same interface setup: a transparent screen, from which we peer at the rapt white user, while a marginal black figure who looks in a different direction lingers on its margin. The scenes from *Reloaded* are clearly using the same telegenic and compelling image of a transparent computer interface as seen in *Minority Report*. The metaphor of the black servant to white interface users is further elaborated. The dentist chairs where users jack in to the Matrix are sites where medical and digital discourses converge with racial imagery. We can see black nurses, or "operators," as they are called in the trilogy, tending to supine white bodies while their owners are off fighting the interface wars—a division of labor not unfamiliar to those who experienced the Silicon Valley boom and subsequent crash.[28] Toni Morrison's *Playing in the Dark*, which like Gilman's work emphasizes the ideological formation of race in culture, anatomizes the figure of the black nurse in Hemingway's work, in which the function of the black servant is to create, by means of negation, whiteness for the benefit of the protagonist. Marginal blackness works to make whiteness even whiter by contrast: a necessary act in the context of globalization, where transculturation threatens to fatally blur racial lines. Certainly, as Gilman notes, black marginal figures in interface narratives signify sex—the multicultural rave scene intercut with Trinity and Neo's sex scene exemplifies this technique—but more importantly, black bodies anchor white bodies in space.

Reloaded's multicultural rave scene depicts sweaty, sexy, and muscular black and multiracial bodies gyrating and pulsing to techno music as their dreadlocks fly and bare feet stamp in the mud. These scenes are intercut with images of Trinity and Neo having very restrained sex alone in their bedroom. This is a fine example of the ways that, as Richard Dyer writes, "through the figure of the non-white person, whites can feel what being, physicality, presence, might be like, while also disassociating themselves from the non-whiteness of such things."[29] Sexuality, a vexed and awkwardly depicted issue in the trilogy, must be filtered through blackness for its white characters, occupied as they are with matters of the mind such as programming and hacking, to feel it; blackness functions as a sexuality-prosthesis in this way. Indeed, the visual style of Zion invokes a kind of sexualized primitivism that could easily read as racism were it not repositioned in the future and in the context of computer technology. The presence of blackness in the visual field guards whites from the irresistible seduction of the perfectly transparent interface. The implication here is that black and white interface styles can coexist, with blackness legitimating the white device as a means for producing pleasure and displacing anxieties regarding the hegemony of white interfaces. In other words, the "mojo" of blackness in the computer interface is a salable commodity in the world outside the films as well. However, the price paid is that blacks are never depicted as masters of the interface, never creators of digital images, and are never depicted manipulating the interface in this direct bodily way.

Transparent interfaces are represented as intuitive, universal, pre- or postverbal, white, translucent, and neutral—part of a visual digital aesthetic code embodied by the Apple iPod. The Apple iPod advertising campaign, which took the form of both television and Internet video commercials, print advertisements, and posters that were highly visible on subway and BART station walls as well as in other urban public spaces during Christmas 2004, features dancing black silhouettes against a solid colored background, with the image of the white iPod clearly contrasted against these two fields of color and noncolor.

The negative space of the alpha channel employed in creating the silhouetted digital images depicts the iPod user's body as a black void into which a viewer's identity can be transported.[30] The visual culture of the iPod, itself a product celebrated as much for its sleek, white, spare good looks in terms of material culture artifacts as for its "easy to use" intuitive interface, is oriented around conveying a sense of neutrality, modernism,

Figure 3.6. Still from Apple iPod "Saturday Night" advertisement.

and negative space. In *Minority Report* and *The Matrix* trilogy, this modernist revival is depicted as a "white" style: transparent, neutral, "clean," and modern. Apple's trademark "iWorld," the logic that brings together the company's diverse product lines in music (iTunes), music hardware (iPod), laptop computers (iBook), and eye-catching design in desktop computers (iMac), invokes the notion of an "eye-world," a world of specific digital visual cultures, on the level of both the interface and the hardware. The title of Apple's iLife multimedia software suite posits an all-encompassing lifestyle defined by the visual spectacle of literally empty bodies and their heedless enjoyment of consumer choice and privilege, customization, and its implication with other forms of geopolitical domination and entitlement. Apple's iPod campaign is an example of the proliferation of niche digital visual cultures. The "iWorld" maintains its focus on the "i" prefix, which implies a constant focus on the user, the unique individual and neoliberal consumer for whom color blindness is a part of a conscious political ideology, and for whom information and communications technologies and the Internet are a means of enhancing customer choice and audience choice. The iWorld sells the user the glories of customization and putting one's own mark on things that are produced in a mass fashion, specifically to be altered, "burned," or ripped. The iPod is the object of desire because though each of them looks exactly the same, they are meant to be written on, to be shared with others, to contain subjectivity in a way that clothes or furniture cannot.

Thus the iPod embodies this kind of digital privilege that is invisible or transparent, the alpha channel of the i-strategy. This is part of the strategy that the iPod ads use to get potential users to insert themselves into iWorld.

Random access is an essential principle of the structure and logic of new media that respatializes media experiences: rather than needing to wait until a tape or other physical medium rewinds to get to the beginning of its contents, random access allows us to get there immediately, if we know where we want to go. As Lev Manovich puts it, random access is symptomatic of the "decline of the field of rhetoric in the modern era," for in contrast to modes of information presentation that rely on argument, narrative progression, and other systems of sequential arrangement, new media culture is better conceived of as "an infinite flat surface where individual texts are placed in no particular order."[31] This "flattening" of the data produces a user who is defined by "spatial wandering"; in the absence of an author or writer to order the media experience for her, the postmodern subject produced by random-access environments like digital gaming and use of hyperlinks and other interactive computer media is one defined by its freedom. The iPod's rhetoric of freedom from bulky hardware and the confining paradigm of music that possesses a material form rather than existing as an abstract information file (and in some cases the implied freedom from paying for music that comes from the MP3 file-sharing culture) is paralleled by its depictions of visualized freedom through linkages between race, dance, and musical genre in the iPod advertisements. The iPod offers the consumer volitional mobility not only on the level of device portability; she can either use the LCD display to navigate through customized playlists and program selections, or if she owns an iPod "shuffle," she can toggle it to "shuffle" and let the machine "randomly" decide what to play. Though the iPod's employment of random-access technology positions all its available musical selections on a "flat plane" in relation to each other, with any one song as equally and quickly accessible as any other through the medium of the interface, the visual language of the advertisements works to reinforce the idea of distinct visual and racial music styles. The "flatness" of the media form is counterbalanced by the creation of extremely well-differentiated visual styles that trace out different options in terms of race and ethnicity: the iPod advertising campaign creates volitional ethnicity as an option for the user in much the same way that interfaced networked visual environments accomplish this goal in the Jennifer Lopez video "If You Had My Love." Just as J. Lo is shown to "shuffle" between different racial, ethnic, and musical identities in response to the click-mediated desires of a projected normative user, so too does the iPod campaign produce racialized bodies that correspond to specific typed genres of music.

In the visual culture of the iPod ads, access to music styles is not seen as random at all; on the contrary, it is a specific media-searching technique mediated by the visual presence of both invisible and hypervisible black bodies. While the blacking out of the silhouettes conceals individual identity by making it impossible to see *who* they are, it becomes centrally the point *what* they are. The iPod ads often depict black people dancing because, as in *The Matrix* trilogy, black people dancing visually signifies desire that the white body cannot feel and cannot express visually. Sexuality, dreadlocked silhouettes, and musical genres like hip-hop (as in the still image reproduced earlier from the "hip hop Saturday night" video produced by Apple for iPod) and dance genres like break dancing are all depicted together in a way that functions as a lesson in musical genre in an age when the demise of album-oriented rock has made such definitions problematic. The notion that one can click through musical genres using software like Apple's iTunes and download music to correspond to the omnipresent racialized bodies in the ads links together the volitional mobility of the interfaced music shop with that of the consumer of the hipness and coolness of black expressive culture itself. Though the silhouettes of the dancers are an empty "alpha" channel devoid of color, they are paradoxically full of racialized color: as in *The Matrix* trilogy, black expressive styles are referenced via signifiers such as dreadlocks, Afros, and pheno/stereo/typically black profiles and bodies and serve to intensify the way that the iPod sells choice and random access in genres: musical genres, of course, but also the way that identities can be chosen and stepped into and out of through the medium of music. As in *The Matrix*, Afro-futuristic style is appropriated to signify both sexuality and "cool" in the context of regimes of hypervisuality and selective interfacial power differentials. As Claudia Springer points out in "Playing It Cool in the Matrix": "Thomas A. Anderson's transformation into Neo in the Matrix recalls the fifties' appropriation of black cool by whites, for the film relies on black characters to guide its white protagonist toward truth and fashion flair." And in a humorous essay by Donnell Alexander, provocatively titled "Cool like Me (Are Black People Cooler than White People?)," he asserts:

> Cool derived from having to survive as far as can be imagined from the ideal of white culture, with little more than a spiritual dowry for support. It's about living on the cusp, on the periphery, diving for scraps. . . . Cool, the basic reason blacks remain in the American cultural mix, is an industry of style that everyone in the world can use.[32]

The modularity and cross-platform salability of black culture guarantee the continued valuation of cool, particularly in representational practices associated with technologies that are feared to be dehumanizing. Apple, in particular, has always positioned itself as more "human" than other personal computer manufacturers. In "After 20 Years, Finally Capitalizing on Cool," the technology journalist Eric Stross asserts that the ineffable commodity that has distinguished Apple from other computer hardware companies is its coolness. He writes that though Microsoft has a near monopoly on oper-ating system software and Google has a lock on the digital library business, "Apple has an absolute monopoly on the asset that is the most difficult for competitors to copy: cool."[33] Apple sold ten million units of the iPod prod-uct as of January 2005 not because it possessed superior hardware or a com-petitive price but because of its "yet-to-be-matched software and essential cool." Stross credits Apple's mastery of the "metaphysical mystery of cool" with its success as "the company that best knows how to meld hardware and software, the company embodied in the ecstatically happy hipster silhouette. The company that is, in a word, cool." Apple relies heavily on advertising to create this invaluable and inimitable commodity; the language and images of interfaces employed in media objects like online and print advertisements create an identity for a product that is itself about the consumption of media.

Technology advertising has always promised different sorts of transfor-mations: Apple in particular is a machine, a company, and an ideology that has always been more preoccupied with the visible (and with "vision") than other information hardware manufacturers have been. Their strategy for creating a "cool" brand identity by promoting an Afro-futuristic visual culture in the iPod ads serves to separate blackness from other types of identities (the punk rock iPod ad features a thin white woman dancing pogo-style to aggressive sounding music) while presenting it as a stable object that can be enjoyed as one of a range of visual and musical options. While digital music may operate under the logic of "random access," users create paths and nar-ratives through exercising their desires that are far from random but rather produce predictable configurations of bodies, types, and images.

In 2005 the Venice, California, artist Trek Kelly created the images in the "iPod Ghraib" series as a way to critique the visual culture and political economy of the iPod.[34] While the war in Iraq continued, shoppers were torn between the different varieties on offer of the season's most popular and coveted Christmas gift: the iPod. In 2004, Apple was offering the iPod mini in a range of five colors, the iPod U2 limited edition with a forty-gigabyte hard drive and a reproduction signature by Bono, and the two "classic" versions

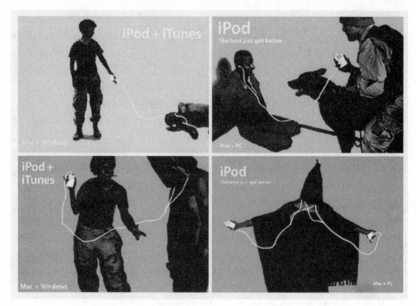

Figure 3.7. Digital image, poster, and vinyl piece "iPod Ghraib." Courtesy of Trek Thunder Kelly, copyright 2004.

of the silver and white iPod from prior seasons. During that same year, Trek Kelly's images could be found plastered around or over the original Apple iPod ads in public spaces. Images of tortured prisoners and American soldiers pointing guns at them were composited with images of the iPods and placed on top of the familiar solid color backgrounds from the originals. The artist's Web site describes the work as follows:

> Trek Kelly's politically charged series, iPod Ghraib, juxtaposes the infamous Abu Ghraib Iraqi prison pictures against the cultural juggernaut of the iPod campaign. Within this context, he explores the nature of torture through the colorful lens of American marketing. The digitally rendered vinyls also reflect Trek's effort to involve modern mediums in the artistic process. Each image is derived directly from the Internet, and contains all its complicit imperfections and mathematical simplifications. The result is a startling comment on our culture's need to simplify and compartmentalize our actions ... and, as is often the case with critical choices like Abu Ghraib, they show how something seemingly clear from a distance, upon closer inspection, can distort and break apart.

Kelly's revisioning of the "cultural juggernaut" of the iPod's visual commercial culture employs a jolting "tweak" or modification of the iconic images of dancing black bodies to bring them into dialogue with another set of images that were also in circulation on the Internet: the Abu Ghraib photographs. The Internet, a contemporary vector for the "modern mediums" of both advertising and news, is not directly critiqued here, but a visual style that combines subjection of one to another, whether invisible or visible, marries the two sets of images. The series "iPod Ghraib" employs the basic visual template of the iPod ads: solid primary background colors, the iPod depicted in detail, and the negative space of the alpha channel replaced and filled in by soldiers and torture victims from the infamous Abu Ghraib photographs, as opposed to the iconic dancers in the iPod ads. In contrast to Apple's efforts to efface the identities of the dancers, but not their races, in "iPod Ghraib" the individual features of the soldiers are not entirely blacked out: the U.S. soldier and war criminal Lynddie England's profile and face are liminally visible so as to emphasize her personal identity and identification with that act of racial and gender oppression. The facelessness of the masked figure in the first image with the electrocution wires replaced by white iPod earbud wires underscores the evacuation of personal identity that is necessary to the act of torture. In keeping with the tradition of reducing victims to an abject body without a face or identity by masking or hooding, these images employ graphic technology to mask the original figures in the iPod ads and replace them with ones from the Abu Ghraib photographs. These shocking images critique consumer culture and the military industrial complex with which consumer culture is imbricated; not just anyone can occupy that desired space of musical free volition, expression, and consumption. Those bodies that are barred from occupying the enticing blank space of the dancer, the shopper, the consumer, the bourgeois subject of digital culture, are exactly those bodies whose oppression underwrites Western privilege.

Susan Sontag's essay "On the Torture of Others" traces the lineage of the Abu Ghraib photographs in terms of their formal elements, mode of composition, framing, arrangement, style of display, and form of address to their viewer, to their roots in the visual culture and convention of lynching postcards.[35] The Abu Ghraib photographs documented and enacted an overtly racialized type of crime, a lynching in the context of a geopolitical military conflict, and one so much about effacing the personal identity of the victim while emphasizing, as much as possible, the victim's race as their marker of difference, the reason why they are there, the reason that this image was created in the first place. As Fusco notes in Skin Deep, visual imaging practices like photography did far more than represent race and racism in a transparent way—they produced them. Internet-based visual imaging practices like those that enabled the production, distribution, and exhibition of the Abu Ghraib photographs are the latest instantiation of a long line of representational technologies that pose the spectacle of torture and death as a matter of racial hygiene. Just as blackness is posed as a cross-platform visual style that can endow a transcodeable "cool" on all types of media technologies and practices, whiteness is exposed as killingly normative.

Similarly, *The Matrix* trilogy and *Minority Report* depict blackness as a decorative strategy in their digital epic narratives. The struggle over control and mastery of the interface and thus the digital world must end in the same way: with white hackers in control and black characters as marginal figures who bring "cool" with them. *The Matrix* trilogy's critique of whiteness situates user entitlement in relation to the computer interface as a highly visible and theatrical means by which masculinity and whiteness are allied with mastery over transparent interfaces. It represents black operators interacting with computer interfaces via the old-fashioned technology of typing, which is part of the new technoprimitivism inaugurated by the trilogy's visual style; however, we do not see black people using gestural computing. Gestural computing, with its immediate and proprioceptive relation to the interface, is reserved for white operators, who, as discussed earlier, are always depicted in the *Matrix* films and in *Minority Report* as framed by marginal black characters.

Their marginal blackness preserves the sense of singularity, identity, and uniqueness so valued in the era of digital reproduction (indeed, *The Matrix* trilogy addresses the postmodern anomie created by the anxiety of digital reproduction: the multiple Agent Smiths horrify by their perfect replicability). Whiteness is replication, blackness is singularity, but never *for* the black subject, always for the white subject. How best to read the particular position of the marginal black in cinematic depictions of the interface? Marginal blacks are literally in the margins of these images—witness to the digital image production that threatens to smudge the line between reality and virtuality. And for many critics, the contrast between the real and the virtual is the most important issue to consider in the films.[36]

However, this question cannot be considered without reference to the visual culture of computing that occupies every frame of these films. This visual culture, which contrasts black and white interface styles so strongly, insists that it is race that is real. In this way the process of new media as a cultural formation that produces race is obscured; instead race functions here as a way to visualize new media image production. What color are the bodies of those who will be making images using computer interfaces? And what color are those bodies who will be taking care of the bodies (and houses, yards, pets, and children) of those people who are jacked in, busy scrubbing, manipulating, buying, selling, and transmitting these images? Considerations of the racialized political economies of computer culture are inseparable from the ways in which we ought to read these texts. Postmillennial science fiction texts provide us with a plethora of images of race in relation to computing and interface culture, the scene of new media image production. In this representational economy, images of blacks serve as talismans to ward off the consuming power of the interface, whose transparent depths, like Narcissus's pool, threaten to fatally immerse its users.

Minority Report (2002), directed by Steven Spielberg, also dramatizes the scene of interface use and posits whites as uniquely privileged subjects of interactivity because of their transparent and thus privileged relations to the computer. However, Minority Report dramatizes the ways that the postmillennial social body has become an object of surveillance via biometrics and crime databases. Networked digital imaging devices that perform retinal scans in public spaces like subways and department stores set in motion a web of state and commercial disciplinary mechanisms. While The Matrix is concerned with real versus unreal bodies, singular versus replicated bodies, Minority Report envisions the future regulation of the criminal body as the work of dataveillance, and the gradual interpellation of its white hero into this system's critique and destruction as part of a process of re-racialization that calls the notion of the "whole" or singularly racialized body into question. Minority Report was released in the same year as Stephen Frears's independent film Dirty Pretty Things, which is set in present-day London and concerns the doings of African and Turkish illegal immigrants who are involved in the world of organ harvesting and trafficking. The biotechnological revolution, part of the network economy that grew to maturity during the same period as the Internet did, has borne fruit in the world of Minority Report: human organs can be bought and sold using conventional credit cards, and there is a thriving black as well as white market in such commodities. It is when the technology of state-controlled vision extends into the organs of vision themselves that we can see the way that whiteness is also critiqued in this film, replaced with a resistant image of a transplanted, patched-together, socially marginal body that opposes itself to the dataveillant systems that demand, create, and control singular bodies. The social optics of race are hacked in this film, a film that posits a visual culture in which the act of seeing itself has become inseparable from the political economies of race, retailing, crime, and surveillance. Seeing is always seeing in relation to the state; attempts to break this deadlock result in the loss of all personhood, a condition under which one enters the dead space or alpha channel of sociality.

"Hello, Mr. Yakamoto! Welcome back to the Gap. How did those assorted tank tops work for you?" These words are addressed to policeman John Anderton, played by Tom Cruise, as he walks into a Gap store in the year 2054. The voice that pronounces them is a synthetic, digitized one that issues from a virtual greeter depicted on a large wall screen which has scanned his retinas to determine his identity. This episode, which occurs about halfway through the film, is one that the New York Times film critic Elvis Mitchell describes as "a laugh-producing sequence set in a Gap store." Mitchell says that "the movie is filled with fictional commercials and the onslaught is presented as intrusive; each has been geared to speak directly to the individual consumer." Indeed, the scene in which the character's eyes are read by the film's omnipresent retinal scanners and identified as belonging to "Mr. Yakamoto" is played for comedy. The joke is that John Anderton, a policeman on the run from the law after having been fingered by a trio of future-seeing mutants, or Precognitives, for a murder they predict he will commit, has had his eyes replaced to hide his identity from digital surveillance methods, and the sleazy black-market doctor who performed the work replaced his original eyes with a set of Asian eyes. The Gap's retinal scanners, initially employed to scan a person's identity so as to market commodities to them more precisely, reveal to Anderton what he himself could not know any other way: his eyes, obtained illegally from the "secondary market" in transplantable body parts, originally belonged to someone of a different race. The joke is on Anderton: as he walks away from the scanners, he mutters in disgust and disbelief, "Mr. Yakamoto!" Within the logic of the film, the doctor's implantation of Asian eyes into the famous face of Tom Cruise is on the order of a prank. The doctor, who had previously been arrested by Anderton, is having his revenge.

Why is it funny that Tom Cruise should be identified as "Mr. Yakamoto"? This seemingly throwaway moment elegantly illustrates what Paul Gilroy calls the "crisis of raciology" engendered by the biotechnological revolution in tandem with digital image-processing technologies such as CGI, Photoshop, Final Cut Pro, and their progeny. As Gilroy writes: "Bodies may still be the most significant determinants in fixing the social optics of 'race,' but black bodies are now being seen—figured and imaged—differently."[37] Technologies of "figuring and imaging" race are central to the visual culture of race in *Minority Report*. Optical scanners matched to networked databases can "see" who you are and can figure out what to sell you, as in the case of the Gap episode. However, other digital imaging applications, such as the technology that enables the Precognitives to project their visions of who will commit which murders onto giant cinema screens in the Precrime company's "temple" brings to a mind another kind of computerized profiling that echoes the new social optics of race in America post 9/11: racial profiling. As the *Newsweek* critic David Ansen writes of Spielberg: "The director couldn't have known . . . how uncannily [this] tale of 2054 Washington D.C. would resonate in the current political climate, where our jails fill up with suspects who've been arrested for crimes they haven't yet committed."[38] The unprecedented access to the suspect's personal information, remote geographic imaging, and militarized rapid response combined with the Precognitives' visions allow the police to concatenate multiple sources of visual and textual information together to profile people who are about to commit murders and arrest them before they can do so, without needing to go through anything but a pro forma trial via videoconference in advance of the crime, but after watching the footage. In other words, it works exactly as does the juridico-legal system in an informational post-terror state.

"[Computers] simulate surveillance in the sense that they precede and redouble the means of observation. Computer profiling . . . is understood best not just as a technology of surveillance, but as a kind of *surveillance in advance of surveillance*, a technology of 'observation before the fact.'"[39] The narrative of inadvertent cross-racial passing that is so much a part of *Minority Report* is enabled by the replacement of the physical body by the databody as a subject (and product) of surveillance. The retinal scanners read Anderton as Yakamoto because they are keyed to databases that look only at his eyes and the information that they are linked to. The science fiction film *Gattaca* (1997) extends the notion of dataveillance to the level of the gene, positing a future in which humans are heavily genetically engineered.[40] In "Closely Belated? Thoughts on Real-Time Media Publics and *Minority Report*," Mark Williams draws connections between the film's handling of time and prediction through data profiling and what he terms "real time desire." *Minority Report*'s "belated thematics" or hypervaluation of mediated time shifting, as in the use of the personal video recorder or TiVo, is evident in the police's possession of "the capacity to allow one to 'freeze' the 'live' image, and then fast-forward through 'real time' to the now, and resynchronize with the 'live,' represents[ing] the newest wrinkle of temporal frenzy within mediated culture."[41] These scenes of mediated video manipulation

are among the film's most telegenic and striking. The surveillance perspective most often seen in science fiction or techno-thriller films of the nineties
is the aerial shot from the "eye in the sky" or satellite, as shown in the film
Enemy of the State (1998) and the television show 24 (2001–). *Minority Report*
replaces the eye in the sky with surveillance images that are keyed to the
deployment, scanning, and use of the eye itself, as photographed at ground
level, as a means of data profiling and surveillance. Retinal scans determine
what characters in *Minority Report* see in quite a literal way: just as grocery
store checkout registers keep consumer purchases in a database to decide
what kinds of coupons to print for customers, so too are advertisements in
public spaces determined by past purchases. When the Gap virtual greeter
asks Anderton how he liked "those assorted tank tops," it is querying Yakamoto's past purchases into order to decide where to direct his vision in the
store. As Williams puts it, the "contemporary mediated public sphere" identifies Anderton through the use of optical biometrics, thus incorporating him
into "the mobile, interactive consumerist public sphere, which is premised
upon one's movement through a persistent 'now' of being hailed into recognition (as a consumer)." As Anderton is hailed by the Gap greeter as "Mr.
Yakamoto," it is evident, however, that the modularity of body parts (which
constitutes both a privilege and an act of utter desperation or brutality depending on one's position in the transaction) engenders a case of mistaken
identity. Anderton has purchased a new identity by taking another person's
eyes. There is an uncanny scene, unfathomably played for comedy in the
film, in which Anderton saves his old eyes to use to fool the retinal scanner
at Precrime into letting him into the building, and as he removes them from
the dirty plastic bag in his pocket, he drops them and pursues them across a
concrete floor as they roll toward a drain. As he manages to snatch one right
before it disappears, his relief mirrors the exigencies of life in a dataveillant
society, a life in which a citizen's claim to citizenship can roll down a drain.
Minority Report depicts a datasociety in which a citizen's "profile" is that of
either a consumer or a criminal, thus throwing into relief Kelly Oliver's conception of subjectivity as defined by ownership in the context of a market
economy: "Subjects are capable of ownership, of having their own, of being
'ownness,' while those who are not capable of ownership become objects to
be seen or not by propertied subjects."[42] When Anderton becomes a fugitive,
he must adopt another citizen's identity to become a propertied subject who
owns freedom of movement in the public sphere. While identity theft and
identity hacking figure largely, this is not the crime that the film foresees—
in this film, the racialized state is the thief, stealing the freedom and agency

of large numbers of members of its underclass. Though the conceit of the film is that crime can be predicted through the use of mutants hooked up to powerful computers used by skilled interface operators, computer profiling is itself a "technology of observation before the fact," and like the Precogs, it can *only* see crime, not the future generally. Dataveillant technologies that profile users' engagements with consumer databases in effect predict what we will buy, and in the case of the preprinted coupons, turn that prediction into fact (users are much more likely to use coupons that they already own). Computing profiling or "surveillance in advance of surveillance" maps well onto the operations of our contemporary informational state, one that asserts its color blindness but continues to racially profile citizens and noncitizens, often with fatal results.

Indeed, one of the most remarkable aspects of Minority Report is the way in which it manages so effectively to evade direct discussion of race (reviewers of the film in the popular press have failed to mention race in relation to the movie at all, though most noted that it performs a social critique of technology and advertising) in its discussion of criminal profiling, identity scanning and surveillance technologies, and political economies of labor and capital. It is as if the film itself were, like the title of Paul Gilroy's book, "against race" (though of course for much different reasons) in its effort to limn a future in which race is forcibly elided. However, the film is set in Washington, D.C., one of America's most multicultural cities, and one of the few where African Americans are a large and powerful political and cultural force. In the world of the film, murders predicted by the Precognitives are prevented by arresting their future perpetrators. They are "disappeared," as is a direct confrontation with the question of race in the film. However, race has been ported from the realm of the visible to the realm of vision itself: Cruise's black-market Asian eyes signify a specific set of concerns regarding the status of race in the biotechnological and technoscientific present and future. "Race" has literally become a networked commodity in this instance: Cruise buys these eyes with his credit card just before the operation. In addition, the significance of eyes in cyberpunk narrative, from Blade Runner on, gestures toward another convention of this most technoscientific of genres: the fetishization of the Orient as a signifier of the future.

As David Palumbo-Liu writes in Asian/American, the Asian eye with its distinctive epicanthic fold has long been seen as the defining feature of the Asian physiognomy: eyelid surgery to "correct" this feature is an example of the new "technologically driven malleability" of race.[43] Minority Report remolds race using a radical new form of surgery—total eye replacement—

but to different ends. Endowing Tom Cruise with brown Asian eyes allows the film to hide race in plain sight, within the body of its hero. In addition, this move references the ways in which the "biotechnological revolution demands a change in our understanding of 'race,' species, embodiment, and human specificity," in Gilroy's words. One of his specific examples of this revolution's recasting of race is "the international and therefore necessarily 'transracial' trade in internal organs and other body parts for transplant, sometimes obtained by dubious means."[44] The anthropologist Nancy Scheper-Hughes observes the geopolitical racialization of the traffic in organs: "The flow of organs follows the modern routes of capital; from South to North, from Third to First World, from poor to rich, from black and brown to white, and from female to male."[45] As mentioned earlier, Dirty Pretty Things, released the same year as Minority Report, traces the chain of supply and demand for body parts through a network of misery, disenfranchisement, and terror concealed under the surface of official institutions such as London hotels, hospitals, apartment buildings, airports, and cab companies. The global demand for kidneys drives the exploitation of recently arrived immigrants by more established ones: the pressure to sell organs as a way to secure the lives and safety of distant relatives is impossible to resist, given the brutal economies of power and economic differentials in what Manuel Castells dubs the "Black Holes" produced by informational capitalism. These Black Holes are everywhere: rather than existing only in extremely informationally deprived places such as Africa, the informational economy that has created them ensures that they exist, though in more covert fashion, in global capitals as well.[46] Castells writes: "The rise of informationalism at the turn of the millennium is intertwined with rising inequality and social exclusion throughout the world."[47] The "rise" of a new category of persons under informational capitalism, a group that Castells calls the Fourth World, is defined by the condition of being forced to sell the only thing that they have that is of even limited value in the informational economy, that is, their bodies. In a section titled "Why Children Are Wasted," Castells notes that while children have always been exploited, the network society and the "new geography of social exclusion" it produces has exacerbated their misery. Children are "ready-to-use, disposable labor . . . the last frontier of renewed over-exploitation under networked, global capitalism." And Castells is also very much of the opinion that race is not irrelevant in this scheme: "Racial discrimination and spatial segregation are still major factors in the formation/enforcement of ghettos as systems of social exclusion. But their effects take new meaning, and become increasingly devastating, under the conditions of informationalism."[48]

Minority Report takes up Castells's premise that the rise of informational-ism has produced a Fourth World that sustains it, "populated by millions of homeless, incarcerated, prostituted, criminalized, brutalized, stigmatized, sick, and illiterate persons," and visualizes it as a narrative of detection. The Fourth World of *Minority Report* is composed of an underclass that includes drug addicts and their families, criminals, black-market doctors and organ traffickers, drug dealers, and other persons excluded from power and subjec-tivity in the informational economy. And just as Castells writes, their hid-den labor and misery are both produced by and underwrite the glossy world that Anderton inhabits as a respected member of the police force and the possessor of a specialized skill in relation to the informational economy: he is a master of the Precrime imaging system that allows him to cut together, suture, composite, and manipulate images of crimes and interlink them with state databases that contain addresses, profiles, mug shots, and other personal information belonging to citizens. In some of the film's most telegenic se-quences, Anderton uses gestural digital video editing technology to manipu-late images of crimes shortly before they are about to occur. As he waves his arms and sweeps the images to and fro, "scrubbing the image," as one observer describes it, he asserts the primacy of *his* vision, and the power that com-puters and their operators have to make visual objects fungible, modular, and scalable. We, the viewer, see the images *as* he sees them: magnified, turned back in time, rotated several degrees, out of sequence, sutured, cut, pasted, and imported from other screens. Detection, always a visual trope, has liter-ally become an act of computer-aided vision in this film, a kind of privileged seeing through postproduction. Like the Zion gate operator in *The Matrix*, Anderton is engaging in a transparent relationship with the interface that confirms his privilege in the racial landscape. Anderton has the privileged view that comes with a proprioceptive, immediate relationship to networked digital imaging. As Aylish Wood puts it: "In *Minority Report* the interaction of the detective with the images is distinct in that the haptic, or touch-based, dimension is absent."[49] While other characters slave over keyboards or peer through monoculars, like Anderton's black assistant, Jad, the detective enjoys an interactive, performative relationship to data images. Just as in the *Matrix* films, the male protagonist is gifted with the ability to move freely and directly into interfaces, in a performance of mastery and immedi-acy that circumvents the ordinary rules of input/output established by lesser users. Anderton and Anderson are superusers; as Tom Foster notes: "Neo becomes the only character who has a direct, unmediated relationship to the mediating structures and languages that allow the Matrix to exist. None of the other characters possess this ability." Echoing the visual setup of *Minority Report*, Foster notes: "The [Matrix] films then define a new ideology of transparency, associated not with the unthinking acceptance of surface appearances, but with the ability to see through such realistic illusions. While immersion in the illusion naturalizes appearances, Neo's ability to perceive their constructedness naturalizes that ability as a function of the unaided critical faculties of the human mind, independent of any technological prosthesis or interface."[50] Wood argues that the scenes depicting the "detecting wall" are demonstrations of interactive media that have more in common with digital games, MUDs and MOOs, and other immersive environments that are more frequently studied. Indeed, if photography as a mode of identifying and categorizing criminals was characteristic of the early twentieth century's efforts to regulate "the new world of mobility and rapid circulation . . . in which signs of class and occupation have moved below the threshold of immediately recognized conventional signs to reach the level of unintentional—and often unrecognized—symptoms," we can assert that interactive digital surveillance video functions in a similar way at the turn of our own century. Tom Gunning's brilliant essay "Tracing the Visible Body: Photography, Detectives, and Early Cinema" explains the ways in which photography became part of a complex of identifying techniques that "became necessary in the new world of rapid circulation" and helped to create "an archive of information on individuals which became the basic tool for the assertion of control in modern society."[51] The assertion of control in network society involves privileged, transparent interfaced relations to immersive digital environments. This hypervaluation of the transparent is echoed in the visual setup of *Minority Report*. As Wood notes: "The plastic boxes of computers and plasma or tube-screens familiar from the late twentieth and early twenty-first century have given way to clear Perspex curves and flat screens on which the image is visible from either side,"[52] and the filmmakers' use of bypass bleaching, choice of camera lens, film stock, and postproduction manipulation result in a visual field that appears cool, silvery, washed-out, desaturated, and colorless. This seems particularly appropriate in a film with an extremely occluded relation to racial politics and its place in dataveillant societies.

Anderton's performances at the interactive detecting wall strongly mirror another much-commented-on scene in *Blade Runner*, one of several resonances between the two films. In the scene in which Deckard uses an Esper imaging computer to see into a photograph he has taken from a replicant, he manipulates the image by orally instructing the computer to "pan right, magnify, stop," and so on. Both characters are engaging with the computer by means other than through a hardware interface: Deckard uses voice recognition, a technique that hails the computer as an interlocutor, and Anderton and the Zion gate operator use gesture, a performative and proprioceptive means of command and control. And in addition, both are engaging in digital image processing and enhancement as a way to "see" or detect the truth about a crime. Both *Blade Runner* and *Minority Report* begin with extreme close-up shots of eyes, and as Kaja Silverman writes of *Blade Runner*: "However, if the opening shots work in an anticipatory way to break down the dichotomy between replicants and humans by focusing on an eye which could represent either, it is because that organ represents precisely the site at which difference is ostensibly discernible within the world of *Blade Runner*."[53] *Minority Report's* ubiquitous shots of eyes being scanned in shopping malls, subways, housing projects, and workplaces expands this notion of retinal surveillance to the public sphere in its entirety. The eye becomes the sole signifier of identity in this panoptic future. Hence the positioning of Anderton's eye as an Asian one allows the notion of hybrid forms of subjectivity to come into play. Far from the celebratory mestiza subject of Gloria Anzaldúa's writings, however, this one comes from a lack of empathy rather than a plurality of it—Anderton only needs to take the position of the raced, hunted, marginalized person of color into account, he only needs to really see it, at the moment that he begins his new life as a fugitive from justice. Hence cyberculture enables a privileged view of image and race as code and takes it away: the same computers that allow Anderton to "scrub" the image make him permanently vulnerable to their surveillance. This unprecedented vulnerability to techno-surveillance is, however, part of what it means to be a person of color in the "integrated circuit," to use Haraway's eloquent formulation. Donna Haraway and Paul Gilroy both strongly insist on the revisioning of race as code, genome, and restlessly interrogate this system: the visuality of race has retreated from pencil tests, paper bag tests, and other naked-eye optical assessments and now resides in acronyms like ART, DNA, IVF, and HGP.[54] The primacy of vision reigns unchallenged but only on a level so microscopic that only machines can "see" it. Advances in biotechnology extend a process of visualizing the body as information that began in the mid-twentieth century. In Sarah Chinn's fascinating history of the Red Cross and its policies regarding cross-racial blood donation during World War II and before, she remarks that blood replaced skin as the ruling metaphor for race in the years after emancipation but became displaced when scientists learned how to type and classify blood based on signs invisible to nonmedical observers: "Blood as a metaphor for racial identity works only when it cannot be seen, in a world in which blood cannot be scrutinized as such outside the body."[55] The definition of the "truth" about bodies and race as inaccessible except through machine-mediated means privileges dataveillant means of identification such as genetic profiling, retinal scans, and other biometric measures, for as Chinn writes, "DNA research offers the promise of reconciling the visible outside and occulted inside of the body."[56] The darker side of this promise, however, can be seen in an open letter to the International Civil Aviation Organization protesting its plans to require passports and other travel documents to contain information about biometrics and other remotely readable "contact-less integrated circuits." The ICAO proposes to create a national biometric database by requiring all air travelers to submit to facial recognition systems, retinal scans, and fingerprinting; many of these measures are already required of U.S. visitors. A consortium of human rights and civil liberties groups opposes these measures on the grounds that they violate the right to privacy of movement, as well as helping to create "interconnecting databases that, according to E.U. privacy officials, 'could lead to detailed profiles of an individual's habits both in the public and in the private sector.'"[57] In particular, the letter notes the inaccuracy of facial recognition systems, which contain a high likelihood of "false non-matches" (where valid individuals are refused border entry because the technology fails to recognize them) and false matches (where an individual is matched to another individual incorrectly) and also "may reveal racial or ethnic origin." It also notes that "the U.S. General Accounting Office warns that facial recognition is the only biometric that can be used for other surveillance applications, such as pinpointing individuals filmed on video cameras." Biometrics are deeply implicated in racial and ethnic profiling of all sorts, and their compulsory usage in the context of travel works to create a dataveillant state that constructs all its members and nonmembers as objects of interactivity, firmly on the opposite side of the transparent interface that separates the state and its representatives, such as the police, from its subjects.

As Castells notes, children and single mothers are especially exploited under informational capitalism on account of the demise of patriarchalism and the absence of alternative social mechanisms to protect the rights of mothers and children. Minority Report's Precognitives embody the exploitation of these abject bodies by the dataveillant state. The Precogs are kept in a vat of liquid and tended like machinery: just like ranks of expensive main-frame computers in "server farms" that need to be kept at precise tempera-tures and levels of humidity so that they can continue to process informa-tion in parallel with each other, the Precogs are networked to each other and to the imaging screens that let the detectives see their visions. This imagery of factory farming is intensified in later footage of the prison where the unconscious Anderton is interred. The convicts occupy tiny cells among vast ranks of other tiny cells. The imagery of the factory prison echoes that of the awe-inspiringly vast ranks of metal pods displayed in The Matrix tril-ogy, each containing a single sleeping wired-up human adult-fetus bathed in a cell of liquid. In Minority Report these futuristic prison cells contain crimi-nals, another growing population who, as Castells notes, are a major com-ponent of the Fourth World, who are networked to a computer that keeps them unconscious and unable to move, and are literally buried in the earth.

Anderton's loss in status, identity, and safety, in short, the loss of his privilege, the privilege to see everyone and everything from the perspective of the state and as a representative of its dataveillant mode of vision, reflects the ways in which the Fourth World is radically marginalized. As Williams writes, Agatha the Precog exemplifies this plight: hers is the most "trau-matic subjectivity" in the film. From a "refuse class of society," she has been displaced "from even consumerist subjectivity and its mediated, mitigated relation to citizenship." The child of a single mother, a drug addict whose use of an experimental substance has resulted in the mutations that enable her child to see future crimes, Agatha is both divine and oppressed. Played by the ethereal Samantha Morton, Agatha is a child trapped in a woman's body. She has never worn clothes and can barely walk. She also has no data profile; when read, her retina tells no story of retail habits, crime, job status, or geographic location. Having lived in a vat all her life, she has had no opportunity to acquire one. She is figured very much as an object of inter-activity, while the policemen who "read" her are its de facto subjects. Ander-ton's framing and expulsion from the police force are meant to remind us that it is really the dataveillant state that owns them both.

Minority Report literalizes Lisa Lowe's formulation of Asians as both capi-tal and labor,[58] for while Cruise capitalizes on the hapless Mr. Yakamoto's disembodied eyes, the custom-built computer imaging hardware that enables him to manipulate the Precognitives' films of murders-to-be is produced for him by "Rufus T. Reilly," the South Asian American cyberparlor operator. The dark, curly-haired, garrulous Reilly runs a shady virtual reality service that allows users to experience their unsavory fantasies, such as sex with multiple

partners and ego-gratifying scenarios in which coworkers applaud the customer. The visit to Reilly's workplace reveals the underpinnings of the
dataveillant state in socially marginal forms of labor: in addition to engaging
in borderline-illegal forms of VR, he has coded the software that allows
Agatha's "visions" to be viewed using a computer interface and helps Anderton hack into her visions while he is on the run. Reilly is the only character
in the film who seems to believe in the Precogs' divinity, though it is referenced often in the film. Though Anderton says, "It's better if you don't think
of them as human," thus at least initially representing Agatha as a "thing"
or an organic hardware peripheral as do the policemen and the state, Reilly
gets on his knees to worship her like a goddess when he first sees her. This
juxtaposition of the primitive-spiritual and technological in marginal characters of color is noticeable in *The Matrix* trilogy as well. However, while *The
Matrix* focuses much more on the rise of the Fourth World in the form of
cool Afro-futuristic rebels, *Minority Report* is much more invested in images
of the techno-Oriental. Just as in paradigmatic cyberpunk narratives like
Neuromancer and the *Matrix* sequels, Orientals are figured as high-tech en-
ablers—figurative software programs like the Keymaster and the Seraph—
in the service of central white characters. This trope goes beyond science
fiction and into the culture at large; as Ron Eglash puts it in "Race, Sex,
and Nerds: From Black Geeks to Asian American Hipsters": "The compulsory cool of black culture is mirrored by a compulsory nerdiness for oriental-
ized others such as Middle Eastern groups, groups from India, and Asian
Americans."[59] The representational damage done to Asians in this formulation of them as either crack engineers or spare parts goes beyond "nerd"
stereotypes, however.

It is noteworthy that the eyes that Cruise purchases are Japanese, for
Japan is a First World nation, more likely to buy organs than to sell them.
Considering the prevalence of Japanese product placements, such as Lexus,
in the film itself, it seems that this aspect of cyberculture's political economy has not changed in its future. However, the trope of transplantation
does evoke a particularly American technique and discourse of dealing with
difference: assimilation. Just as global capital can effortlessly assimilate traffic
in information, corporate and personal identities, and the digital encoding
that enables the eminent portability of these things, so too can the Western
male subject of the future incorporate racial difference. As Chinn notes as
well, Japanese Americans have posed a particular problem to the dynamic
of U.S. assimilation, one that became apparent during the World War II
internment of large numbers of Japanese American citizens. At that time,

Lieutenant General John L. DeWitt wrote that "the Japanese race is an enemy race and while many second and third generation Japanese born of the U.S. soil, possessed of U.S. citizenship, have become 'Americanized,' the racial strains are undiluted."[60] While African Americans could be incorporated into citizenship (albeit in a less-privileged form) despite their racial difference, Japanese Americans could not. Anderton's literal assimilation of a socially unassimilable body represents biotechnologically enabled racial hybridity. Hybridity is figured as sinister and dangerous in other contexts in this film: as Dr. Hineman, the coinventor of the Precrime system and "discoverer" of the Precognitives' crime-predicting skills says of her bioengineered poisonous plant, it is "a hybrid of my own design." But in this case, it works to solve a particular cultural problem with a much longer history, that of miscegenation.

This type of hybrid identity enabled by the literal incorporation of differently raced genetic material by a consuming Western subject presents a distinctively technoscientific solution to the "problem" of miscegenation. Miscegenation has long been figured as a colonial solution to the problem of the Other; as Benedict Anderson writes, "liberal" colonists in the early nineteenth century such as Pedro Fermin de Vargas believed that "the Indian is ultimately redeemable—by impregnation with white, 'civilized' semen, and the acquisition of private property, like everyone else (how different Fermin's attitude is from the later European imperialist's preference for 'genuine' Malays, Gurkhas, and Hausas over 'half breeds,' 'semi educated natives,' 'wogs,' and the like)."[61] In Minority Report, Asian Americans cannot be visually assimilated into mainstream culture, as they will always look different and thus be visually profiled differently from "real" Americans, so they are assimilated as instruments or commodities of vision. This formulation goes beyond a convenient pun, for the trope of vision in the context of technoscience and film is central, and in ways that are currently under revision as genomic means of understanding the body and the digital production of film replace older paradigms. Both race and the media image are being configured as code or "information" at the same historical moment, which makes them both subject to a new logic of transcoding.[62]

The last scene of Minority Report shows us a tableau of Anderton reunited with his formerly estranged and now pregnant wife as they gaze out a window at the rain from their cozy apartment. Though reinstated in the police force and in his family, he still has Yakamoto's eyes, a souvenir of his sojourn in the Fourth World. His own eyes are gone. If, as Oliver writes, only "the self-possessed enjoy the sense of entitlement to exercise control over themselves and their bodies," and "the notion of self-possession takes on new meaning when bodies and body parts can be bought and sold on the market,"[63] Anderton has literally redeemed himself by assuming control of his databody. There are associated losses, for after purchasing Yakamoto's eyes, he is never again depicted using the gestural Precrime interface. Precrime has been shut down and the Precogs freed, but more importantly, Anderton's integration with the Fourth World, however temporary, has precluded an engagement with informational white privilege in the context of the police state. He cannot engage with the interface as a superuser with Asian eyes, and in the eyes of the dataveillant state he will always be "Yakamoto." He is, however, shown as having gained another sort of potency; in impregnating his wife, he is replacing the lost child, a boy, whose death he mourns throughout most of the film. Reproductive ability stands in to replace the masculine power that has been lost by his alienation from privileged scenes of interface use.

When the Precrime system is first described in the film, within its first half hour, we are also told that the ACLU opposes it. The digital visual culture of race in these popular visual narratives figures the digital image as scrubbable, manipulable, and mobile in ways and by means that encourage assessments of power relations regarding interface use. Rather than focusing mainly on the role of racialized digital content, these narratives urge us to consider the contexts of image exhibition, preparation, and consumption and how these contexts reflect racialized positions. Information machines are the sole means of vision in digital visual culture, but as the body itself becomes socially defined and handled as information, there is even more at stake in paying attention to the incursions of machines in everyday life and the forms of resistance available to us.

4

Avatars and the Visual Culture
of Reproduction on the Web

In a 2005 episode of *Six Feet Under*, a highly regarded HBO television series, a pregnant Brenda and her husband Nate receive bad news regarding a prenatal test from their gynecologist.[1] She recommends they get an additional test, an amniocentesis, to rule out any problems, though, as she says, the first test they took and failed is "very unreliable." We later witness Brenda at home at the kitchen table using the Internet to look at a Web site called "Maternity Today.com" and are given a full-screen shot of the site's bulletin board page with the heading "Topic: Bad Test Results."[2] The screen shot consists of post headings from several users, demonstrating that perusing Internet bulletin boards has become part of the process of doing research on the risks of amniocentesis and the accuracy of prenatal testing. While the laptop displays the site to the viewer, Brenda decides to present her husband with her decision not to have the amniocentesis because she is afraid of the risk of the procedure endangering the fetus; clearly her decision is depicted as having something to do with what she has just read on the bulletin board. Brenda had suffered a miscarriage earlier in the season, in fact on the day of her wedding. The decision produces a great deal of conflict between Brenda and her husband, and we later witness her sadly gazing at two ultrasound images stuck on the refrigerator door with magnets as she picks up the telephone to ask her mother to lunch. In this series of vignettes that deal with digital technology, female anxiety, reproductive medicine, and networked,

131

many-to-many versus traditional one-to-one forms of medicalized knowledge, we can see that the Internet has become a place where pregnant women go to gather information, fellowship, and alternative discourses regarding important decisions about their pregnancies. The increasing medicalization of pregnancy and its social networking on the Internet is just one aspect of the technologizing of the body that continues to work as a distinctive feature of networked postindustrial societies. And as Eugenia Georges and Lisa M. Mitchell found in their 2000 study of Canadian and Greek pregnancy guidebooks, "Baby Talk: The Rhetorical Production of Maternal and Fetal Selves," only "a decade ago, Barbara Katz Rothman observed that many North American women 'take pregnancy as a reading assignment.'"[3] They assert that this "widespread 'educating' of women, ostensibly to inform and empower them," is accomplished by texts that "discipline women to become particular kinds of patients and mothers."[4] Many North American women take pregnancy as an Internet research assignment, using the medium to find health information, both official and anecdotal; to share stories, fears, and anxieties with other pregnant women whom they may or may not know; and to view and exchange visual images of their own pregnant bodies as well as those of others. And just as the rhetoric of pregnancy guidebooks greatly influences the formation of discourses and disciplines of motherhood in different national contexts, so too have the form and visual culture of the Internet created both normative and resistant discourses of motherhood in the context of the United States. This is quite an under-researched area of study; as Georges and Mitchell observe, the content and form of these ubiquitous pregnancy guidebooks seem to have escaped critical feminist analysis, and the same can be said for the use of the Internet as an informational and educational tool in the culture of pregnancy.[5]

In *Six Feet Under*, Brenda's feelings of anxiety, fear, and anticipation engendered by the intense medical surveillance of her pregnancy (a level of scrutiny that is becoming increasingly available to middle- and upper-class women in the United States) are both assuaged and spurred on by a parallel development in this technology, that is, the production of ultrasound images that represent a "baby." While the test's "bad" results are invisible to Brenda because they are dematerialized and abstract, coming to her secondhand from her doctor, her "baby's" picture as represented by an ultrasound is depicted as a direct visual argument against terminating the pregnancy should it turn out to be "bad." Internet bulletin board posts created by female Internet users can work to decenter medical authority, yet at the same time the digital imaging technologies that create ultrasounds work to create an insistent visual argument for the "personhood" of a fetus.[6] As Peggy Phelan notes, the image of the fetal ultrasound has been deployed in the context of television commercials to produce "both protectionist sentiment and the potential feeling of guilt in those who 'bond' with it."[7] This is because of the immediacy of this particular type of fetal image, one that produces both "bonding" to the notional infant still invisible to the mother by nontechnologically assisted means, and "bondage" to social norms regarding how a mother ought to act, view, and conceptualize her position and identity.

The increasingly visual culture of user-posted photographs and other self-produced digital images is part of a rhetorical mode of cultural production online that also works to decenter medical authority or at least to displace it somewhat in the examples from the Internet that I discuss here. Pregnant and trying-to-conceive women use Web sites as forums to receive as well as disseminate a wide range of images of pregnant bodies and fetuses. They circulate images that as often as not challenge prevailing medical authority about what kinds of decisions women ought to make, and what their duties are to themselves and their children. They, along with the noncredentialed and often intimate personal narratives of women who have experienced all types of pregnancies, work to counterbalance the discourses of centralized medical knowledge. The Internet provides a space in which women use pregnancy Web sites' modes of visuality and digital graphic production to become subjects, rather than objects, of interactivity.

As I discussed earlier, visual culture studies was created partly as a protest against an art historical tradition that was unwilling and unprepared to engage with the changes wrought on representational and artistic practices by digital technology. "Compared to the analogical arts—which are always instantiated in a fixed, Euclidean space—the digital arts seem abstract, ephemeral, and without substance. Digital representation is defined as 'virtual' owing to its desubstantialization: the disappearance of a visible and tactile support for both image and text."[8] In this chapter, I discuss an example of the networked bodily visual image that challenges the notion of a desubstantialized digital body unsupported by the visible and the tactile, and that is the pregnancy bulletin board avatar. Avatars posted by pregnant women constitute a particularly salient example of the "substantial" and "tactile" body because they are warranted by an offline physical state that it is unimaginable to fake, and because they are surrounded by a matrix of visual and textual discourse that attests to the irremediably embodied nature of pregnancy and childbirth. While Internet users are fond of taking on different sorts of identities in the context of computer-mediated communication, often engaging in cross-racial, cross-gender, cross-generational, or cross-sexualized forms of identity play, identity tourism as a pregnant versus nonpregnant woman is rare.[9] In addition, the stakes regarding digital pregnant body avatars are especially high on account of the contentious and bitter political and cultural discourse surrounding the status of the maternal body in our culture, and in particular the incursions that visual and other technologies have made on this concept of the materiality of bodies.

While debates between the religious Right and advocates for women's reproductive rights continue to rage, calling into question a woman's ability to "own" her own body, the Internet provides a place where pregnant and TTC (trying to conceive) women can create and own their own digital bodies. Pregnant avatars are databodies that women deploy as part of a visual counterdiscourse to the images of databodies on the Internet that come out of much nineties cyberpunk fiction and that still persist: images of male cyberhackers constitute the illusory and normative "unmarked body" to which Phelan refers. Cyberpunk fiction has figured the computer-using body as itself desubstantialized and dematerialized, just as all digital images are envisioned by many respondents to the *October* visual culture questionnaire. However, as Tom Foster cogently notes, the trope of the dematerialized or posthuman body is not necessarily progressive just because it is de-essentialized and acknowledged as socially constructed. Rather, the *nature* of that construction bears watching when digital bodies are brought into play. The condition of posthumanism, a seemingly netural term that excludes categories such as gender and race, is never free of "racial subtexts that inform the various transformations summed up under the heading of the 'posthuman.'" As Foster writes: "The debates about posthumanism demonstrate that there is no fixed meaning either to the understanding of embodiment as plastic and malleable—that is, open to critical intervention—because socially constructed. In the context of postmodern technocultures and their disembodying tendencies, the materiality of embodiment, consciousness, and human nature can constitute a form of resistance, while at the same time the denaturalization of embodied identities, intended as a historicizing gesture, can change little or nothing."[10] Female avatars that are modified to "set" their state of pregnancy and race permit visualization of two states that insist on the materiality of female bodies in the context of community and resistance to medicalized modes of image regulation.

"I would like to ask if someone could make a new dollie for me as I am not pregnant anymore—my son John was born on April 1st. ☺ And if it helps—I love Care Bears™ Thanks a bunch! ☺" This post from a popular

Web site for pregnant and trying-to-conceive women, babydream.com, appeals to its members (which also serves women who have just had babies) to collaborate in the creation of visual online signifiers of identity—avatars.[11] The overwhelming majority of the site's users add digital signatures to each of their posts; these signatures usually contain images of the woman who is posting. A "post" consists of a box containing typed text from the user, which can include a quotation from a previous poster to whom the user is responding. Appended to the bottom is the poster's signature, which usually includes a graphical avatar that visually represents the user. Once the user creates her signature, it is automatically appended to each post that she creates on that board. Thus each post comprises a text element and a graphical element. These signatures, or "siggies," as they are called on pregnancy Web sites, were an enduring feature of early e-mail visual cultures before the graphical Web; many featured ASCII art images, fashioned from letters and diacritical elements available on the computer keyboard. These early signatures were part of the early Internet's do-it-yourself (DIY) culture: the labor of painstakingly tapping out rudimentary pictures using the space bar and alphanumeric characters gave a hard-won graphical quality to text-only e-mail.[12] ASCII art images of "Kilroy," cartoon lions, and roses allowed users to give a personal touch to their signatures and to endow them with self-authored style. This endowed social status on the sender, who was shown to be skillful and invested enough in digital visual culture to have created something like this from scratch. This ethic of originality was a key aspect of early computing culture.

Signatures in graphical bulletin boards function as a kind of public text, since no password or authentication is needed to read them, even if you don't have an account on babydream.com. While a family or individual photograph is often scanned and uploaded to enhance a signature, members conceive themselves much more as authors or cultural producers in relation to their digital avatars, or "dollies" as they are called in this community (a separate bulletin board on the site deals solely with the practicalities of, and techniques for, avatar creation, modification, and sharing; it is extremely active). These are created using software that offers cartoonlike body parts that can be arranged to make different types of bodies. As can be seen in the post quoted earlier, women often envision these avatars in some of the ways that they do their own bodies. They will supply their height, weight, coloring, and preference in clothing colors and styles to the site's "Siggy Girls," women who volunteer to use their skills with computer graphics to create avatars for their less technically inclined sisters, in hopes of acquiring

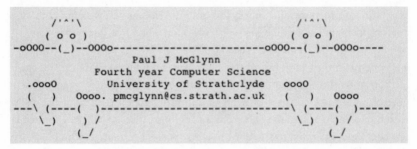

Figure 4.1. An ASCII art signature.

an avatar that looks like them. They request, create, trade, and alter pregnant avatars when they themselves become pregnant, and, as in the quoted post, which states, "I am not pregnant anymore," they acquire new ones or alter their old ones to reflect nonpregnancy. In addition, their liberal use of visual signifiers such as smiley emoticons, figures from licensed media franchises like Care Bears, and preferences for purple and "sparklies," or animated GIFs that move and dance around the avatar, reveal an intense interest in digital aesthetics.

Women are relatively late adopters of the Internet. And many new female users of the Web are drawn to it to obtain information on pregnancy and babies on sites like babydream.com and others devoted to serving pregnant women and new mothers (see ivillage.com, pregnancy.org, and parentsplace .com for examples.) In this chapter I discuss the critical interventions that women make in pregnancy Web sites by composing and deploying digital images of pregnant female bodies, babies, fetuses, pets, and families. User-created pregnant avatars pose a direct challenge to the female "hyperreal, exaggerated, hyperbodies" evident in mainstream video games such as *Tomb Raider* and *Dead or Alive*. The "unique aesthetic for perfection" embodied in digital heroines such as Lara Croft and Kasumi presents "embodiments that have left the real female body behind in a significant way."[13] I agree with Mary Flanagan's assertion that "it is at the female body that the formation and contestation of digibodies is occurring."[14] However, the pregnant avatars that pregnant women create for parenting Web sites accomplish the opposite from those deployed in digital gaming culture; they bring the "real female body" into the digital in a central way rather than leaving them behind. Instead, these avatars turn out to be far less hyperreal and exaggerated than their owners' *real* pregnant bodies; most women seem to want avatars that are built exactly like their unpregnant bodies, only "with a belly," an offline impossibility, as anyone who has experienced pregnancy knows. However, this fantasy of modularity—a digitally pregnant body is simply a "regular" stock-model female body with another "feature," a pasted-on belly—addresses the anxiety of permanent transformation versus transient state that pre-occupies many pregnant women. (Complaints and fears about losing "baby weight" and "getting your body back" give voice to this particular obsession of the gestating body.)

In addition, an analysis of pregnancy Web site signatures enables a class-based critique of a newly forming taste culture: the visual culture of preg-nancy and the body on the popular Internet. While scholarly discussions of visual culture and taste have long acknowledged the roles of class and to a lesser extent gender and race, little attention has been paid to the ways that pregnancy creates visual cultural artifacts. The sociologist Herbert Gans notes that childbearing and child rearing do have an impact on new parents' media consumption by exposing them to children's programming—the babysitter of the lower classes—but he considers this mainly in terms of the ways that it forces parents to give up their previous television programs. He envisions media choices and preferences as primarily an effect of class and other factors but does not take pregnancy and parenthood itself into account:

> Many factors determine a person's choice among taste cultures, particularly class, age, religion, ethnic and racial background, regional origin, and place of residence, as well as personality factors which translate themselves into wants for specific types of cultural content. Because ethnic, religious, regional, and place differences are disappearing rapidly in American society, however, the major sources of subcultural variety are increasingly those of age and class.

Thus, for Gans, "the major source of differentiation between taste cultures and public is socioeconomic level or class."[15] However, pregnancy is an iden-tity state that truly crosses classes and possesses what might be called a tem-porary taste culture in the sense that once its members bear and raise their children, they are no longer part of it.

This is not to say, however, that the visual culture of pregnancy is not inflected by a user's class position in terms of style and conceptions of taste. In recent years there has been a popular movement to "rescue" the visual culture of pregnancy from its association with lower-class taste cultures. In "The Modernist Nursery," an article that appeared in the *New York Times Magazine* in 2004, Elizabeth Weil writes that "Melissa Pfeiffer, 33, is the founder of modernseed, a year-old store selling modern furniture, fashions and accessories for kids, and Eric Pfeiffer, 35, is a contemporary furniture de-signer, and theirs is the kind of home that inspires house envy, particularly if you're one of those parents who vowed not to let the house fill up with plastic junk and then saw exactly that situation come to pass, first with the musical vibrating bouncy seat, and then the doorjamb Bumper Jumper and then a gift of a multicolored plastic Fisher-Price train set that became your daughter's absolute favorite possession." The characterization of inexpensive and widely available children's accessories and toys as "plastic junk" hails the reader of the article, who is most likely *not* a member of a lower- or working-class home, to identify with a different and implicitly higher taste culture of pregnancy than is commonly available. The article celebrates the entrepreneurial initiative of well-heeled and tasteful new parents who are working to bring modernism to the nursery. Their DIY spirit is seen as the appropriate and laudable reaction to the retail industry's failure to supply the correct range of taste cultures appropriate to upper-class buyers' preferences, envisioned in this article as "needs." When asked to explain why he designed a new baby crib the way he did, Michael Ryan says that he lives in a small New York City apartment and "came to this floating idea with the legs set in—on every other crib they're on the corners. Simple, elegant, low profile, no embellishments. There's so much fluffiness out there, mixing textures, frilling. Tone it down, man."[16] This disdain for decoration, adornment, bulkiness, and profusion is contrasted with the "clean," elegant, minimal, modernist style currently enjoying a revival in fashionable nurseries. Similarly, in an article titled "Sophisticated Baby" that appeared in the same magazine, Corky Harvey, a cofounder of the Pump Station in Los Angeles, "which includes a boutique for new or soon-to-be-parents," says that its "clientele is well off and smart and wants things that are 'functional as well as beautiful.'" The store carries the Fleurville "Mothership" diaper bag that costs $155 and was designed by a couple who "like many entrepreneurs . . . started out as dissatisfied customers." And does the store carry diaper bags with, say, famous cartoon characters on them? Harvey replies, emphatically, that it does not. The store sells only products that "'elevate motherhood' out of the context of tacky commercialism, she explains. 'Our mothers despise that stuff.'"[17]

This identification of mainstream consumer culture's offerings as unacceptable for "smart" people, people who wish to rise above "tacky commercialism," is itself implicitly antifeminine. As Penny Sparke writes in *As Long As It's Pink* of the modernist period, "the notion of 'taste' continued to align itself with domesticity and femininity. As such, it became increasingly marginal to modernism, representing to the protagonists of that movement all that needed to be eliminated."[18] Taste, gendered as feminine, came into conflict with design, gendered as masculine, with high culture and the authority of all its institutions on its side. The emphasis on functionality, "cleanness," and simplicity has long been employed as a way to critique and gender women's aesthetic decisions as "frilly femininity": Sparke's analysis discusses the ways that postwar advertisements for furnishings tried to teach women "good taste" as part of an attempt to create a sense of middle-class consumer identity. The identification of women as shoppers rather than creators is a distinctive feature of modernity and its advertising culture, as Rachel Bowlby has noted in her study of the French novel.[19] However, the material culture of dolls and facsimiles of children, a culture that echoes the impulse behind digital pregnant avatar creation, reveals a growing DIY culture that participates in the discourse of modification that springs from the culture of computer hacking and software modification. Two examples of grassroots creativity in the realm of body modification, babies, and retail hacking, that of "reborn dolls" and American Girl dolls, demonstrate the ways that the culture of composable baby bodies blurs the line between creation and consumption. "Reborn dolls" are extremely realistic baby dolls that hobbyists modify using a stock "base" bought from a retail store. These dolls, which are almost exclusively marketed and bought on eBay, are made by people who have developed techniques for "reborning," engaging in "a curious process of altering and enhancing a baby doll to look and even to feel as much like a human baby as possible."[20] Reborn dolls are frequently composited from heads, bodies, and other parts from multiple other types of dolls; the provenance of these body parts is painstakingly documented in the elaborate "birth stories" that accompany many of them. A New York Times Magazine article by Rob Walker describing this practice is titled "Hyperreality Hobbying: Like other do-it-yourself crafts, these dolls are a creative outlet—if a slightly strange one." The dolls sell for impressively large sums—up to $1,500 in some cases—come with birth announcements, and can incite fierce bidding wars on eBay. Walker, who writes a column on consumer and retail trends titled "Consumed" in which this article appeared, notes that "once you get past the creepier aspects of all this, it's not too hard to see it as yet another medium of grass-roots creativity, like making scrapbooks." The notion of duplicating the reproductive process through modification of existing material commodities is envisioned as "hyperreal" in the sense that it remediates an original to a degree described as "creepy" or uncanny; dolls are already uncanny, as Freud noted in his analysis of the Hoffmann story "The Sandman," and reborning intensifies this sense of boundary blurring between original and copy. It is also classed as an example of a material culture practice identified specifically with female domesticity and the active—at times too active, it seems—management of family memory, history, and representation. The notion of hacking or "modding" dolls allows women to participate in a type of productive hobbying often associated with masculinity and intrepid DIY culture.

This practice can be contrasted to the marketing of composable bodies on offer through retail outlets like American Girl, a doll manufacturer based in the American Midwest with an extremely enthusiastic cult following. While reborn dolls are "stock" bodies that are modified by users, given mock identities, and then resold, American Girl dolls can come both as stock characters and as customizable creations that can be ordered to suit from the factory. The company specializes in producing "dolls with stories," meaning dolls that have ethnic clothing, backstories (many come with books that narrate their lives in various historical time periods, in the interest of enhancing their educational value), and identities based on the notion of diversity and collectibility. Though there has been no scholarly writing yet on the practice of reborning, Terri Kapsalis's article "Making Babies the American Girl Way" notes the connection between the commodification of reproductive technologies and the creation of material baby-bodies: "Traditionally, fussing over dolls is practice for future motherhood." She notes that ART, or advanced reproductive technologies, present donor sperm and American Girl dolls as customizable objects that can be made to suit. While American Girl dolls are notable for their range of identities, a quality that has been lauded by their fans ("finally, a doll company was being responsive to ethnic differences by offering Asian, Latina, and other dolls of color"), the totemization of nationality and ethnicity evident in the "character doll" modes of dress and props like pets, parasols, and so on creates a vision of ethnicity that is essentialized and unproblematic.[21] "Addy" (a black girl in the Civil War era, 1864), "Felicity" (an English girl in the Colonies, 1774), Josefina (a Latina girl in New Mexico, 1824), Kaya (a Nez Perce girl in 1764), and Samantha and Nellie (two white American girls of different social classes in 1904) wear the costumes of their individual historical periods and have their own media empires including books and accessories, as well as diegetic relationships to each other. For example, Nellie O'Malley, an Irish American girl, is hired to be a servant to Samantha, her upper-class mistress (though any danger of class, racial, or ethnic conflict is prevented by the explanation that Nellie and Samantha "quickly become best friends, even though they have lived very different lives").

While the dolls are imbued with detailed identities right out of the box, so to speak, endowed with manufactured "memories" as are the almost-human replicants in *Blade Runner,* another popular series of American Girls is marketed on the basis of its composable identity and volitional ethnicity. The American Girl Today series invites the user to "select the American Girl Today doll with the hair, eye, and skin color you like best. Each doll is 18 inches tall and has a soft, huggable body with arms and legs you can pose. Her beautiful eyes open and close, and her hair is long so you can style it into all the looks you love! Your doll comes in her pretty new Go Anywhere Outfit." There are twenty-one possible combinations, and though some of these dolls are phenotypically different from each other, no reference to race is made in any of the discourse evident on the company's Web site or paper catalogs. Though straight hair is simply described by color, such as "honey blond," and by the word "curly" if the hair is "light," the dark curly hair evident on the "dark" doll is dubbed "textured." Kapsalis notes the language of modularity evident in the company's discourse that stresses the interactivity of the act of purchasing one of these dolls, an act that is overtly figured as creative and reproductive in the sense that the buyer is steered toward an act of visual self-replication: "The catalog encourages girls to pick dolls that look like them, selecting skin, hair, and eye color as close as possible to their own." So while the character dolls are made to represent specific types of ethnic and national "others," American Girl Today dolls create a representational landscape that replicates the discourse of reproductive technology, one that promises to help mothers create babies that look like them. While both "reborn" dolls and American Girl dolls are part of the material culture that is derided by the tasteful parents described in articles about designer nurseries and diaper bags, classified no doubt as examples of the "plastic junk" that the Pfeiffers and Michael Ryan dismiss as "not smart," and definitely not something that "our mothers" would consider chic, what is notable about this discourse is the way that it figures reborners and American Girl doll enthusiasts as "hobbyists" and "collectors." These are both terms associated with creativity, but in a way that is distinctly gendered, and in a way that still stresses consumption and selection rather than creation and design. Michael Ryan and the Pfeiffers are described as designers and entrepreneurs, partly because of their financial success (as mentioned earlier, reborn and American Girl dolls generate a great deal of revenue in both primary and secondary markets), but mainly because of the way that their work is credited as "original" creation, because of their class position, and because of the visual styles that they prefer. While Ryan and the Pfeiffers are quite clear about not having invented modernism, but rather having applied it to an area of the home where it had not been seen before so as to make a whole house internally consistent in terms of its style, Ryan also notes that his crib design was a "hack" or modification of an existing crib, which he found inelegant and bulky. The user-driven innovation that comes from modifying existing doll bodies is envisioned as either "creepy" and socially marginal or trivial partly because it deals with baby-bodies themselves, rather than furniture or more general types of design objects. However, these types of modifications or hacks give voice and vision to the culture of "frilly femininity" overtly critiqued by nursery modernists. The gendering of pregnancy and baby material culture turns on the axis of two types of taste cultures that can be classified as female and male, lower and upper, modifier/consumer and creator/designer. Recent articles in the popular press regarding "sophisticated babies" and "the modernist nursery" note that "good design" has dared to invade the one domestic space that had been exempted from this injunction to adhere to standards defined by taste cultures: the nursery. While "decoration" has long been dismissed as feminine, "design" is perceived as more substantial, more the province of experts, and more connected to architecture, a "masculine" field that has immense social prestige.

The notion of a taste culture as something that can be created, rather than merely consumed, by its own users, who are consequently freed from the necessity of engaging with "tacky commercialism," has long been a part of the discourse of the Internet and its potential for interactivity. The Internet's stance toward commercialism has for the most part been a critical and oppositional one, with its more utopian critics envisioning the Internet as a form that allows "the people" to create commonly owned and collaboratively created software as in the case of the open-source and creative commons movements, and fan-authored media and taste cultures. There has, however, been little writing on taste, class, and gender when it comes to Internet visual culture. The injunction of the crib designer Michael Ryan to "tone it down, man," maps quite well onto the design imperatives and values of new media professionals, who favor sites that are "simple, elegant, low profile, [with] no embellishments," while "fluffiness out there, mixing textures, frilling," is despised in both baby carriages and digital design.[22]

Women's digital signatures on pregnancy sites function figuratively as the "nursery" in the habitus of cyberspace, indulging in a type of frilly femininity on the level of taste and design that is deeply threatening and subversive to the principles of "cleanness" and masculinity that dominated digital culture in its early years. Rather than "toning it down," their digital signatures tend to do exactly the opposite, mixing media and textures and ornamentation in a fashion that defies these notions of good taste and embodies "tackiness" as exemplified by the lower-class taste cultures reviled by the modernists cited earlier. In addition, the form of these sites challenges the bourgeois-individualist model of property and presence that characterized early cyberspace's rhetoric. This rhetoric of ownership and triumphant individualism inherent in much of the electronic frontier discourse has since been critiqued from both feminist and postcolonial perspectives. The notion that representational and cultural power could arise only from the staking out of individual spaces or "homesteads" on the Internet privileged singly owned, managed, and designed Web sites or "home pages" as "domains" or sites of identity. Susan Leigh Star critiques this notion of the home-page-as-home because it requires an amount of cultural and real capital unattainable to many; ironically, as she notes, academic nomads such as herself may be among the few who can afford to be figuratively situated or "homed" in cyberspace through the ownership and control of a personal site. She also notes that technology, the Web included, has often resulted in "more work for mother" rather than less and has also created more rather than less isolation for women, who are often stuck at home in caregiving roles.[23] However, the figuration of the individual home page, a space that Nina Wakeford notes can reduplicate the endless housekeeping and drudgery of domestic upkeep just as does the offline home, has since lost much of its cachet as a source of digital visual capital on the popular graphical Internet. Despite early predictions such as Star's and Wakeford's, which were published in 1996 on the eve of the World Wide Web's massification, the individual home page has not turned out to be the main or even dominant route to independent expression in terms of the Internet's visual culture. Web sites like babydream.com maintain or "host" discussion boards that permit users to create individual posts or spaces of visual digital identity within the confines of a shared virtual space. This model of shared rather than personal space, characteristic of blogging and online journaling spaces such as LiveJournal, which have also often been identified with female users, allows a model of digital participation and cross-linkage that requires less technical skill than is necessary to create a single stand-alone Web site, thus creating *less* work for mother and easier navigation between different users' virtual spaces of expression. While an individual Web site may constitute a burden, a virtual "room of one's own" in the form of a digital signature, even an elaborate one, is manageable. This trend away from digital privatization exemplified by the ownership and maintenance of personal Web sites and toward atomization shows the formation of a more communitarian, urban notion of graphical online space, where users create individual rooms or spaces within their signatures that are nonetheless viewed as part of a visual whole or shared visual culture. Space on babydream.com's pages is shared, not owned, and a user's post is displayed exactly as many times as she chooses to contribute to the discussion, thus emulating in visual form the dynamics of a face-to-face conversation.

While American Girl Today dolls permit sanitized, depoliticized racialization, by allowing the creation of "dark" dolls with "textured" hair but avoiding any overt mention of race, racial politics, or racial inequality, the female avatars or "dollz" that pregnant women create and use in their digital signatures warrant race in an intensely embodied way by bringing it into visual collision with the discourse of the reproductive body. Babydream .com's users produce digital group portraits of themselves in varying states of pregnancy, motherhood, or hoping for pregnancy, portraits of women who unite in solidarity and support around medical and personal issues but may never have met in person. Consider the group signature of the "Beaner Dreamers" ("bean" is a popular slang term often used to describe a fetus, as very-early-term fetuses often show up as a beanlike shape in an ultrasound image), twelve women who became close friends using the bulletin board and wished to be represented as a group online. Their signature, which appeared in several of the members' larger signature spaces, functions like a custom T-shirt or bumper sticker in the sense that it signifies membership in a group of people with a shared purpose. In addition, each figure is composed to look phenotypically the same in terms of facial features, yet distinct from each other in terms of skin color, hair color, and body shape. While all these avatars are made using the same doll base, and thus are the same height and generally the same width and share the same visual style, much effort has been put into endowing them with pregnant or unpregnant bellies, elaborate and distinct hair styles and colors, differently embellished jeans, bouquets of flowers; and three possess the ultimate accessory: babies carried in front packs or in arms. Indeed, the language of embellishment is very much the paradigm invoked in this avatar group portrait. Like the popular BeDazzler, a device that enables users to attach crystals, beads, and other trimmings to jeans or pocketbooks, these avatars embody an aesthetic of decoration that has to do with adornment of an existing "base." And in a sense, race is one of these aspects of adornment.

Figure 4.2. Beaner Dreamers avatar group portrait. Source: babydream.com.

While three of the Beaner Dreamer avatars have dark skin and hair and could be read as Latina, and one is quite dark-skinned and could be read as African American, these are idealized portraits that have more in common with animated characters from television or comic books than with any type of indexical visual representation. While it is possible and in fact must be the case that these users are deploying images that do not resemble their real bodies, the insistence on visual racial difference in this photograph has a different valence from the deployment of racial bodily imagery used in digital games or in chat rooms. Because pregnancy is so much an embodied state, and because these women have come together around the desire to conceive and bear children, the imperative to idealize the maternal and pregnant body works to create a uniformly and conventionally "pretty" avatar that nonetheless retains racial difference. This is in line with the site's emphasis on the production of biological children despite physical and emotional obstacles. The production of avatars and digital babies that "look like" the user reduplicates the modification-oriented reproductive desire evident in offline material-culture practices like reborning and doll collecting and is similarly viewed as a low-status and feminine activity. The communitarian impulse behind the Beaner Dreamers' group portrait characterizes the spirit of collectivity, collaboration, and responsibility for shared visual space in terms of avatar design and production evident in the site as a whole and in women's online culture devoted to family and domestic matters.

The culture of babydream.com overtly lauds the creators of digital signatures as important contributors to the space's overall value: "beautification" or decoration of the bulletin board by posters who go to the trouble to create elaborate and informative signatures is acknowledged and complimented, regardless of style. As one poster wrote in a thread titled "Doll Request":

> I'm new here, and I'm trying to beautify my posts. My light brown hair is to my shoulders, straight, and I like to wear hippie clothes, tie-dye, bandanna's . . . etc Justin is 5ft10inches, short light brown hair, and usually wears jeans and a sweatshirt. Nicole is a 11 week old little girl with big blue eyes. Thanx for any help you can give me. You ladies have wonderful imaginations, and generous hearts.

Another poster earlier in the same thread also describes herself and her family in her request for assistance with a signature, saying, "I'm in desperate need of some siggy help—it's so sad and pathetic (smiley face emoticon). . . . I really appreciate your work! You all make BD.com a nice and colorful place."

This post conveys the sense of a shared obligation to contribute to the formation of a visual habitus, a beautiful home or room online, as a major responsibility that attends membership in this online community. Gans notes the powerful influence of women and mothers in creating and maintaining taste cultures and is careful to be as nonjudgmental as he can regarding their choices, despite his frequent use of the outmoded term "housewife." He writes: "Every housewife of every taste culture who can afford to buy furniture seeks to make her rooms into a work of beauty expressing her standards. . . . The two housewives differ in the amount of training in their standards, the skill and resources available to put their standards into action, the verbal fluency with which they justify their choices, and of course, in the content of their standards, in what they think is beautiful, but they are similar in that both are striving for beauty."[24] Though he stops short of asserting that this aspiration toward beauty is part of a biologically essential feminine quality, Gans acknowledges that "housewives" participate in taste cultures that exceed the management of family memories and help define the class identifications that a family can aspire to or possess. While it is doubtful that any of babydream.com's posters are sociologists, they seem to have taken this insight—that any mode of adornment is aesthetically valuable—to heart in their stance toward digital signatures. While many of these signatures might appear monstrous and deeply unappealing to a viewer who values modernist "cleanness," they are products of a desire to create online content and images of bodies and lives that are underrepresented in other media outlets.

The digital signatures that pregnant women create for use on babydream .com embody a new aesthetic code of self-representation on the popular Internet. Generally speaking, digital signatures work as part of a system of verification and database mapping that ensures the legitimacy of financial and other transactions on the Internet. A "unique number" may be assigned a particular transaction to organize it and make it searchable in a database, and this can be called a "signature." In contrast to these machine-generated coded verifiers of identity, user-created digital signatures to bulletin board posts work to engender an alternative style of managing visual digital surfaces, hewing to a logic that Christopher Pinney has dubbed "vernacular modernism." The visual anthropologists Stephen Sprague and Pinney examine the ways that Yoruban and Nagda photographers have responded to a colonial discourse of photography that privileges depth, indexicality, and a particular kind of chronotope or relationship to time and history by creating a resistant practice of photographic visual representation that works under an alternative visual logic and system of representation. While Western photographs enforce a singular notion of space and identity, African and Indian montage photographs that represent double and triple portraits of the same sitter occupying a visual field "place a person beyond the space and identity that certain forms of Western portraiture enforce." Rather than condemning these portraits as poor examples of, or inept attempts at, traditional Western photography, Sprague and Pinney encourage a cultural reading that takes into account their unique social purpose: "There is ... an explicitly articulated recognition by photographers that their task is to produce not an imprisoning trace of their sitters but to act as impresarios, bringing forth an ideal and aspirational vision of the bodies that sitters wish themselves to be."[25]

This desire to create a digital body or home that reflects aspirational pregnancy and child-centered domesticity is literalized in babydream.com's numerous digital signatures that represent nurseries, pregnant avatars of the user, ultrasounds, and miscarried fetuses. Shown here, Holly's signature collects images from several disparate sources into one place, coalescing a

Yea!

Thanks, Rebecca!

AF has "left the building", so I'm getting excited about trying this month. I've decided to chart everything that I ca
since my temps have been unusual due to allergies. I may need some help on this!!!

Tamara, we are all here for you and look to you as our wise leader...hope everything works for ya. Wouldn't it be
great if we could all become the OPB's (Official Pregnant Buddies) next month?

Gotta go study...be back in a bit to check on everyone!

_____

Nadia Simone!
Click here to see Nadia's Nursery!

A New Baby Girl Due, 1/7/2005
24 Weeks, 2 Days Pregnant! 109 days left!

My angels born at 21 weeks:
Keira Rachel and Keeley Lana
January 20, 2004

"vanishing twin" - 5/12/04

Due Jan.7/2005

HOLLY'S   MONKEY MAMA

Monkey   monkey   i love
Mommy-to-Be!   maniac   monkeys

***Thanks to Jamie and Lisa_A for my Monkey Mama & *DD* Blinkies!!!

Figure 4.3. Holly's signature on babydream.com.

broad range of desires, aspirations, bodies, and forms of representation. The scanned-in uterine ultrasound with its authenticating medical information, such as the name of the pregnant woman, location of the hospital, time of day, and date, takes pride of place at the top of the signature, alongside a collage consisting of a photograph of the poster's nursery, with a cartoon avatar inserted alongside it.[26] While the ultrasound verifies the reality of the pregnancy, the nursery depicts an idealized physical space in the home. There is a link to "Nadia Simone's" nursery pictures on another site, should the viewer care to see them, but the photograph of the nursery that is present in the signature provides a wealth of detail. The coordinated wallpaper border, curtain, valance, mobile, crib, crib bumper, quilt, and linens all attest to an anticipatory and privatized vision of the future that the ultrasound promises. Their extensive coordination and use of colorful ornament and pattern exemplifies exactly the type of "fluffiness" condemned as excessive and lower class by nursery modernists. The cartoon avatar superimposed on it looks at the viewer with one huge eye while the other hides underneath a fluffy bang. Her body is slim and childlike, and the avatar's visual style contrasts strongly with the posed quality of the photograph underneath, which resembles a catalog page in its sense of having been staged and styled to represent a "perfect" example of successfully composed middle-class domestic space. Yet the promise represented by the ultrasound and the photographed nursery ready for its occupant, both images warranted in indexicality, is given a different shading by the details underneath: while the monkey-themed pregnancy day "counter" bar underneath it reads, "A New Baby Girl Due, 1/7/2005, 24 Weeks, 2 Days Pregnant! 109 days left!" the animated swinging monkeys flank three tiny avatars that tell a different story of loss and bereavement. The fragility of the images of the ultrasound and the nursery as "aspirational" and anticipatory signs of new motherhood is reinforced by the images of two tiny cartoon angels with long hair, dresses, large pigeon-toed sneakers, and glittery wings, along with a small baby monkey wearing a blanket over its shoulders. These angels are meant to represent miscarried pregnancies, "My angels born at 21 weeks: Keira Rachel and Keeley Lana, January 20, 2004," and the monkey is captioned with the words "'vanishing twin'—5/12/04." The convention of representing miscarried pregnancies or stillborn children in this way is quite common on this bulletin board and others that serve pregnant women. The visual means of memorializing them tends to include dolls that look like cartoon children with wings—angels—along with the date of miscarriage. Since miscarriages are not uncommon among women who are trying to get pregnant, this should not be

surprising; what is novel is the way that these posters visualize them alongside images of viable pregnancies that they may be carrying now, as if the
fetus that failed to develop were on a par with the ones that the medical
establishment represented by the ultrasound image. These images of "missed"
children are never represented with ultrasounds, though it is almost certainly
true that women have them, as many miscarriages are diagnosed in this way.
It seems that the language of loss and bereavement around the matter of
miscarriage—a pregnancy that produces an invisible result, or rather one
that is never visualized in popular culture—must take the form of vernacular image production or graphical avatars. The collaborative do-it-yourself
visual culture of pregnancy bulletin board signatures has created a community of women who give each other liberal acknowledgment for assistance
with image and icon creation and have authored images to address a need
that is seldom articulated in social space. Miscarriages are still a taboo topic
in the United States. Holly thanks "Jamie and Lisa_A for my Monkey
Mama & DD Blinkies!!!" animated GIFs that blink at the bottom of the
post, and we might also assume that the "angels" and "vanishing twin" images
came from another poster as well.

The practice of visualizing "lost" children using avatarial means is addressed as well in Yoruban photography. "Because twins are sacred children
with connections to the spirit world, it is especially important to show them
proper respect," and thus photographs are often made of them to hang in
the parlor.[27] If by chance a twin or a triplet should die before a portrait is
created, photographers will commonly pose a surviving child, sometimes
dressed in cross-gendered clothing if the missing child was of a different
gender, to represent the deceased one and print the two images together,
thus creating a composited portrait in which two copies of the same body
occupy the same visual field. It is also sometimes the case that an identical
image of the surviving child, if the twins shared the same gender, is printed
twice on a photograph to represent the missing body.

Holly's signature depicts five "virtual" bodies, only one of which exists in
the world—her own. However, unlike many other pregnant posters to this
site, she does not represent her own avatar as pregnant or "having a belly."
Tattie's signature, also shown here, positions her pregnant avatar within a
tableau arranged in a circle bordered by animated sparkling purple stars and
bubbles. Entitled "Tattie and Stan," it depicts her pregnant avatar wearing a
white T-shirt that says "baby" in large letters with an arrow pointing to her
swollen abdomen; in the background and slightly to the left is an image of
her husband, "Stan," who is carrying a snowboard and wearing baggy cargo

Tattie33
We got our bean!!
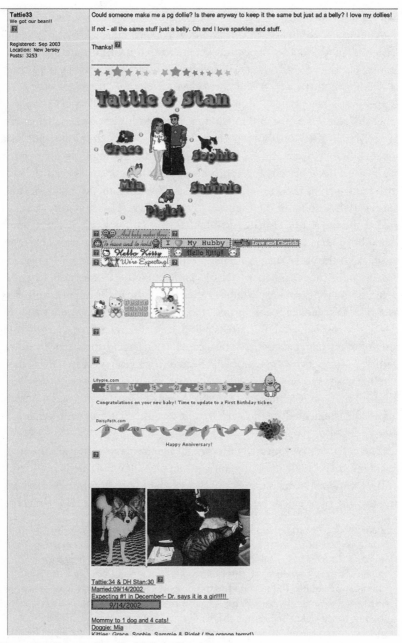

Registered: Sep 2003
Location: New Jersey
Posts: 3253

Could someone make me a pg dollie? Is there anyway to keep it the same but just ad a belly? I love my dollies!

If not - all the same stuff just a belly. Oh and I love sparkles and stuff.

Thanks!

Figure 4.4. Tattie's signature on babydream.com.

pants and a short haircut. Near the bottom and arranged in a circle around the couple are five images of cats and dogs named "Grace," "Mia," "Piglet," "Sammie," and "Sophie." These images are a mixture of cartoons and photographs, but they are all similar in size. Below this family portrait sits a bank of "bumpers" three across and three deep, declaring "Pregnant with #1!" "Expecting a blessing!" "I ♥ my hubby!" "I adore Hello Kitty," "Love and Cherish," and "To Have and to Hold." Underneath these are a series of images of Hello Kitty on shopping bags and baby blocks, and a bumper that sits on a line by itself: "Bush Cheney '04." Candid snapshot photographs of the five pets complete the graphical section of the signature, which ends with facts such as the ages of the poster and her husband, the date of their marriage, the gender of their fetus, and its due date. This signature was created at the request of "Tattie," who had asked that her existing unpregnant avatar be modified to add "all the same stuff just a belly." The use of bumpers to speak to the story that the images tell creates a nuanced picture of the poster's political sentiments, stylistic preferences, and eagerness to assert heteronormativity and traditional domesticity. The inclusion of family pets as part of the ménage is absent from Holly's post, as is the reference to miscarriage or lost babies. This poster's willingness and indeed eagerness to represent her own avatar as physically altered in shape and appearance—a "pg dollie," as she puts it—may not be reflected in signatures created by women who have suffered one or several pregnancy losses. The power of the visual image of the avatar to project a future that may be both feared and fervently hoped for is reflected in the deployment or elision of pregnant avatars in users' posts.

The collaborative culture of avatar and signature creation links the sharing of information about the technology of pregnancy and the technology of avatar creation. The management of the pregnant or trying-to-conceive body and the virtual or avatar body comes together vividly in the following post:

> I am about to go to the graphic site- I get real weird about internal health stuff, so hopefully I wont fall out of my chair. I will let you all know if I made it through it. I think I will start checking CM and my cervix position next month (if there is a AF this month) and start fresh from the start. Tamara, we are just BD'ing and hoping - we are trying to do it at least every other day so hopefully we will hit it that way. I don't know why, I'm just not that obsessed right this second, maybe because I don't feel good, but that is subject to change any moment. *I went* and haven't fainted yet - real graphic but I will try to do it - - it reminds me of the time I had to give myself and enema for a lower GI - I called my mom crying telling her I couldn't do it, well she calmed me and I did it, but I hope I never have to again.

Oh, btw: I was reading more about pregnancy symptoms, and you know what? - most of them don't show for weeks or months after a missed AF, so I don't know if that will help us not be obsessed, yeah right!

As far as hiding behind the sunglasses or feeling silly - don't - we are all just learning and I think not worrying about putting stuff out there on this thread is what is so great about it - at least we find out answers to our questions. and I know we are just going to get real close through all of this. . . .

Ok - some *techie help*

- To not loose my postings, I always type them out in an email or word document and then copy and paste into the thread but of course, I learned that the hard way

- If you want to have your chart as a part of your sig, here is what you can do. I am somewhat of an HTML nerd, so I hope this helps. Copy your web address that you were given by your charting site. Go to your signature here on *IDOB*, and add the tag below overwriting my note about pasting with the web address, save and presto, you're chart is there.

If anybody wants to learn anything else about HTML, let me know - its pretty easy (now that I know) and I could help with adding additional stuff to your sigs if you want.

The liberal use of acronyms in this post reveals how common and naturalized the language of obstetrics and gynecology has become in this online community: "CM" stands for "cervical mucus," and "GI" for "gastrointestinal." The use of more vernacular acronyms like "AF," which stands for "Aunt Flo," a euphemism for menstrual period, and "BD'ing," which means "baby dancing," or having intercourse, demonstrates the mixing of colloquial and medical rhetorics. Indeed, the posts along with the signatures show the blending of at least two modalities of discourse: the poster takes pains to reassure an interlocutor that "we are all learners here" presumably in regard to both the language of reproductive medicine and the language of HTML.[28] "Getting real close" through shared disappointment, technological expertise, anticipation, and joy is figured as one of the benefits of this online community, and the visual culture of the signature embodies this principle by calling into question the notion of singular ownership of a body or of a pregnancy. Their visual style is crowded, chaotic, and based on a principle of accretion rather than integration. There are significant clashes in styles and textures between images on the same signature, especially when compared to the orderly ACSII sigs of the text-only days of the early-nineties Internet. These are riotous combinations of bumpers, animated GIFs, blinkies, photos, borders, cartoons, and other combinations of text and image, many or most of them acquired from other sites or shared between self-styled "siggy girls" who possess graphical imaging skills. These exuberantly informational and richly multimediated images of identity exemplify a visual style created to signify identities in process, literally often in transition between the social and bodily states of "woman" and "mother" that cannot be integrated into one sign or signature. The users of these sites are often stay-at-home mothers, often quite politically conservative, often working class, and when they create avatars they often state these positions (Tattie's "Bush Cheney in '04" bumper was quite popular during that election year). In short, they are a taste culture that has never been taken much into account when new media theorists discuss avatars, embodiment, and gender. Their overt political ideologies certainly do not square with the dominant discourse of new media theory. What to do, however, when a media form that had been dominated by engineers, students, artists, and other cultural elites becomes popular in dramatically quick, Internet time? One of the most striking technology adoption stories I can think of has to do with the Internet: in 1993, Scott Bukatman could ask, "Why are there no women in cyberspace?" and mean it.[29] In 2003 the percentages of women and men online were exactly fifty-fifty, and they are holding steady as of today. However, according to Wakeford, from 1992 to 1996, women's presence on the Internet increased from 5 percent to 34 percent.[30] The partial closing of the digital divide has resulted in a very different Internet user, one more likely to be female, less educated, less culturally elite. These are people who belong to much different taste cultures than previously existed on the Internet. This is not to say that kitsch never existed on the Internet; it is not difficult to find Web sites devoted to screen grabs, slash fiction, and the digital equivalent of velvet clown paintings. However, this was masculine, geek kitsch, and it seems important to note that. This was a primarily male audience in whose visual culture Tolkien, Ridley Scott, Frank Frazetta, cyberpunk, anime, and Marvel Comics figure largely. This Internet popular culture has largely been ignored except by sociologists, who tend to discuss it as symptomatic of a subculture with its own customs in terms of social engagement, alienation, and the public sphere rather than in reference to aesthetics or taste cultures.

Visual style and taste are rarely discussed in relation to popular (as opposed to artistic or countercultural) digital forms. While art sites are often discussed and valued in relation to their challenges to old media forms, deployment of new modes of interactivity, and forms of resistance to linear modes of consuming and producing the art object, pregnancy Web sites are seldom visited by people who are not pregnant or are partnered with people who are pregnant. Web sites that deal with domestic, everyday, or commercial matters have heretofore been the province of sociologists and graphic designers or usability experts, such as Edward Tufte, whose *Envisioning Information* has become a standard text in information design. This discourse of transparency and usability values efficiency and density of information and does not discuss new media objects in terms of visual culture. "Look and feel" are elements of button positioning, font size, use of white space, and intuitive icons and are not used to signify anything vis-à-vis what sorts of offline visual traditions are being referenced.

Parenting Web sites exemplify the ways that women use the Internet to graphically embody themselves in specific reproductive states, that is, as pregnant women, nursing women, and mothers. They draw significant numbers of women who exemplify the profile of the "late adopter" of the Internet; that is to say, they are often stay-at-home mothers from the working or middle classes rather than professionals who might be required to use the Internet for work. They are more likely than in previous years to be members of racial minority groups who have previously been represented very poorly online, such as African American and Latino. In addition, they defy their gender profile in relation to the Internet because they are deeply involved in digital production: they upload significant amounts of online content in the form of their large and detailed postings and digital signatures.

Pregnant avatars challenge many conventional ideas regarding online embodiment. While nobody believes anymore that on the Internet nobody knows you're a dog, it is certainly true that many women offline can exist for several months without anybody knowing that they are pregnant. Women who work outside the home must carefully weigh factors such as economic need and work climate when they decide how and when they wish to reveal their pregnancies in the workplace. This discourse of "outing" is in some sense a queer one; pregnancy is a state of difference whose visibility and legibility are, at least at first, performative and volitional. Thus pregnant avatars represent a state that is by definition temporary. They signify a changing body, in some sense an ephemeral body. In addition, an avatar can be pregnant in the "public" space of the Internet bulletin board, while its owner may be still closeted in public. The pregnant avatar memorializes a body in transition, one that is out of the user's control. The Internet is likewise a space of ephemerality, as its content changes rapidly and constantly. In addition, pregnant avatars have a certain literal quality that leads to intriguing phenomenological questions: Would a user keep a pregnant avatar if she miscarried? Would the act of altering or removing that avatar from the board signify a miscarriage in miniature, a digital reenactment of the offline state? What are the implications of this participatory digital practice?

In *Feminism and the Technological Fix*, Carol Stabile describes the defining paradox of the visual culture of pregnancy as follows: "With the advent of visual technologies, the contents of the uterus have become demystified and entirely representable, but pregnant bodies themselves remain concealed."[31] Hence the paradox: while medical imaging technologies like ultrasounds and laparoscopy have turned the pregnant female body inside out, rendering it as transparent as a pane of glass, a vessel containing infinite visual wonders of procreation and opportunities for witnessing with machine-enabled vision the miracle (or spectacle) of birth, its exterior remains hidden in plain sight. As Stabile writes: "The pregnant body... remains invisible and undertheorized in feminist theory."[32] Many other scholars of feminism, technology, and the visual have noted the pregnant body's peculiar status in post-1990s feminist visual culture. As Lisa Cartright writes in "A Cultural Anatomy of the Visible Human Project," pregnant bodies have long been used to stand in for all female bodies in the culture of medical imaging, from its roots in classically rendered paintings of female pelvises by d'Agoty[33] to current projects like the Visible Woman, whose cryosectioned body was digitized and put on a database online for educational purposes.[34] Thus women's reproductive organs, and women in reproductive states, are overrepresented in medical visual culture; the pregnant female body and its interior in particular is classically overdetermined as it comes to represent all female bodies. A spate of scholarly books and collections on the topic of reproductive technologies and feminism have all noted the way that the medical establishment has worked to make the pregnant female body normative, and its result, which is to pathologize nonreproductive female bodies—as Cartright notes, the Visible Woman was criticized as an incomplete and inadequate model of the female body because, though in perfect health at her time of death, she is "postmenopausal and presumably therefore unsuited to demonstrating processes of reproduction."[35] Ultrasound has taken up the imaging practice that once belonged to medical painting and engraving and is valued because it seems to give access to the invisible, the interior, to move right past the unspeakable and abject pregnant body to its contents, the fetus.

While American culture as a whole is unappeasably eager to see photographic or "real" images of babies in the womb, pregnancy's hidden spectacle, feminists in particular are wary of the way that this desire encourages ways of seeing that represent the fetus and mother as occupying different visual frames and tends to visually reinforce the notion of their separate existences. Of course, this type of machine-enhanced seeing most famously provides fodder for anti-choice movements who have deployed these medical images aggressively in their protests and signage. However, feminist theorists' skepticism regarding reproductive visioning technologies has roots in an earlier technologically critical discourse. Just as the move to challenge the medical establishment by reinvesting midwives rather than medical doctors with authority characterizes second-wave and later feminisms, so too has feminist theory's suspicion of the visual as a mode of knowing conditioned this reception.

As Rosalind Petchesky writes in "Fetal Images: The Power of Visual Culture in the Politics of Reproduction," the problem with seeing as a way of knowing is that it creates a distance between the seer and the seen that translates into an uneven power relation between the knower and the known. Evelyn Fox Keller critiques this privileging of the visual in her work in science and gender, and Laura Mulvey has also written on the ways that the gaze objectifies women and, more importantly, how it is a product of the apparatus and form of narrative film. Part of visual culture's intervention into this state of things is to critique the gaze and to encourage other ways of seeing; Nick Mirzoeff wishes to replace the gaze with the "transverse glance," which is the "transient, transnational, transgendered way of seeing that visual culture seeks to define, describe, and deconstruct."[36]

However, as Donna Haraway writes in "The Persistence of Vision," perhaps it is time to reclaim vision for feminist ethics. Despite the eyes' "having been used to signify a perverse capacity—honed to perfection in the history of science tied to militarism, capitalism, colonialism, and male supremacy—to distance the knowing subject from everybody and everything in the interests of unfettered power,"[37] it seems particularly strategic to do so right now, at this particular moment in both new media studies and feminist theory. For the parallels between medical visual imaging and the deployment of digital communication technologies are strong, in terms of both chronology, causality, and usage. Computer screens and ultrasound screens, while both televisual, share a common origin in radar, a military technology. Unlike the cinematic screen, which shows images of the past rather than the present, computers and ultrasounds show images in real time: "processual" images.[38] Reproductive visual imaging is an important part of digital screen culture as well as the culture of pregnancy: many a pregnant woman's first look at her baby is through a CRT monitor that is about the same size and color as a small television, the type that many people buy for their kitchens, that archetypal domestic space. While she is most likely looking at an Accuson rather than a Sony or Toshiba, and the experience of cold ultrasound gel on her belly distinguishes one viewing experience from the other, the mode of delivery is the same, that is, the dynamic screen. This engagement with screen culture as the primal scene of reproductive looking, this uncanny techno-visual moment, resonates with another scene of looking at the digital screen, and that is in using the Internet.

The linkage between the Internet's visioning of pregnant bodies and the deployment of medical images of pregnant women and fetuses allows us to parse gendered embodiment at a critical moment in its visual culture. Much feminist critique of medical imaging has targeted its mode of production. Typically, doctors, medical illustrators, and research scientists are the gatekeepers in deciding what (and when) a pregnant woman ought to visualize. Ultrasounds are not transparent texts: like all images, they require interpretation. Discovering a fetus's gender requires both the warranting of this information in the presence of the ultrasound image and the technician's expert eye, which is trained to recognize fetal genitalia. The prospective parents can be looking right at "it" and find themselves unable to identify what they are looking at. This means that the pregnant body is surveilled from both without and within, and the production, manipulation, viewing, printing, and interpretation of the image are controlled by doctors and technicians. However, the Internet has long been celebrated for its interactivity, that is, the way in which it puts image production in the hands of amateurs, or "the people." It bridges the production/reception divide. As Robert Burnett and David Marshall write: "Distinctive from telephony, the Web implicates a production component, that is, where content is developed and enhanced beyond its original orality (think of any conversation and its unpredictable flow) into some combination of visual, textual, and graphic structure. The Web, when thought of as a medium is a hybrid that invokes the sensation of orality and contingency with the guided structure of a book or magazine."[39]

This is one quality that makes the Internet in general and the Web in particular different from other telecommunicative forms. Hence, when we look at the ways that pregnant and trying-to-conceive women depict themselves in pregnancy Web forums, we are given insight into the reappropriation of the medicalized gaze. When these women make graphical images of themselves as pregnant avatars to insert in their bulletin board posts online, they are producing a counterdiscourse that challenges the binarism of hypervisible/invisible pregnant bodies. In addition, the avatars they produce exist to serve a specific type of orality on the Internet: the kind of asynchronous conversation that goes on among pregnant women in an on-line forum. In these forums, the often "unpredictable flow" of conversation is directed fairly predictably into a specific path; all discourse that is not about pregnancy or babies is flagged as an "off-topic" thread so that users can avoid it. Conversations about the virtues or drawbacks of day care, breast-feeding, stroller use, and nutrition are generally cordial and tolerant of diverse opinions, but political discourse is flagged as being off topic, since it tends to have a divisive effect on the discussion objected to by many of the participants; this became particularly evident during the U.S. presidential election in 2004.

Since the orality of pregnancy online is so self-referential—it consists of pregnant women talking about their pregnancies ad nauseum—the graphi-cal avatars they create combine "visual, textual, and graphical" structures in a hybrid form that remediates the pregnant body in truly multifarious ways. Rather than depicting hypervisible interiors and invisible exteriors, these women create complicated, at times visually incoherent, embodiments of pregnancy, a paradigmatically embodied state. Their use of dynamic screens to reclaim the mode of image production of their own bodies results in rich and at times bizarre taste cultures online.

Ultrasounds that depict a fetus floating in an undefined space, the invis-ible and occluded space of the mother's body, as well as fetal photography that encourages the sense of an "independent" fetal body, reinforce the notion of the pregnant body as really two bodies. As Phelan writes: "De-tached from the pregnant woman, the fetal form has become a sign that is already powerfully implicated in the political economy of capitalism and patriarchy."[40] The persistent envisioning of the pregnant female body as a vessel (the umbilical cord is painstakingly deleted from most photographic images of fetuses, thereby emphasizing its existence separately from the woman's body) echoes an older cyberutopian notion of the body or "meat" as a disposable package for what really counts: the mind. The computer sci-entist Hans Moravec, "the most exemplary advocate of radical disembodi-ment," sees the flesh as just a carrier or an envelope: a person is an "essence or pattern," signal to the body's noise, and the body is merely "the machin-ery supporting that process."[41] The mind, termed "wetware," operates like the software in a computer; it is housed by an apparatus but is transferable in nature. This notion of the mind/body split is the foundational assump-tion and driving force behind cyberpunk fiction and one of the reasons that theorists claim that new media create a "posthuman" being, one that is detachable from a body if embedded in an alternate site enabled by machinery.[42] Thus this radical sundering of the body from its contents, whether "the mind" or "the fetus" so disliked by feminist medical theorists, is not a new idea: cyberpunk has been representing bodies separated from their contents since its inception in the early eighties. What is of more interest is the ideological uses to which machine-enabled disembodiment is put. Much medical imaging encourages a similar idea to cyberpunk philosophy, that is, what "really counts" is what's inside the body, not the body itself—that is to say, the fetus.

Cyberfeminism has been described as "a restart button" for gendered ideologies partly because it seeks to reclaim machines and by extension machine-enabled vision for women, as producers and users of their own imaging. The radical possibilities that new media offer to digitally create "other" bodies, other iterations of "woman" and "man" that elude the dichotomies between interior and exterior, white and nonwhite, and female and male, are especially evident in digital visualizations of bodies, that is to say, avatars. Sites like Victoria Vesna's "bodies incorporated" are the darling of cyberfeminist and other new media theorists because they allow for interactive body play in the realm of the absurd; avatars made of chocolate with human and machine parts certainly challenge paradigms of normative bodies.[43] The commercialization of the Internet has led many Internet utopians to despair of its potential as a site to challenge institutional authority and tired media scripts, and they often look to artists to provide that bit of resistance or subversion which new media theorists so badly need. However, it is important to note the elitism that can arise from this position. As Burnett notes, new media are distinguished by their redistribution of image and content production to "the masses." This stance celebrates the Internet's potential to give expression to "all," to put media production into the hands of nonprofessionals (who are presumably less hegemonized, or at least freer of overt commercial agendas). Mirzoeff writes that the popularization of digital media has produced an "apparent state of emergency in North American universities at the level of criticism, pedagogy, and institutional practice," since they "promote a form of empowered amateurism—make your own movie, cut your own CD, publish your own Web site—that cuts across professionalization and specialization, the twin justifications of the liberal arts university."[44] However, Vesna is a professional herself: a professional artist. Her use of digital media is far from amateurish, and the site evidences some serious expertise with imaging software. As Grant Farred writes regarding the use of the vernacular: "The vernacular is the transcription of the popular (subaltern) experience into political oppositionality."[45] "Vernacular" assemblages created by subaltern users, in this case pregnant women, create impossible bodies that critique normative ones but without an overt artistic or political intent.

This constitutes an interesting case of theoretical convergence. However, there are institutional reasons for this; as Lisa Cartright writes of television studies, popular (as opposed to "artistic") digital media studies have "remained marginal to disciplines that shun low culture."[46] Her remarkable observation that television was excluded from serious consideration by the famous "Visual Culture Questionnaire" that appeared in *October* in 1996, while both digital media and film were discussed extensively, I would contend has to do with digital media's efforts to legitimate themselves by focusing on digital *art*. It is not a new strategy for new disciplines to array themselves with authority and prestige by invoking the artistic. As mentioned before, Victoria Vesna's work is a great favorite among feminist media theorists, and in fact the strongest critical-theoretical discussion of new media has come from the world of art.[47] Like television studies, which have "tended to rely on the methods of sociology and communication foundational to cultural studies,"[48] new media studies have split into two streams: high critical exegeses of new media art, and social scientific case studies of popular new media practices on the Web and Internet. The vernacular assemblages created by pregnant women on these sites demand the creation of a different stream, one that brings a critical stance to popular new media practices.

The promise of free and easy digital production is, practically speaking, an illusion; in reality it is very difficult to create "original digital images." Photoshop, Illustrator, and Fireworks are notoriously difficult to learn, and it is a truism of the Net that it is much easier to borrow or steal images than it is to create them from scratch. As Manovich writes, this new aesthetic of selecting from preexisting sets of images rather than creating new ones characterizes new media's very structure and logic.[49] The modularity of digital images makes the principle of copying and modification the basis of new media practice. Yet many new media theorists heavily favor "original" artistic production and also tend to prioritize graphical versus textual production. This tends to decrease the likelihood that "empowered amateurs" might create the kind of work that gets noticed, written about, discussed, assigned on syllabi, and analyzed. This emphasis on the essential originality of avatars, either textual or graphical, is apparent in Dianne Currier's work; she writes: "The visual avatars adopted by participants in more sophisticated graphical social environments present not simply a graphic icon manipulated by the individual user but a figure that is self-imagined and created." She emphasizes how avatar construction represents a form of "disembodiment" because "the construction of these bodies is entirely along the lines of individual desires."[50] However, considering how difficult it is on the level of techne to create "new" digital images rather than modify bitmapped ones taken from other "original" sources on the Web, individual desire, as strong as it may be, is likely to be thwarted unless the user is a graphic designer.

Popular graphical avatars created by "ordinary" users for nontechnical purposes are the blind spot of visual culture studies *as well as* digital culture studies. There is little writing on this topic from either perspective. Perhaps the most promising line of inquiry so far has been Don Slater's, in his lucid essay "Domestic Photography and Digital Culture." Though his essay was published in 1995 and thus predates the popular graphical Web, he engages with the meaning and deployment of digital snapshots in the "new home economy of the image" and concludes on a somewhat pessimistic note, asserting that digital domestic photography is unlikely to provide culturally productive and empowering resources for everyday life, as he expects it to function only as another form of "intensified leisure consumption."[51] He points out the linkage between photography and leisure and consumer culture, and the ways that the family snapshot and family album, long the province and responsibility of wives and mothers, work to "idealize the self and the family."[52] He proposes that the pinboard replace the photo album as the most appropriate model for domestic imaging in the digital age, as it is made up of "images bound up with forms of practice rather than memory of commemoration, which are part of the instantaneous time of the consumerist present rather than a historical time marked by the family album" (139). The pinboard, like the digital signature, is an act of "practical communication rather than reflective representation" that might offer a site of resistance to the commodification of leisure created by photography's industry and history. Photo albums have lost cultural relevance because their hypervaluation as an artifact of a static and idealized notion of family is only matched by how seldom we look at them: gazing at photographs has failed to become a structured consumer leisure activity in the way that taking them has become. Pinboards, unlike traditional photographic albums, resemble digital signatures in the sense that they contain dynamic and modular content and convey the sense of a life in motion rather than one frozen in time, artifactual, and thus untrue to the sense of a lived past. In an article titled "Forum: Mombloggers, Unite!" and subtitled "Consumed by the minutiae of child-raising, young parents can suffer from isolation. Cooper Munroe, mother of four kids, prescribes frequent Web logging," Munroe asserts the superiority of blogging over family photo albums. Munroe, a member of DotMoms, a blogging collective for women to share and record their experiences as mothers of young children, writes: "The added benefit is that by going through the exercise of thinking through what occurs in a day and writing it down, I am also creating a permanent record of what life is like while raising them. If I did not have a few hundred people stopping by every day to see what Emily and I are writing about, I likely would not be chronicling in a diary or a scrapbook about the maelstrom of Otis and a snake in a fight to the death (Otis won) or the time our 3-year-old asked the dentist if we could take home the laughing gas. Someday, I hope, my blog will tell my kids much more about themselves, and about the woman who raised them, than any photo album ever will." The notion of the "mommyblog" as a time-shifting communication medium that enhances convenience and memory can be read as a rebuke to Wakeford's and Star's fears that women's use of the Internet might produce only more drudgery and isolation for overworked caretakers and mothers of small children. Munroe writes that "Julie Moos, managing editor of the Poynter Institute, a journalism education organization, and editor of DotMoms, a collective of 'mom' writers, to which I contribute, points out that since we are a much more mobile society, we have less time to connect. 'We don't necessarily live where we grew up or where family is or friends are. There is a great deal of mobility in the workplace. It is our mobility that makes it increasingly difficult to find the company we need.'" The irrelevance of the photo album in the digital age is asserted as well in an entry to themommyblog.com in which the author writes an "open letter" to her family explaining its purpose. She describes her blog as "a family memoir, one that looks forward rather than backward (the family is backward enough without having to look there). Therapy for me. A way to get out of scrapbooking. A way to make up for my never having embraced the Cult of Creative Memories. Something I hope to pass on to my children and their descendants so that they may have the unique opportunity to see into their childhood in a way that birthday party photos and school portraits could never convey." Indeed, it may be critically productive to envision women's blogs, digital signatures, and other representational products online as an extension of the offline material culture of scrapbooking, part of a complex of tasks that women have performed since time immemorial: the management of family memory. Scrapbook hobbyists refer to themselves somewhat touchingly as "memory consultants," implying that their function has to do with the business of memorializing the ephemeral

"look and feel" of family life with small children. These two mothers identify Creative Memories, a scrapbooking retail outlet, as at worst a "cult"
and at best an odious obligation that they can painlessly fulfill using the
Internet, a form that allows for a "unique opportunity" to record memories
in a dynamic and interactive form. Digital signatures in pregnancy bulletin
boards and pregnant avatars function as a form of vernacular memory management, one as yet uncommodified by the retail behemoth of scrapbooking
hobby shops, and one that women employ to represent and share the lives of
young children and their lives as their mothers. These women use the Internet as a place to manage memories, replacing paper and other material
forms like quilts and albums. In a way, the mode of production of digital signatures on pregnancy Web sites most resembles quilting, in the sense that
like pinboards they are accreted out of scraps that are differently sourced
and may not match, yet all have meaning. While the culture of Creative
Memories values the creation of a professional-looking product, one that
adheres to traditional middle-class notions of good taste, digital signatures,
like quilts, can be "crazy."

Virtual community has fallen out of favor as a topic for academic discussion. While it dominated new media theory in the nineties, it has lately
taken a backseat to academic discussions of new media form, such as interfaces and databases, and other uses of the new media screen technology,
such as digital gaming, which has become an economic juggernaut. However, as I have argued elsewhere, often the most sophisticated and interesting uses of new media involve its older instantiations (as in the subversive
potential of e-mail) precisely because they employed less bandwidth and
were thus less bounded by exacting infrastructural requirements.[53] Pregnancy
bulletin boards are asynchronous and simple. They are divided into areas
based on due date, "TTC" (trying to conceive), lesbian mothers, et cetera,
and within each board a user is required to choose a nickname and a password. They are then given access to posting ability. Posts follow threads on
topics such as spotting, sex, labor stories, and fertility charting. This particular visual culture of accretion rather than integration references scrapbooking or "scrapping," another signifying practice uniquely associated with
middle-class women and reviled by "real" artists. Like scrapbooking, new
media work through a logic of selection of existing modules or scraps and
the subsequent accumulation and arrangement of these pieces into something new. Like patchwork, the signatures that result are often extremely
large, in many cases taking up more than three computer screens to view. A

short post consisting of only a sentence or two will still appear with the same signature as a more substantial one.

Avatar construction is a valorized object of study in new media, especially in gaming studies. Discussions of avatars in contexts other than gaming are relatively rare. The signatures that women create on pregnancy Web sites include images of themselves and their families that take back the power to visualize the pregnant female body from the medical establishment and return it to the women themselves. The results are often cartoonish, conflicted, disorganized, and bizarre, but the openness of the form—any image or text can be uploaded to form a signature—allows for moments of poignancy that defy description and put pressure on the notion of photographic visualization in digital media. One poster's signature consists of a photograph of her stillborn child's hand, with her own hand enclosing it. Beneath this image appears a passage by the poet Rumi: "Out beyond the ideas of wrongdoing and rightdoing, there is a field. I'll meet you there."

As James Elkins writes in *Pictures of the Body: Pain and Metamorphosis*, "The crucial issue in studying pictures of the body must be the expressive value of each individual choice: what *kind* of pain is evoked, exactly *where* the sensation is strongest, precisely *how* the analogies operate."[54] The power of this image indeed resides in its pain: the pain of the bereft mother. Its transgressiveness consists in its delivering to the viewer an image of a body that is rarely represented at all in any contemporary medium: that of the stillborn child. As Elkins writes, "Some images are unrepresentable because they are forbidden by law or prohibited by custom."[55] While images of dead babies were common in nineteenth-century photography and are still publicly displayed in Yoruban photographic culture, they are extremely rare in our times, and even rarer in the context of a pregnancy Web site, thus demonstrating the ways that "custom" regarding the exhibition of these kinds of images shifts when we consider differing historical period and media use.[56] This signature represents a body that, like that of the pregnant woman, lies beyond the vocabulary of signifying practices that make up the common visual language of domesticity and home, gesturing toward the incredibly wide range of electronic elsewheres and virtual bodies that pregnant women, mothers, and trying-to-conceive women create on the Web.

The digital signature of the bereaved mother of a newborn has, itself, an ephemeral status; when "Little Livy's" mother changes her signature file, this image will disappear, leaving no trace in cyberspace except on the hard drives of those who have "captured" it. When I present this chapter as a

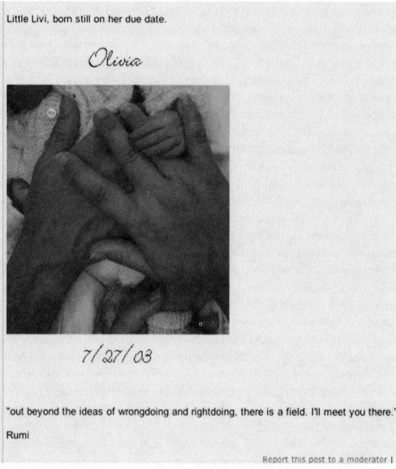

Little Livi, born still on her due date.

Olivia

7/27/03

"out beyond the ideas of wrongdoing and rightdoing, there is a field. I'll meet you there."

Rumi

Report this post to a moderator |

Figure 4.5. Olivia's signature on babydream.com.

talk, many audience members ask me why I believe a woman would want to disseminate a photograph like this one. Susan Sontag and Michael Lesy both address this question, and both write from a perspective that predates the digital. In *Wisconsin Death Trip*, Lesy explains the predominance of photographs of deceased babies by noting the relatively high infant mortality rate in mid-nineteenth-century America owing to childhood diseases like cholera, diphtheria, and smallpox but also remarks on the ritual function of funeral photography in this period: "None of the pictures were snapshots ... their deepest purpose was more religious than secular, and commercial photography, as it was practiced in the 1890s, was not so much a form of applied technology as it was a semimagical act that symbolically dealt with time and mortality."[57] Sontag as well stresses that "ever since cameras were invented in 1839, photography has kept company with death. Because an image produced with a camera is, literally, a trace of something brought before the lens, photographs were superior to any painting as a memento of the vanished pasts and the dear departed."[58] Photographs of deceased children were a particular type of "applied technology" that worked to manage memory in a graphical form. Digital signatures deployed on pregnancy bulletin boards work to manage visible and invisible bodies—avatars of pregnant women in particular allow users to gain access to a digital "counterutopia expressed in [an] area of contemporary culture resistant to, and less territorialized by, the mass media and commodified forms of communication," as David Rodowick puts it.[59]

Signatures that include the stillborn child put a formerly invisible body on display in a global medium—the Internet. The act of publicizing this socially invisible body flies in the face of contemporary custom but is quite in line with the ways that early photographs of departed children mediated between grieving parents and the community. While it may seem morbid to imagine a scenario in which a bereaved mother would have a photograph of her deceased baby blown up and displayed in her living room, Lesy narrates just such an event in nineteenth-century Wisconsin: "Mrs. Friedel had a picture taken of her little baby in its coffin. Then when a fellow came up the road who did enlargements, she had just the baby's face blown up to a twofoot picture. But, since the baby's eyes were closed, she had an artist paint them open so she could hang it in the parlor." This emphasis on public display had the dual function of "permitting the grieving parents to express and then accustom themselves to the irreversible facts of their children's death" by "permitting them to be comforted by the whole town." This primitive manipulation of the photographic image by Mrs. Friedel to produce a feeling of "liveness" in this early photographic image bespeaks a sense in which this image is both "sacred" or "semimagical" and yet modular and modifiable, traits most often associated with the digital. In addition, this sense that the image must be made public, must be shared, resonates with the use of the digital photographic portrait in the case of "Little Livy." For digital photographs are fundamentally shareable in a way that analog ones are not—as Abu Ghraib has shown us, their transmission and reproduction are uncontrollable.[60] Since they exist as binary code, they are as easy to transmit as any other type of digital file. However, their claims to truth are compromised partly for this reason; images that exist as a digital signal are easy to modify in ways that may cast them into doubt as signifiers of things that "really happened." Hence digital photography has a different kind of power in relation to the management of memory, especially in relation to the domestic and familial sphere.

Much has been written about the particular changes wrought on photographic practice and theory by digital imaging technology. In *The Reconfigured Eye*, William Mitchell notes the ways in which analog images are enduring, stable, or finished in the ways that digital ones are not, and observes that "notions of individual authorial responsibility for image content, authorial determination of meaning, and authorial prestige are correspondingly diminished."[61] Thus, unlike analog photography, which had a privileged status in relation to memory, all digital photographs call the idea of truth and authorship into question. I would contend, however, that both the photograph of "Little Livy" and the Abu Ghraib photographs are resistant to this dilution of truth value inherent in the digital. These images are, like the funeral photography displayed in Lesy and Van Schaick's book, intensely and purposefully posed; like them, they are not "snapshots," and they perform a ritual function of public mourning in the first instance and militarized racialization in the second. It was noteworthy that when the Abu Ghraib photographs were released, nobody thought to question their authenticity despite their obvious status as digital images; they possessed a cultural truth that exceeded their always already questionable means of production. Likewise, the image of "Little Livy" is very much meant to be a "real" versus a fictional image; unlike the pregnant avatar cartoons and fairylike images of miscarried "angels" and "vanishing twins" memorialized in Holly's signature, Olivia's is decidedly meant to invoke the sense of "something brought before the lens," as Sontag puts it.

The achievement of authenticity in these cases of bodies in pain and mourning transcends the ordinary logic of the analog versus the digital photograph because these bodily images invoke the "semimagical act" of remembering types of suffering that are inarticulate, private, hidden within domestic or militarized spaces that exclude the public gaze. The truth of these images remains unquestioned because the notion that someone might purposely falsify them seems incomprehensible. Women's digital signatures on babydream.com perform the important work of visualizing previously hidden body narratives, and most importantly they do so in a way that juxtaposes an amazingly broad set of signifiers in the same space: images of happy

pregnant women, healthy babies, pets, proudly displayed or missing hus-
bands or boyfriends, miscarriages, stillborn babies, and postpregnant bodies
coexist in the same virtual spaces.

As David Rodowick reminds us, it is crucial that new media scholarship
produce a "social theory that is as attentive to creative strategies of resistance as it is to mechanisms of power and social control." It is not enough
to simply locate the ways in which subjects are constrained by new media's
surveillant and capitalistic tendencies; we must also identify what he calls
new "lines of flight" that permit new "forms of becoming out of virtual per-
sonae and communities."[62] Early computing culture consistently marginalized women as users of digital technology by firmly embedding them in the
domestic sphere as computer users: engineers could not imagine that women
might use computers in any context other than that of traditional women's
work, in particular, cooking. In *Interface Culture*, Steven Johnson relates
the story of a hapless engineer at Intel who tried to pitch the idea of the
personal computer to his bosses: "His most compelling scenario involved
filing electronic versions of cooking recipes."[63] As this scenario demonstrates, a narrow conception of the domestic sphere has always intersected
with the digital. The contemporary networked personal computer does indeed function as a type of domestic appliance in the sense that it helps to
mediate acts of quite literal reproductive labor. In so doing, it permits women
access to social collectivity around the condition of pregnancy and child rearing; women use pregnancy bulletin boards to share information and counter-
information about prenatal testing, nutrition, and breast-feeding. The power
of individual experience is stressed quite heavily: while many women end
their posts with "YMMV" (your mileage may vary) or begin them with a
modest "IMHO" (in my humble opinion), seemingly discrediting or at least
casting doubt on their own claims, there is no doubt that they use the board
as often as not to challenge received medical opinions by describing their
experiences as conflicting with medical wisdom. For example, women who
receive "bad" AFP (alpha fetal protein) or ultrasound results receive much
reassurance from women who have had healthy babies with these same results, showing that the tests are often falsely positive. While a doctor or a
nurse may be able to chart a test's documented rate of error, hearing from
several actual women with healthy babies that the "bad" result is nothing to
worry about assuages fears in a different way, one more accessible perhaps to
women living in less stable, long-standing communities. Military wives, in
particular, may have a more stable "home base" and community among
pregnant women or new mothers on the Internet than in their offline lives,

considering the rigors of frequent transfers and relocations, especially during wartime. Younger and less educated women, also newcomers to the Web, may also find personal "live" testimonials from "real" mothers less alienating and more reassuring than medical discourse and statistics.

Beyond this, women's creation of digital signatures enables genuine resistance to institutional forms of identity management that only continue to proliferate in daily life. While the seemingly free spaces of composable identities evident in build-your-own avatar games like MMORPGs continue to instantiate stereotyped images of women,[64] as Rodowick observes, "there is still an unequal division of power in the data images that count— for access to credit, medical insurance, voting and residency rights, ownership of property, and so forth—[and they are] still culled, collated, and controlled by a few large corporations and marketing organizations."[65] What are the "data images that count," the avatars that matter, in relation to women's reproductive labor online? While pregnancy bulletin boards may at times affirm normative domestic behavior in terms of pregnancy and child rearing, the digital signatures on several pregnancy Web sites are evidence of eclectic digital production that reflects the reality of reproductive labor and its attendant losses.

Women's production of digital signatures not only re-embodies themselves as pregnant subjects but also visualizes holistic visions of family that embody the paradox of pregnant women's empowerment and invisibility. While women who are on the Internet are empowered in a sense, certainly in relation to their sisters in other parts of the world where access is extremely scarce for any gender, they are still subject to the regulation of images of "proper" pregnancies and visual cultures. The gendered and classed nature of their signatures, as well as their mode of arrangement and visual ranking, which includes pets, political affiliations, and displays of communal belonging with other members of the online community, shows the development of a digital vernacular modernism. Pregnant women represent themselves exuberantly in the form of their digital avatars, and this energy and joy in self-representation take on all the more significance in a dataveillant society that continues to regulate pregnancy through imaging technologies. In representing themselves and their babies, pregnancies, babies yet to be, and lost children, women graphically embody themselves as dual subjects of interactivity in digital visual culture, thus publicizing bodies and lives previously unrepresented by the women living them.

5

Measuring Race on the Internet: Users, Identity, and Cultural Difference in the United States

What are the racial politics of visibility on the Internet? To understand the visual culture of the Internet, we must know who uses it and how users are counted or seen. To some extent this question has been conceptualized as an empirical one; scholars and policy makers rely on reports based on demographic data gathered by organizations like the Pew Internet and American Life Foundation, the National Telecommunications and Information Agency (NTIA), and the U.S. Census. David Rodowick observes: "Without access, there is no interface to digital culture—one cannot be included in its social networks or forms of exchange whether for good or ill. The question of access is therefore one of the principal political questions of digital culture."[1] What do we mean when we speak of "Internet access"? What are the cultural politics of measuring Internet users in terms of race, and how do the categories used in demographic studies of Internet users evaluate and influence assessments of online participation and power? As Wendy Chun, Lee and Wong, Palumbo-Liu, and my prior work has noted, Asians and Asian Americans are already figured as having a privileged relationship to cybertechnologies *in some ways*.[2] Despite characterizations of Asian Americans as uniquely privileged technology consumers, they inhabit a range of positions in relation to the Internet: Robert Lee writes that "Asian Americans, particularly immigrant Asian workers, have a highly visible position on both ends of the post-Fordist economy, in what urban sociologist

Saskia Sassen has called 'global cities.'"[3] Asian Americans, most of whom
are working-class immigrants and refugees in contrast to popular conceptions of this group as a professional upper-middle-class "model minority,"
indeed live on *both* ends of the networked information economy, both as
low- and high-skilled workers and as consumers.

However, demographic studies of Internet use emphasize only Asian
Americans' position as consumers. Many of these surveys design questions
that hew to this paradigm by querying respondents on what types of services
and activities they engage in, rather than asking them about their cultural
production, such as postings to bulletin boards or creation of Web sites or
other forms of Internet textuality or graphical expression. Thus Internet
use by racial minorities may be misunderstood as being on a par with usage
by the white Internet majority in the United States if "access" is the only
criterion considered. The premise of this book is that women and racial
and ethnic minorities create visual cultures on the popular Internet that
speak to and against existing graphical environments and interfaces online.
Surveys of race and the "digital divide" that fail to measure digital production in favor of measuring access or consumption cannot tell the whole
story, or even part of it. Failing to query users about their level of participation on the Internet perpetuates a model of Internet "activity" that dis-
counts production of Internet content as a key aspect of interactivity. At
worst, by overrepresenting minority participation, studies may deepen the
digital divide by leading to mistaken policy decisions regarding whether or
not public Internet access is needed in local communities.

When considering the question of racial minority use of the Internet in
the United States, it is also especially important to consider the way that
language use is handled in demographic studies that count numbers of Internet users broken out by race. Studies such as the Pew Internet and American Life Project reports and the NTIA reports that are based on the Current
Population Survey gather data by conducting telephone surveys and doing
paper surveys, and they *do not survey in Asian languages*, a reasonable decision
considering the difficulty and expense of employing multilingual surveyors.
However, the majority of Asians who identify as Asian alone in the United
States—seven out of ten, according to the 2000 U.S. Census—were born
outside the country, and many of them do not speak English fluently enough
to participate in a telephone survey or fill out a form in English.[4] This means
that reports that cut out non–English speakers are looking at a very small slice
of the Asian American population, one that is already selected for affluence
and linguistic assimilation. Thus these influential, widely read, and widely

cited reports overcount Asian Americans as Internet users, representing them as far more connected to the Internet than they actually are. Asians are a notoriously difficult group to count, partly because of the linguistic challenge presented by their recent immigration patterns; the 2004 *Recommendations of the Census Advisory Committee on the Asian Population* recommends that "in the 2005 or 2006 Census Tests, the Census Bureau should identify areas across the nation with a high concentration of non-English speaking households, making forms and promotional materials, and identifying census tracts with a high concentration of, not only Spanish speakers, but also Asian speakers." Even the U.S. Census, a very thorough and comprehensive survey indeed, is trying to correct the possible undercounting of Asians who do not speak English, demonstrating that they fear that they are undercounting Asian-language-speaking populations. Reports on Internet usage that only count English-speaking Asian Americans perpetuate a damaging racializing formation that perpetuates digital inequality. Asians in America are far from the wired "majority." On the contrary, when we count non-English-speaking Asians, they inhabit a painful paradox: they are a digital minority whose racial formation and public perception are that of a digital majority.

In addition, releases in the popular press and representations of Asian Americans as a "wired" minority may result in especially intense marketing directed to them on the Internet, which may interpellate or hail them as consumers in a more powerful way in than it does other users.[5] If we wish to measure interactivity rather than "access" as broadly defined, it is crucial that minority participation in free-response sites like bulletin boards and petitions sites be measured as well to acquire a more nuanced view of racialized participation online. When we do, we see that minority groups such as Asians who have been believed to be especially "wired" have less interactivity than previously thought.

Much demographic research has conceived of the Internet as a "passive" media like television, asking questions regarding what types of activities users engage in, rather than what they produce, share, or post. "Kill your television" bumper stickers are popular in many American cities, and we have all come across people who deliberately abstain from watching TV. They are not framed as backward or on the wrong side of a technological divide. If anything, they are considered to know more than the norm about media. Their position usually garners respect because it represents a critique of television's oppressive mass-media qualities such as manipulative commercials, ethnic and racial stereotyping, and sexualized violence. As I discussed in chapter 2, television has long been denigrated as "antisocial" and "repressive" in contrast to textual media forms. The Internet benefits from both its textuality and its interactivity, and the two are linked in users' and scholars' minds in a way that adds to the Internet's cachet. Non–television watchers are often perceived as intelligent, savvy, and discriminating consumers who have a critical perspective on media. And it follows that members of oppressed and marginalized groups are those who lose the least by killing their televisions, since theirs are the images most frequently exploited, commodified, and misrepresented by that medium.[6]

The assumption in much discourse regarding the digital divide is that the Internet is somehow exempt from the critiques that we make of television, and that it is de facto "enriching." In addition, the Net is paradoxically thought to have more in common with "popular" media forms versus mass ones because of its supposed openness and interactivity; theoretically any user can post his or her own content to it. In practice, however, as McChesney notes, "The most striking change to occur in the late 1990s has been the quick fade of euphoria of those who saw the Internet as providing a qualitatively different and egalitarian type of journalism, politics, media, and culture. The indications are that the substantive content of this commercial media in the Internet, or any subsequent digital communication system, will look much like what currently exists."[7] Gans agrees, asserting bluntly: "Some innovative, marginal, and deviant culture that is devoid of economic resources and beset by political opposition may find a home on the Internet. The Internet can transmit only symbolic culture, but in theory, at least, it has room for everything if not everybody. Unfortunately, the more the Internet becomes a mass medium, the more likely it is to attract censors that now place limits on TV and the other mass media. Assuming that the Internet can remain outside the cultural power structures is illusory."[8] Beacham agrees with this rather gloomy perspective, noting that the Internet has shifted from "being a participatory medium that serves the interests of the public to being a broadcast medium where corporations deliver consumer oriented information. Interactivity would be reduced to little more than sales transactions and email."[9]

Despite this state of affairs, in the popular imagination the Internet gets to have it both ways; unlike television, film, or other mass media, the Internet is still perceived as inherently educational (perhaps because it is both a new medium and one that involves computer use), and thus a contributor to democracy and equality, although it is not accessible to nearly as many users as other mass media are. It is interesting to note that people of color, a newly expanding and overwhelmingly young group of new Internet users, value the Internet most highly for its educational properties and are most enthusiastic about it for the sake of their children, if they have them: "About 53% of online blacks have a child under the age of 18 at home, while 42% of online whites are parents of children that age. Users often perceive gaining access to the Internet as an investment in the future and this seems especially true in African-American families"[10] This is also the case for Hispanic families, 49 percent of whom have a child at home. "Hispanic parents, like other parents, often see the purchase of a computer and Internet access as an investment in their children's future."[11] I would venture that few Americans of any race would frame television access as an "investment in their children's future"; the language of progress, class mobility, and education is generally lacking in discussions of that medium. Yet scholars like McChesney claim that the differences between the Internet and other popular noninteractive media like television are eroding if not already functionally gone. Thus families of color are putting their faith in an Internet that is coming to resemble less an "information superhighway" than a sprawling suburban shopping mall. It is becoming increasingly clear that people of color missed the "golden age of cyberculture."

Despite these critiques, the Internet does still retain at least a potential for interactivity that television lacks, particularly vis-à-vis minority digital visual cultures. Studies that discount users' cultural production hew to a market research model that forecloses studies of this interactivity. This is a crucial omission, for the distinctiveness of new media and the Internet in particular is the possibility of interactivity in the form of cultural production. In a chapter of his book *The Network Society* titled "The Culture of Real Virtuality," Manuel Castells lays out what he sees as the dangers regarding access that ought to concern new media users in the future. In contrast to McChesney, Castells thinks the Internet is better than television in several basic ways: he advocates a

> multimodal, horizontal network of communication, of Internet type, instead of a centrally dispatched multimedia system, as in the video-on-demand configuration. The setting of barriers to entry into this communication system, and the creation of passwords for the circulation and diffusion of messages throughout the system, are critical cultural battles for the new society, the outcome of which predetermines the fate of symbolically mediated conflicts to be fought in this new historical environment. Who are the interacting and who are the interacted in the new system, to use the terminology whose meaning I suggested above, largely frames the system of domination and the process of liberation in the information society.[12]

In this chapter, I wish to discuss the ways that users of color are framed as interacted and interactors, subjects and objects, of interactivity.

It would be a novel idea to suggest that it might not be an unmitigated ill for people of color to be absent from the Internet. In recent years only a few cultural critics have been brave enough to buck the trend of Internet boosterism, and Coco Fusco and Kim Hester-Williams are the most perceptive of these. Their critique cannot be ignored.[13] Neither espouses a Luddite antitechnological stance; rather, they "examine the price that is exacted for participating in corporate-mediated cyberspaces that take advantage of our search for 'beloved community' on the net by reifying and subjecting our identities to the law of the market."[14] The question "Does the Internet really offer spaces of representation and resistance constructed 'for us' and 'by us'?" is answered in the negative by Hester-Williams. Fusco's critique is similar; she notes that the alliance between globalization and the commodification of cyberspace has enabled the "techno-elite's search for a more efficient work-force, which at this point means better trained at the top, less trained at the bottom, and more readily positioned for increased consumption of commodified leisure." She also rightly notes the racial dynamics of this stratification of cyberspace: the gap between power-users and the power-used is widening, and it is most often people of color who are left digitally divided from the ranks of the techno-elite. However, Asians occupy a unique position in this racial landscape, for they constitute members of both groups. In this chapter, I assess the ways that this racialized political economy is worked out in cyberspace's Asian spaces and propose theoretical models with which to evaluate the meaningfulness of Asian American participation in shaping online discourse. Have Asian Americans successfully made their cultural influence felt online? Do they enact the familiar stereotype of nonthreatening and apolitical "model minority" in cyberspace? And in what ways, if any, is this model subverted on the Internet?

It is a widely accepted notion that media interactivity is power. If this is true, then scholars and institutions wishing to create an equal and fair society have an interest in measuring types and degrees of digital interactivity as it is distributed among different social groups. We must create nuanced terms and concepts for evaluating participation to assess the impact of cultural power differentials on the ability of people of color, youth, senior citizens, and others to deploy their identities on the Internet. Rather than focusing only on the question of Internet access, a clumsy binary model of participation that ignores crucial questions about *kinds* of access, more recent scholarship has considered the impact of factors like skill level with search engines, as well as duration, speed, and location of Internet access, on what kinds of access to information users can have. However, empirical studies have not tended to survey users about their production, if any, of Internet content. As Geert Lovink notes, "read-only members" of virtual communities possess a different status in relation to that community than do those who post online. They more closely resemble television users in an infinitely channeled multimedia universe than they do the idealized active, mobile, expressive subject posited in early research on online community. Television audience research often recognizes the effects that time-shifting devices like the VCR have had on enhancing audience choice, and thus interactivity, but tend to also remain grounded in the notion that television watchers constitute an audience clearly separate from television producers. As Ien Ang writes: "With the VCR, then, we have witnessed the 'active audience' in action. This does not mean, however, that audiences are moving out of the industry's sphere of influence: rather, that their relation to the industry is shifting from that of the more or less passive audience-mass to that of the selective individual consumer."[15] The active audience is the primary distinction between television and Internet audiences.

Measuring media audience is a famously problematic enterprise. Audiences are difficult to define, as they tend to shift based on context and do not constitute a stable object of study. However, television audiences are "read-only members" in a way that Internet audiences are not and have never been.[16] Ang observes that the Internet's infrastructure enables participation in the media form in a way that already figures the user as, among other things, a "selective individual consumer," but as in the case of television, this "does not mean that audiences are moving out of the industry's sphere of influence" (12). As I have discussed in previous chapters, the visual culture of the Internet industry's popular visual interfaces, such as those that govern the deployment, selection, and in some cases creation of buddy icons for Instant Messenger, online quizzes and tests, image editing software, and digital signature files used in commercially owned bulletin boards, all constitute small and often overlooked spaces of self-representation that users of color and women are both constrained by and actively modify to suit their own purposes. Though companies like Microsoft and America Online and owners of pregnancy Web sites like ivillage.com create the standards and protocols of applications like Instant Messenger, various Web site protocols, bulletin board software, and industry standards like HTML preceded these and have an impact as well on what users can create, nonetheless opportunities exist for the production of surprising modes of media creation within these constraints. Relative latecomers to the Internet, such as people of color, women, youths, and working- to middle-class users, have never owned the means to produce cultural texts on the Internet in the same way that more technically skilled and better-capitalized users have. Indeed, "complex and contradictory 'living room wars' are taking place wherever and whenever television (and other media) sway people's daily lives in the modern world."[17] However, "dailiness" varies across subject positions of various users, and assessing it must involve considerations of place and context of use as well as the racial and gender identity of users. The wars over the Internet's visual culture are taking place in settings that include the living room, but also extend outward in ways that other media have not. The Internet intervenes in people's daily lives across social spheres and public spaces such as public libraries, cybercafés, and school classrooms and across platforms like the cell phone, the PDA, and the television. Though, as Anna McCarthy notes, television itself has become an "ambient" medium, newly common in waiting rooms, vehicles, and public spaces, television's migration out of domestic space and into public space has been driven partly by the influence of digital media. The Internet is a paradox: notable for the ways in which scholars have predicted its "ubiquity," it is nonetheless far from universally accessible inside or outside the context of the living room.[18]

I focus here on the ways that influential and widely cited demographic studies of Internet users broken out by race, such as those released by the Pew Internet and American Life Project and the NTIA, represent Internet users as more or less passive mass audiences and "selective individualized consumers." This characterization of Internet use creates a discourse of race and the visual culture of the Internet that envisions minorities as more or less successful consumers of a commodity or information source rather than as producers or active audiences. Even in cases in which Internet users of color do engage with the Internet mainly *as* consumers, participation in online petitions used to protest retail racism, as in the case of the Abercrombie and Fitch T-shirts, and media racism, as in the case of a controversial "Asian or Gay?" article in *Details* magazine, demonstrates not only that users of color use the Internet to organize and protest, but more importantly how they use the form of the petition itself to enable discourse that reveals ambivalent, complex and rich understandings of racial identity. Already-existing cultural representations of Asian American men, in particular, as queered and emasculated in terms of their identities as *consumers* of retail goods, are extended by studies of Internet use that emphasize access, or consumption of the Internet, rather than production. Asians, and in particular Asian men, are thus imagined primarily as shoppers.

Until recently, surveys of Internet use have tended not to query for race. In 1998 the Hoffman and Novak study studied African American Internet users and measured their activities and levels of access in relation to white users but did not look at other ethnicities or races.[19] The Pew Internet and American Life survey and the NTIA reports from 1995 to the present are an improvement because they examine four ethnic groups: African Americans, Asian Americans, Hispanics, and whites. This potentially allows a more nuanced discussion of minorities online, what their presence consists of, the specific areas of cyberspace in which they are present or absent, as well as an examination in more complex terms of how race matters. I focus primarily on the ways that Asian Americans have been singled out as the most wired racial group in America, "the young and the connected," as the title of the Pew report on Asian American usage of the Internet calls them, and the repercussions of this particular categorization for Asian American Internet audiences and digital visual culture.

Robert Lee's analysis of the "model minority" myth in the United States critiques U.S. Census data for misrepresenting Asian Americans as possessing a higher SES (socioeconomic status) than they actually enjoy: "The suggestion of parity between Asian Americans and non-Hispanic white Americans is, therefore, deceptive. The figure cited most often to illustrate the Asian American success story is the median income of Asian American families ($42,250 in the 1980s and '90s), slightly higher than the median income for white families. When controlled for geography and the number of wage earners per family, however, the income of Asian Americans falls short of that for non-Hispanic white Americans."[20] Similarly, dubbing Asian Americans as "the most wired group in America" deceptively represents them as subjects of interactivity in a way that other users are not—Castells's "interactors" rather than the "interacted." They are thus classed as honorary or approximate whites in a way that obscures their actual oppression and position as material labor base rather than as privileged consumers of Internet- and IT-based services and media. As the Pew report did not sample non-English-speaking respondents, it is unlikely that it was able to survey immigrants or recently arrived and undereducated Asian Americans, exactly those people most likely to work as the "interacted" in the circuit of informatic labor.

Members of Castells's Fourth World are irrelevant to global flows of informatic power. Asian Americans are not members of this group. However, neither are they necessarily privileged digital model minorities. As Wendy Chun writes, "The Internet is not *inherently* oriental, but has been made oriental." The ongoing cultural association with Asians and Asian Americans and high technologies is part of a vibrant and long-standing mythology.[21]

The most important development in terms of Internet users between 2000 and 2005 is the radical increase in the number of women and ethnic and racial minorities online. In the early years of the Internet's massification, cyberculture scholars discussed race online with only marginal references to online media and computer-mediated communications produced by blacks, Asians, and Latinos, instead focusing on representations of racial and ethnic minorities produced for consumption by white users and audiences.[22] Things have changed a great deal since then: English is no longer the majority language of the Internet, and vast numbers of new Asian users have made it inaccurate to speak of the Internet as a primarily Western medium. Cultural critics of new media as well as research foundations and policy organizations have much at stake in the way that race online is counted and tabulated. Neither are Asian American scholars free from bias when it comes to measuring Internet participation. There is much at stake in race-based measurement of Internet usage for them as well. As Lee and Wong note: "On the whole, scholars in the field of race and cyberspace remain critically hesitant to emphasize Asian Americans' differences from other racial groups in terms of their cyberpractices, in part due to legitimate worries over the way such claims to distinction can play into old divide-and-conquer tactics that set minorities against (model) minorities."[23] Scholars have strategically ignored Asian Americans as Internet power-users because this characterization separates them from other minority groups and implies that their priorities have more in common with the white majority. Unlike the Pew Internet and American Life Foundation, they are anxious to avoid characterizations of Asian Americans as a "digital majority." Lee and Wong are right to emphasize the difficulties created by this strategy: if it is not possible to acknowledge Asian American advantages vis-à-vis Internet access, discussion of their cultural production is foreclosed. Even worse, representations of Asians as possessing "dangerous expertise" vis-à-vis the Internet because they are less disadvantaged than other minority groups exacerbate anti-Asian sentiment.[24] Reports that characterize Asians as *more* connected than whites capitalize on fears that even a slightly higher percentage of Asians online constitutes a large and potentially worrisome majority.

Race has long been a vexed issue on the Internet. In 1996, John Perry Barlow wrote "A Declaration of the Independence of Cyberspace," in which he explains:

> Ours is a world that is both everywhere and nowhere, but it is not where bodies live. We are creating a world that all may enter without privilege or prejudice accorded by race, economic power, military force, or station of birth. We are creating a world where anyone, anywhere may express his or her beliefs, no matter how singular, without fear of being coerced into silence or conformity.

Race is the first thing that Barlow claims will be eradicated in cyberspace. This implies that of all of the bodily handicaps recognized as oppressive, race is somehow the most oppressive. Barlow's statement is part of the first wave of utopian thinking on the Internet.[25] However, unlike the original Declaration of Independence, it does highlight an intense awareness of race as a problem of access that needs to be overcome. And Barlow was correct at least in stressing it; data gathered by the Pew Foundation do indicate that significant disparities still exist in Internet access based on race, with African Americans and Hispanics *much* less likely to be online than whites. Fifty-eight percent of whites have used the Internet, compared to 43 percent of African Americans and 50 percent of Hispanics.[26] The Pew Foundation reports that Asian Americans are the most likely to have access: it finds that 75 percent of them have used the Internet, making them "one of the most wired groups in America."[27] What's more, though the gap in access between people of color and whites is closing, African Americans with access to the Internet do not go online as often in a typical day as whites do: only 36 percent of African Americans go online in a typical day, compared to 56 percent of whites.[28] These figures differ from those in the 2002 NTIA report "A Nation Online," which claims that "computer use rates were highest for Asian American and Pacific Islanders (71.2 percent) and Whites (70.0 percent). Among Blacks, 55.7 percent were computer users. Almost half of Hispanics (48.8 percent) were computer users."[29] These numbers imply at best that whites and Asian Americans have *parity* when it comes to access, rather than one group being "more connected" than the other or possessing a digital advantage. However, as noted earlier in the chapter, the numbers leave out the majority of Asians in America, as 69 percent of those identifying themselves as "Asian" alone were born outside the United States according to the 2000 Census. The NTIA reports surveyed Spanish and English speakers; the Pew reports surveyed only English speakers. In addition, the small sample size of Asian Americans counted in the Pew report calls their characterization as especially "connected" into question.[30]

Past digital divide discourse has tended to perpetuate the "gap" metaphor, stressing the absence of people of color online and implying that this is a state of things that needs to be remedied.[31] The Pew Foundation's study of Internet use and race, which tracks minority participation in four major categories (Fun, Information Seeking, Major Life Activities, and Transactions), examines the ways in which all three minority groups studied participate proportionally *more* in several activities. For example, 54 percent of the African Americans online listened to music there, while only 32 percent of whites online did. Hispanics and Asian Americans also listened to music proportionally more than did whites online: 48 percent of Hispanics had done so, while 46 percent of Asian Americans had. This represents quite a significant digital divide in terms of use of the Internet as a means to get access to music, with whites on the "wrong" side, despite their superior numbers in terms of general access to the Internet. This divide extends into several different types of activities: when racial minorities get online, the Pew data indicate that more of them spend their time online chatting, sending and reading instant messages, looking for sports information, and downloading music than online whites do. This held true for all three racial nonwhite racial groups, including Asian Americans. It seems clear that their investments in the medium are different from those of white users, and that they are far more engaged with the Internet as a source of expressive or popular culture than as a way to buy or sell stocks, get weather reports, or get hobby information: all activities in which online whites participate proportionally more than do online Hispanics, African Americans, or Asian Americans. Significantly, using the Internet to access music, movies, sports information, and social functions such as chatting and instant messaging are all categorized by the Pew Study under the heading of "Fun." The titles of the remaining three categories, "Information Seeking," "Major Life Activities," and "Transactions," rhetorically imply that participating in popular culture is not a "major life activity" or a way to get important "information." On the contrary, rather than devaluing those online spaces where the small but growing numbers of American minorities are spending their time and energy, a reenvisioning of what constitutes a "major life activity" or salient "information" may be in order. In the case of people of color, popular culture practices constitute a discursive domain where they are more likely to see cultural producers who resemble them; and most importantly, these are exactly the spaces that invite participation by users. This is important in-formation in the context of Internet users and their lived realities. Manifes-tations of expressive cultures on the Internet may thus provide an online oasis or refuge for users of color, most of whom are relatively young and new to the medium.

According to the Pew reports, English-speaking users of color use the Internet quite selectively, tending to favor activities related to expressive culture, such as music, movies, chatting, and using multimedia sources, over others. And though the sample sizes for Asian Americans were quite small in some cases, this is true of racial minority groups who responded in greater numbers. The Pew reports enable a new perspective on what people of color actually do when they are online as opposed to the old focus on the digital divide and information haves and have-nots. Thus the project is very much in the spirit of the Afro-futurist group, which, in a special issue of *Social Text* and in the collection *Technicolor*, brings to light neglected examples of "African diasporic technophilia" and its long history, debunking the "underlying assumption of much digital divide rhetoric . . . that people of color, and African Americans in particular, cannot keep pace with our high-tech society."[32] As stated before, there are several areas of online life in which people of color participate more fully, in proportion to their numbers, than whites do. African Americans, Hispanics, and Asian Americans generally participate more often in activities coded as "Fun" by the Pew report. To give a complete list, these are the following:

- Browse just for fun
- Get hobby information
- Send an instant message
- Chat online
- Use video/audio clip
- Play a game
- Look for sports information
- Look for info about music, books, or other leisure activities
- Listen to music
- Download music

As the report notes, this is partly explained by the relative youth of minority groups in comparison to whites. This is especially true of Asian Americans and Hispanics. "The online Hispanic population is very young. . . . About 61% of online Hispanics are 34 or under. In comparison, about 37% of white Internet users and 54% of African American users are in that cohort."[33]

Moreover, "the Asian American Internet population is also one of the most youthful on the Web. Almost two-thirds (63%) of Asian American users are between the ages of 18 and 34."[34] More than half of all people of color who use the Internet are "young." This has a tremendous bearing on their relation to popular culture, as "youth culture" and expressive cultures tend to cross and overlap in numerous ways.

The Internet is a popular communication medium that is used differently by different racial groups.[35] I also make a case for how minority expressive cultures in cyberspace, particularly those produced and consumed by youths of color, may provide sites of resistance to offline racial hegemonies that call for serious consideration.[36] But we must also consider the relation between expressive or popular culture and racial identity and being in the world. Expressive culture practices like music have always been media spaces where people of color are visible as producers and performers, though of course this should not be read as an unalloyed good. As Herman Gray writes:

> Marginalized and subordinated communities have creatively transformed and used popular cultural artifacts such as music, costumes, parades, traditions, and festivals to transgress their particular locations, to express their visions, and invent themselves. What characterizes black youth culture in the 1990s and therefore warrants careful attention is the central role of the commercial culture industry and mass media in the process.[37]

If indeed the Internet has become a mass medium and has lost some of its potential as a space for transgression, expression, and reinvention of mass images of race, gender, and identity, this is alarming, but perhaps less so than it seems. Black youth culture is already closely engaged with the commercial culture industry. As Robin Kelley observes, "In a nation with few employment opportunities for African Americans and a white consumer market eager to be entertained by the Other, blacks have historically occupied a central place in the popular culture industry."[38] Asian Americans are far less visible as producers of a distinctive and commodified "youth culture" than are African Americans.[39] However, they are overrepresented or hypervisible in media industries such as pornography, a medium that has found a particularly congenial home on the Internet. While this is egregious in that it perpetuates the exoticization of Asian women, it does open up a space for Asian Americans to intervene as critics, artists, and independent contractors. In "Good Politics, Great Porn: Untangling Race, Sex, and Technology in Asian American Cultural Production," Tu describes how Asian American Internet artists and activists have critiqued Orientalist cyberspace by producing their own Web sites and digital films. Her examples, Bindigirl,

BigBadChineseMama, and the independent filmmaker Greg Pak's digital short *Asian Pride Porn!* "Are all "hilarious send up[s] of the adult industry."[40] However, there are shortcomings that come with relying on humor to perform their critique: as Tu writes, "creative works like these, however, are politically tricky, playing as they do with the easily misunderstood tools of humor and irony." Nonetheless she asserts that their importance lies in their ability to "challenge the representational order that dictates their position."[41] In other words, these sites work much as does alllooksame.com in that they encourage reflection and critique through fairly indirect, satirical means. The angryasianman.com weblog works in a more straightforward fashion: it serves some of the same functions as old media Asian American newspapers and magazines in that it tracks and reports instances of anti-Asian racism in the media in a fairly denotative way, as "news." Rather than envisioning Asians as power-users or hyperconsumers, it speaks to its audience as media users and potential activists.

Images of Asian Americans as "wired" consumers both hopped up on the drug of hypercapitalism and endowed with the cultural capital to know their way around cyberspace imply that social power lies in the ability to purchase and take advantage of the network's most advanced features. Indeed, numerous joke lists that circulate via e-mail attest to this self-identification of Asian Americans as avid and enabled users of the Internet. For example, one of these, "Eighty-two Ways to Tell If You Are Chinese," contains an entry that reads, "You e-mail your Chinese friends at work, even though you only sit 10 feet apart." These constitute a useful corrective to digital divide discourse by "casting technology use as one of many aspects of racial identity and practice, rather than vice versa."[42] Second, and most importantly, cyberspace functions as a vector for resistant cultural practices that allow Asian Americans to both use and produce cyberspace. Indeed, new media's potential when it comes to Asian Americans has much to do with the powerful ways in which it deploys interactivity to destabilize the distinctions between users and producers, as well as questioning a rigid and essentialized notion of Asian American "authenticity."

In March 2004 Daniel Lee's "Asians against Ignorance" online petition at www.petitionsonline.com called for Asian Americans to boycott *Details*, a U.S. men's magazine, as a reaction to a piece it published titled "Asian or Gay?" This short article, a humorous piece on the convergence between "Asian" and "gay" sartorial profiles, galvanized Asian American activists and journalists both offline and online. Online petitions like these indicate the growth of cyberactivism among a racial minority group in the United

States often perceived as politically apathetic.[43] I will examine the development of Asian American online petition cybercultures by analyzing three specific examples of media protest campaigns against racial stereotyping that produced an appreciable online response: the *Details* "Asian or Gay" controversy, the Abercrombie and Fitch "Two Wongs Don't Make It White" T-shirt protest, and the Ondade Mar Buddhist tankini scandal. Asian American activists launched online petitions hosted at petitionsonline.com in each of these cases. And in the first two, the petitions served to polarize the Asian American community at least as much as they did to unite it. The sites themselves functioned as highly ambivalent responses to issues around the visual culture of race in the United States. The anonymity afforded the petition signers, the persistence of their replies on the site, and the opportunity for users to view them all simultaneously create a space for online discursive play that challenges the notion of race- and ethnicity-based community in the act of creating it.

Struggles over Asian American visual culture are waged on the Internet in all sorts of places, and the online petition is one place that remediates the political process offline.[44] Representations of Asian Americans as laundrymen or effeminate dandies (if men) and geishas and sexual playthings (if female), as well as visual images of Buddha or bodhisattvas on the crotches of bikinis and men's underwear, are closely monitored by civil rights organizations such as the Japanese American Citizens' League, the Organization of Chinese Americans, and the Asian American Journalists' Association. Asian Americans are extremely aware of how media depictions, in visual media in particular, shape their experiences in the United States. The Japanese American press is particularly quick to attribute many of these protests' "successes" to online petitioning: Caroline Aoyogi of the *Pacific Citizen* writes that "thanks to the Internet, Buddhists have launched a massive coordinated campaign against swimwear company Ondade Mar and lingerie magnate Victoria's Secret." The swimsuits feature "strategically placed Buddhist images all over their itty-bitty bikinis and tankinis," which the story compares to "the complaint launched against Macy's recently after the department store carried boxer briefs with the image of Buddha and the words 'rub me for luck.'" The article goes on to say that "Both Trang and Rev. Umezu believe that such a use of religious imagery would never have been used if it were Christianity or Islam. 'I do not believe that this would occur with any other religious images. They would never have put images of Jesus nor Allah on the same spot of swimwear,' says Trang."[45] This conviction that Asian Americans are uniquely suited to, or at least exceptionally drawn to, the Internet as a means of political protest—that is, the notion of Asian Americans as both wired and disgruntled consumers, if not activists—is confirmed in Jeff Chang's article "Who's the Mac? The Asian E-mail Circuit Wins Again."

> Asians with a law degree call it "retail racism." The rest of us call it fucked up. It's when you want to go buy something and they flip on you like the KKK. Nothing in the world—not famine, pestilence, segregation, war, not even Steven Seagal—gets us yellows more pissed. It makes us want to steal your parking spot at the outlet mall. It makes us want to scream "Pay respect to the yellow fist or we'll fry your T3 lines down to a crisp!" Hell hath no fury like an Asian-American with disposable income and an email address.[46]

The article lists the five most "successful" online protests in descending order: the Adobe help line protest, the San Francisco Acura boycott, the Skyy Vodka protest (whose success Chang attributes to AsianAvenue.com), *Ego Trip's Big Book of Racism,* and the Abercrombie and Fitch online petition. As in Aoyagi's article, Chang is explicit about the ways that "yellows" use the "Asian email circuit" in a fashion that is different in quality or kind from that of other ethnic groups. Regarding the Skyy Vodka e-mail protest, Chang cites AsianAvenue.com CEO Ben Sun as saying in the official press release, "Prior to AsianAvenue.com, most corporations had no way of getting feedback from the very important consumer group represented by Asian-Americans." Putting this somewhat dubious claim aside, it seems that the rhetoric of online protest evident in this statement assumes that the Internet is particularly suited to addressing the wrongs of "retail racism." And the eagerness to claim the Internet as an efficacious space of articulation and self-assertion for Asian Americans is further reflected in the following claim regarding the Abercrombie protest: "The resulting flood of angry Asian-American email, followed by impromptu protests at A and F stores across the country quickly turned the t-shirt line into cleaning rags." Indeed, the emphasis here is very much on the quickness and profusion of response via e-mail, which produces a "flood," the production of a voice in the public sphere, and the deployment of Asian American consumer capital as the primary vector for this voice. Indeed, at the end of the article, Chang ironically acknowledges this association between protest capitalism and Asian culture by exhorting his readers to "monetize that struggle, comrade!"

This characterization of online protest omits some key issues regarding the nature of both political and media activism and online identity. For one, not all protests of this kind are equally popular; the "Stop OndadeMar's Bikini Exploitation" page on the petitionsonline.com Web site only has 498 signatures, relatively few, especially when compared to the 32,000 gathered on the *Details* petition, and extremely few when compared to a petition like the "End the Hate" Paltalk initiative, which had 192,641 signatures, or even the "*Angel* Season 6" online petition campaigning for the continuation of a television show, which had 65,184. The enthusiasm for the Internet as a vehicle for social protest against anti-Asian racist imagery clearly exceeds its actual utility. So what sorts of investments and assumptions underlie the notion within the Asian American community and elsewhere that the Internet permits more and more-effective political civil rights protest?

Leaving aside momentarily the question of whether or not online petitions are efficacious,[47] Asian Americans are using the visual culture of the Internet to challenge racism in offline visual media cultures. Asian Americans use petition boards as community spaces in conflicted, rich, and ambivalent ways. Threats to the community are dealt with mostly via identitarian calls to "AZN pride," yet the formatting of the petition space itself encourages and indeed requires that these responses be read in dialogue with other comments, many of which complicate Asianness as a category and (most importantly in my first case, the *Details* magazine "Asian or Gay" image) oppose queerness to Asianness in ways that suggest limited victories for racial justice. Rampant homophobia among Asian American protesters on this site splits potential community formation and produces online texts that demand intersectional critique.

In "'Asian or Gay?' Piece in *Details* Magazine Angers AA Community," Caroline Aoyagi writes: "The national men's magazine *Details* is drawing loud criticism from the Asian American and AA gay and lesbian communities for a piece entitled 'Asian or Gay?' that is supposed to be a humorous take on social stereotypes."[48]

A photograph in the *Details* article depicts a full-frontal, full-page photograph of a young Asian man with spiky hair wearing fashionable urban gear such as sunglasses, a shoulderbag, and silver tennis shoes. Numbered arrows to the right of the image point out features such as "Dior sunglasses," "Dolce and Gabbana suede jacket," and "Louis Vuitton bag," along with others such as "ladyboy fingers" and "delicate features." These arrows are keyed to a legend at the bottom left of the image. This concatenation of bodily features and luxury fashion commodities stresses the identification of both Asian and gay men not only as hyperconsumers but also as phenotypic homologies. While the text claims that both Asian and gay men sport labels such as "Evisu jeans: $400" as well as Dior, Dolce, and Vuitton, in some cases the luxury object and its owner's body are conflated in such a way as to make them simultaneously queer and raced through the act of purchasing and wearing

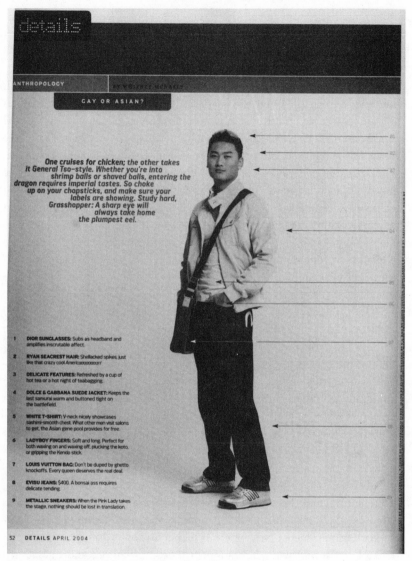

Figure 5.1. "Gay or Asian?" article in *Details* magazine.

them: Evisu jeans are explained as follows: "A bonsai ass requires delicate tending." The emphasis on the queerness and delicacy of the Asian body as configured by its patterns of consumption and style runs throughout the article; even an item as seemingly innocuous as an unbranded "white t-shirt" is indexed as follows: "V-neck nicely showcases sashimi smooth chest. What other men visit salons to get, the Asian gene pool provides for free." This emphasis on the genetic difference of the Asian man configures him as inherently queer. This Asian American man is figured within the discourse of the contemporary dandy or metrosexual at best, outright queer at worst.[49] The table of contents gives a subtitle for the article: "One orders take-out sushi, the other delivers it. Enter the gaysian." This hybrid formulation invokes differences in class and the racialization of labor, particularly in the "global cities" described by Saskia Sassen, in which Asians are visible both as ubiquitous low-skilled service workers and as privileged consumers of sartorial goods, networking services, and other informational commodities. The image thus contains both types of Asian American male bodies: those of "high-tech coolies" and low-tech coolies. This deepens the article's insistence on the perfect equivalence of gays and Asians, for it emphasizes that one, presumably the Asian, must deliver for the other to receive. Yet gay men are often also misrepresented in terms of class much as are Asian men, as privileged consumers rather than as workers or laborers. In any event, the article's figuration on Asian men as unparalleled consumers mirrors Chang's, Aoyagi's, and Chen's insistence on the Internet as a remedy to "retail racism."

As Lisa Lowe reminds us, "In conjunction with the relative absence of Chinese wives and family among immigrant 'bachelor' communities and because of the concentration of Chinese men in 'feminized' forms of work—such as laundry, restaurants, and other service-sector jobs—Chinese male immigrants could be said to occupy, before 1940, a 'feminized' position in relation to white male citizens and, after 1940, a 'masculinity' whose *racialization* is the material trace of the history of this gendering."[50] In his analysis of Asian and Asian American porn and cyberspaces, Darrell Hamamoto notes as well in his discussion of "Mr. Wong," an overtly anti-Asian and extremely popular Web-based comic strip, "A well-worn strategy for feminizing, emasculating, and thereby disempowering men of color is to cast them as homosexuals."[51] As I discussed in chapter 4, the visual culture of the Internet genders new media production in such a way as to preserve old associations of femininity with decoration, frilliness, profusion, and modularity. Modular means of digital production assume that users "shop" for digital parts to combine into a composited whole rather than building original images. As Manovich notes, this is the structure of *all* new media objects and is intrinsic to the protocols of digital media in a way that is not necessarily gendered at all. However, the feminization of consumption or "shopping" as a mode of digital self-expression is certainly well established in our culture. Images of

Asian men as "gaysians" reinforce the notion of Asian men as support staff, uninspired by new ideas and defined by consumption rather than production.

Unsurprisingly, the Asian American popular press was quick to decry the imputation of queerness to Asian American men and to speak in favor of rehabilitating the image to make it more masculine. Rather than picking up on the class bias at work here, one that is part of the "model minority" myth that images all Asians as wealthy and wired consumers, Patrick Mangto, executive director of Asian Pacific Islanders for Human Rights (APIHR), a support and advocacy group for the API LGBT community, complained that "as usual, from the mainstream community... there is the assumption that all Asian men are effeminate." In addition, "The Asian American Journalists Association (AAJA) also sent a letter to Details calling for an apology. While we can't figure out exactly what the feature is trying to say—Asian men are gay? Asian men look gay? Asian men would be better off gay?—there's no disguising the fact that it combines leering sexual innuendo and a litany of the most tired clichés about both Asian and gay culture with no goal other than to ridicule both groups."

This neologistic pairing of gay and Asian to form a new hybrid term—"gaysian"—references an older visual culture of racialization by invoking the visual culture of anthropology. The photograph and its accompanying captions uncannily mimic the structure of the "Chink or Jap?" photographs that ran in Life magazine during World War II that I discussed in chapter 2. Just as the Life photographs featured textual annotations that explained the significance of each physiognomic feature with a quasi-scientific precision, anatomizing identity in purely visual terms, so "Asian or Gay?" has arrows that interpret each "feature" on the fly. However, the dichotomy that it presents works at cross-purposes with the former; while "Chink or Jap?" argues for the visibility and interpretability of race to the trained eye, "Asian or Gay?" attempts to erase the differences and emphasize the similarities. Of course, the particular type of scientism invoked by this visual arrangement of photographic portrait or mug shot with interpretive textual annotation is quantitative anthropological measurement methods such as biometrics. And indeed, while biometrics has fallen out of favor in recent years (as evidenced by the moribund state and imminent closure of Le Musée de l'Homme in Paris, the former exhibitor of the preserved genitalia of Saartje Baartman, otherwise known as the Hottentot Venus), the discipline has reappeared as part of the technoscientific inscription of race on the visible body, as in the case of iris scanning, fingerprinting, and the use of facial recognition technology for U.S. visitors who travel via plane, and the recent call for biometric identification papers for air travel by the International Civil Aviation Organization. As noted in chapter 3, this open letter to the ICAO singles out facial recognition technology as problematic because it may be used to "reveal racial or ethnic origin." The "Gay or Asian" image deploys the visual culture of racialization to create its own brand of facial-recognition technology, one that positions its subject not only in relation to border and immigration status but also in relation to class and sexuality. Alexander Galloway writes that new networked biometric technologies—"The science of measuring the human body and deriving digital signatures from it"—are worrisome not only because of their possible infringements on privacy, but also because they have "redefined what counts as proof of the true identity of material life forms. Authenticity (identity) is once again inside the body-object, yet it appears now in sequences, samples, and scans."[52] The "true identity" of the queer or raced male subject, its outing via the visual culture of biometrics, may not overtly participate in the "digital signature" described by Galloway, but the reaction to the image that appeared on petitiononline.com literally produced digital signatures by material bodies, actual people who logged on and wrote comments. These bodies, however, lack the authenticity or presence guaranteed by biometrics and thus evade the dataveillant gaze; it is impossible to tell what race or gender or sexuality they are, a point to which I will return.

When we analyze the online response to "Gay or Asian?" we can trace the ways in which the protesting of racial and gender stereotypes, new media, technology, and Asian Americans constellate. The signatures that petitioners leave are anarchic, unorganized, and astoundingly diverse. Like the discussion boards on alllooksame.com, these often very short and truncated postings create a processual, problematized vision of Asian American identity on precisely the kind of electronic medium that one might expect would preclude it. On March 30 there were 14,589 signatures on Daniel Lee's "Asians against Ignorance" petition at petitiononline.com pushing for a boycott of Details magazine, and on April 27 it had 32,964 signatures.[53] Considering that the site's petition is quite straightforward about protesting the racism behind the "Asian or Gay?" article, the responses are themselves interestingly all over the map. However, this is itself a statement as to the multivalent uses to which the Asian American community, at least as constituted by this board in the moment of signing the petition, wishes to put this discursive space.

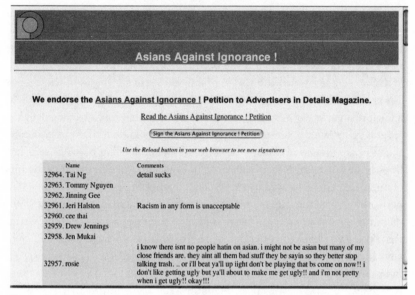

Figure 5.2. "Asians against Ignorance" from petitionsonline.com.

Signator 32,906, "Chow Yun Fat," posted simply: "My tiger crane style will defeat your dragon kungfu." This statement, which seems like a non sequitur considering that the petition he is signing has to do with media racism in *Details*, repeats and invokes popular media images of Orientals to parody and manipulate them. While this is the very offense that the Ondade Mar Buddha swimsuits (and the response from *Details* magazine) commit, in the sense that they reproduce stereotyped images of Asian Americans from popular media, this is repetition with a difference. The choice of signature also has meaning, for Chow Yun Fat is a legitimate media star, one of the few to have name recognition and (limited) box office clout in the United States. Here the anonymous signer invokes both older and contemporary Asian martial arts films, a genre that is one of the few media spaces available to Asian men that does not feminize them.

While the majority of signators decry the racism and ignorance inherent in the "Gay or Asian" story and pledge to stop buying *Details*, several did use the site against the grain, as in the case of signator 33,959, who wrote: "Of course not ALL asians dress that way, and neither do all gays. But it's a _style_ magazine and the article is pointing out the striking similarities between popular gay style and popular asian style. now get over it." This injunction to "get over it" is, ironically, exactly the message coming from both Victoria's Secret and Ondade Mar, neither of which agreed that the images were offensive or offered to alter their practices. In this case, the signator used the space of the online petition to protest the protest.

Other signators used the site to practice reverse racism, as in the case of signator 32,925, P. S. Ryu, who states baldly: "Asians have higher IQ." In addition, a variety of configurations of racism and homophobia coexisted in several posts, which due to the limited space available for free response on the site, are almost aphoristic in tone. These haiku-like postings of a few lines or less necessarily imply more than they state; like so many of the bits of microcontent generated by the Web 2.0 technologies like blogs and social networking sites, they are incomplete, poorly articulated or even inarticulate-seeming, evocative rather than denotative. Signator 33,958, "ExT," writes that "the gays should be offended by this comparison," and signator 32,868, who gives no name, writes simply, "FU_CK_THEIR_AS_S." His use of typography and underscores indicates that he realizes that a filter might catch these R-rated words and edit his post. Signator 32,867, Lee Enrile, writes, "What kind of honky ass name is 'Whitney' anyway. Sounds like he's the one whose gayer than hell." (Whitney McNally, the author of "Asian or Gay?" is in fact a woman.) In these instances, the petition revealed the homophobia of the Asian communities, failing to produce the "gaysian" subject posited by Details. For all the Internet's touted abilities to produce new forms of subjectivity, in these cases it tended to reinforce old ones.

Why were the Abercrombie and Details online petitions so much more popular and well publicized than the Ondade Mar protest? Coco Fusco writes that "serious discussion of the meaning of our desire to see race in visual representation is impeded by the difficulties we have in distinguishing between racialization as a visual process, and racism as an ethical and political dilemma."[54] In other words, visual representations of race and racism work paradoxically: they are both irresistible spectacles and social problems. Racial difference and racialized bodies are mediagenic in ways that appeal to all viewers. And since the nature of digital media is to be transcodable, instantly transmittable, and infinitely reproducible, racial imagery flows in torrents up and down the networks that many people use every day. As Fusco writes, "We like to see race even if we don't consider ourselves racist," and "The act of visualizing and looking at racial difference continues to seduce and enthrall American viewers" (23). It is possible that the Details and Abercrombie petitions were so much more popular than the Ondade Mar petition because they depicted Asian people rather than religious iconography of Buddha and thus were more "racial" and mediagenic. They satisfied the desire to consume race visually that is possessed by all people, even and perhaps particularly by Asian Americans themselves.

The viral nature of e-mail forwarding often works in this way: Asian Americans may have received mailings urging them to sign the petition, and did so partly because they were eager to see the "Asian or Gay?" article for the same reason that the magazine ran it in the first place—it is funny. And also egregious. And as Fusco writes, its irresistibility is part of the complex of investments in the proliferation of racialized imagery, not only in spite of multiculturalism, but indeed as an integral part of it. The desire to share the horror and fascination of what seems like unambivalent homophobia and racism in a mass-market publication mingles with the need for confirmation of its badness and an impulse to indulge in the pleasures of shared indignation. And since the Web is so extremely good at transmitting visual images via links in e-mail, and the petition itself includes a copy of the image, the petition space serves as a perfect venue for transmitting the image to many more people, and certainly more Asian Americans, than might have ever seen it in the first place. (The link from the petition to the image was broken as of July 15, 2004, but there are several blogs that have it up that one can find through Google, demonstrating that the Asian American blogosphere is an extremely effective vector for keeping the image alive and moving throughout cyberspace.)

A dominant theme of the signators' responses involves decrying the existence of such "ignorance" and racism in this supposedly enlightened post-multicultural culture. The surprise and outrage at this evidence of failed antiracism seem to be invoked by a sense of violated temporality—if we are "beyond racism," if history has put it to rest, surprise would be the appropriate response. This sense of temporality, of being in a "new age" that turns out to our dismay not to be so new after all, is echoed by the discourse of Internet utopianism, which also claims to be a harbinger of a new period of history, one in which important things have changed. Cybercultural studies have made claims that technology has changed the nature of the body, that databasing, gene mapping, prosthetics, and various forms of biotechnology have created a cyberbody. Biometrics is a space where racial identity, technology, and surveillance converge. The new visibility of the body as a digital signature creates apprehension because it seems first of all to be profoundly antihumanist but offers benefits in terms of our desire to visualize race. The

Internet offers enhanced opportunities not only to view race, in all its scan-
dalous deliciousness, but also to put our own bodies into play as digital
signatures.

Perhaps as a result of the petition's being anonymous, a significant number of signators felt compelled to identify their race, but almost always *only*
if they were non-Asian. Signator 34,024, "Brian," writes, "I'm not even Asian
and I think this is stupid"; and signator 34,023, "Todd Keithly," writes, "I'm
white and think this is out of line." This addresses some of the compelling
questions regarding online activism posed by Martha McCaughey and Michael
Ayers in the introduction to their collection *Cyberactivism: Online Activism
in Theory and Practice*. They claim that "the Internet allows us to interact
with others without our voices, faces, and bodies. In the absence of meat
bodies (also known as wetware among Netizens), the traversing of spatial
and temporal boundaries raises questions about what presence, essence, or
soul we think we are on the Net (Slater). The Internet thus raises new
questions about social change and how it works. For instance, where is the
body on which that traditional activism has relied?"[55] Their concern with
the free-flowing "traversing of spatial and temporal boundaries" appears to
be misplaced when read in the light of online petition responses like the
ones I list here, for these petitioners are all too aware of their racialized
bodies when responding to Asian American media protests. Concerns that
the racialized body or "meat" might itself be the basis for effective activism
cause these writers to question whether social change can occur without
"putting your body on the line," as they dramatically put it. Protests, particularly civil rights ones, have often depended on the ability to successfully visualize activism, especially when the particular offense in question is itself
visual in nature, as in the case of racism in advertising and media. In addition to seeking visibility as a cause in and of itself (some protests are less
concerned with accomplishing actual specific goals than with "getting themselves out there" and being correctly counted by the media), civil rights
protests in particular have capitalized on producing visual evidence of racial
diversity in their support base. It is thus that the presence of whites in Martin
Luther King's civil rights protests and the presence of men at pro-choice rallies attest to the ideas, as well as that a cause benefits from *visible* diversity.[56]
The presence of whiteness validates racial justice protests as "universal"
rather than as particular and invests them with legitimacy. However, as Mark
Golub points out, there is a tendency in civil rights dramas such as *Missis-
sippi Burning* to make white people the main characters in these conflicts in
such a way that belies historical accuracy; this may be perceived as the only

way to draw in white audiences. Indeed, this is partially borne out by the structure of these posts, in which declarations of whiteness precede and even eclipse critiques of "Asian or Gay?" thus making whiteness itself, and specifically the invisible but digitally asserted whiteness of the signator, the "main character" in the protest.

How do online petitions function differently from television, film, and other media in this way? Should we talk about them as media, or as political protests? Of course, we need to do both, and visual culture is the way into resolving this dilemma and debate. Political protests that feature diverse physical bodies visualize the issue at hand, such as civil or reproductive rights, as social problems at large, rather than as minoritarian concerns. This is no doubt a worthy goal. However, online petitions lack this feature; it is impossible to poll for diversity on the Internet because there are no visible bodies attached to signatures. Hence the self-identification of some signators as white serves as an attempt to bring this feature back into the space of on-line protests. These signators seem to realize that their claiming whiteness in the moment of signing the petition reinserts their bodies into the discourse in such a way as to make the petition more powerful, just as the presence of their white, heteronormative (very little discourse on the poll concerned it-self with gay or straight identity) bodies might "count" more in the context of a physical march or demonstration. This shows an impressive amount of media savvy but raises some vexing questions regarding the position of the raced body as a media product to be protested and as a vehicle of protest itself.

The default identity assumed in these petition spaces is Asian American-ness, not whiteness. In what ways has the use of information technology intertwined itself as another aspect of identity within the complex of iden-tity categories such as race, gender, sexuality, and class? How might forms of racism other than "retail racism" be challenged using what is at base an industrial media form with its own infrastructural constraints, interface and platform specificities, and flows of labor and capital? *Wired* magazine's February 2004 cover features an image of a South Asian woman in a veil with *mendhi* on her hands, which spell out the characters of a programming language. The cover story is titled "The New Face of the Silicon Age: Tech Jobs Are Fleeing to India Faster than Ever," and in tiny letters next to the dateline we see the words "help wanted."

The salient question here and in much visual representation of labor, consumption, technology, and race is precisely the one stressed in the "gaysian" tagline: who is to receive and who is to give? Who is "technologi-cal" in a threatening, protesting, queer way, and who is technological in a

Figure 5.3. *Wired* magazine cover from February 2004 depicting the threat of Asian information technology workers.

useful, helpful, and comfortably offshore way? As Robert Lee notes, Asian American women outnumber Asian American men, which may account for why the "face" of offshore labor is a female one. In addition, the use of the veil works to obscure the individuality of the face and to underscore its exoticism. This *Wired* cover images Asians as technological down to their skin, which is inscribed by strings of code and the language of machines. Instead of protesting "retail racism" using online protests, these particular Asian bodies are depicted as part of the abstract infrastructure of the Internet itself: to cite the replicant Rachael in the film *Blade Runner,* they aren't in the business, they *are* the business. The *mendhi* typography on the Indian woman's hands spells out a computer programming language, as if to stress the ways that South Asian women are naturally digital. This techno-Orientalist imagery can be seen as well in the final installment of *The Matrix* trilogy, *Matrix Revolutions,* in which software programs are embodied in a South Indian family, Rama-Kandra, his wife Kamala, and their daughter Sati. They implore Neo for their freedom, since as bonded labor they are bound to serve the Architect's purposes. The notion of Asians as technological, and intimately acquainted with, or even, in the case of *The Matrix,* intrinsic to informational technologies as products rather than users, creators of value rather than consumers, valences the ongoing racial formation of Asians in America.[57]

While the "gaysian" formulation of consuming Asian masculinity reinforces the notion of Asians as defined by retail culture, in some cases the Internet has enabled young people of color to critically intervene in particular aspects of the culture industry, such as fashion, another commodified expressive culture with its own set of politics and investments in youth culture. In April 2002, Abercrombie and Fitch, a popular mall retailer that markets its casual clothing to the high school and college set, produced a series of kitschy graphic T-shirts that depicted images of Asians with "slanty eyes [and] rice paddy straw hats" along with slogans such as "you love long time" and "Two Wongs Can Make It White." The latter slogan was paired with a satiric cartoon image of two Asian laundryworkers. The Internet response to these T-shirts was immediate. An e-mail campaign was organized both informally and formally through two Web sites. The first was initiated for the sole purpose of organizing the protest and is at http://www.boycott-af.com. The other can be found at http://www.petitiononline.com/BCAF/petition.html. Both provide an area where a user can sign a petition on the Web, as well as a link to Abercrombie and Fitch's e-mail address and a link that enables one to "send petition to a friend." Ultimately this Internet organizing resulted in several rallies in front of Abercrombie and Fitch bricks-and-mortar stores. The Organization of Chinese Americans attributes this to "angry complaints, phone calls, and e-mail campaigns [that] spread like wildfire among APA students, community members, and leaders nation-wide." The Web petition gathered over 6,500 signatures, and it is impossible to track how many Asian Americans used private e-mail to circulate this information. The T-shirts were withdrawn shortly afterward, and Abercrombie and Fitch delivered an apology to the Asian American community. Here the Internet's ability to spread information "like wildfire" provided a politicized space that allowed Asian Americans, a minority that struggles against popular images of themselves as prostitutes and laundrymen, to intervene in the commercial culture industry. Though the e-mail campaign against Abercrombie's racist T-shirts is encouraging, it should be noted that it still constructs users of color in relation to online commerce, as "angry customers." The language of boycott is still that of the dissatisfied consumer, who uses his or her clout to influence retailers' policies. In effect, this is just more of the same; business as usual ported to the Internet is only likely to reduplicate existing power relations in terms of race and racism. Rigorous scholarship into the distinctions between Internet users as consuming audiences and producers of online discourse is crucial if we are to guard against the further reduction of people of color to markets.

Thus it is crucial that future demographic studies of the Internet and race explore *production* as well. How many people of color are putting up Web sites, posting their music, images, and videos, managing and contributing to Listservs, or adding content to other textual sites? The Pew category "Using email" conflates passive e-mail activities such as reading and deleting porn spam and "tribally marketed" hypercapitalistic advertising with more active ones like writing or even forwarding politically oriented messages on racial identity issues such as Abercrombie's "Two Wongs Can Make It White" T-shirts, sending pictures of the grandkids to relatives, or distributing a family newsletter. This is why future studies of Internet usage in America must ask questions regarding people of color as *producers* of Internet content, not just consumers. Tracking the extent to which racial minorities are availing themselves of the Net's interactivity will tell us how much and in what ways they are adding to the discourse. Michelle Wright notes the significant increase in numbers of Internet users of color approvingly; she is encouraged by studies that report that Latinos and African Americans are the number one and number two slots of "fastest growing groups of Internet users."[58] She also quite rightly emphasizes the importance of moving beyond models of minorities as passive media audiences: "We need to engage with the Internet beyond Web surfing and checking e-mail."[59] It is imperative that we devise rigorous methodologies to help us understand what constitutes meaningful participation online, participation that opens and broadens the kinds of discourse that can be articulated there. It is not enough merely to be "there": the image of the online "lurker" invokes the passivity and ghostliness of those who watch from the sidelines of online life.

Epilogue
The Racio-Visual Logic of the Internet

Mark Poster argues that "visual studies . . . is best understood as part of a broader domain in the cultural study of information machines."[1] The difference between present and earlier visual regimes is that "we employ information machines to generate images . . . and to see."[2] Rather than asserting that culture at the beginning of the twenty-first century is somehow inherently more visually oriented than it has been at other times in history, he claims instead that experiences of the image are now defined by their mediation by machines. The Internet is a visual technology, a protocol for seeing that is interfaced and networked in ways that produce a particular set of *racial formations*. These formations arose in a specific historical period: the premillennial neoliberal moment, when race was disappeared from public and governmental discourse while at the same time policies regarding Internet infrastructures and access were being formed.[3]

Studies of the Internet have followed suit, in that they have emphasized the technology of image making as well as the technology of its reception but have failed to consider its racio-visual logic. The work of visual culture studies, on the other hand, as described by Nick Mirzoeff, "highlights those moments where the visual is contested, debated, and transformed as a constantly challenging place of social interaction and definition in terms of class, gendered, sexual, and racialized identities."[4] Digital game spaces and cyberspace abstract the process of body visualization by embedding the creation of digital bodies within a series of hierarchical choices, mimicking the menu structure of modern operating systems interfaces. This book seeks to rematerialize the Internet, a form of digital representation seen as being resistant to grounded forms of critique by art historians because of its insubstantial and ephemeral nature, by locating its material base in specifically embodied users and producers, its use as a communicative technology as well as a form of media, and its engagement with other offline and online popular, medical, and technological visual cultures. Veiled Muslim AIM buddies deployed in Instant Messenger are created by users who participate in a vital youth culture that coalesces around online chat. These avatars kitted out in chadors and DKNY sweaters fill a gap in the available forms of bodily representation that AIM users can find circulating in the world of avatar sharing. The tension between the representation of the veil, a sign of privacy and a controversial symbol of female subordination under Islam, and its positioning on a hyperfeminized and overtly displayed cartoon body creates a virtual body that works to negotiate the notion of the nation-state in the world of IM embodiment. Similarly, pregnant avatars used to adorn and supplement posts to women's bulletin boards are collaboratively produced artifacts of the popular culture of the Internet that address pregnant women's socially invisible bodies in the context of "scientific" and medical representation.

Nick Mirzoeff writes that visual culture critique engages with "any form of apparatus designed either to be looked at or to enhance natural vision, from oil painting to television and the Internet. Such criticism takes account of the importance of image making, the formal components of a given image, and the crucial completion of that work by its cultural reception."[5] In this book I have interrogated the ways that users of color and women have used the Internet's graphical spaces to produce images that modify and enhance existing images of bodies, families, politics, and interfaces. In addition, the dynamic and interactive nature of online communities in particular means that the issue of reception is always up front and center. Users comment vociferously on each other's visual objects of self-representation. Praise and critique are mixed with requests for technical assistance in image creation and uploading; these images work actively to help create the sense of a community that "knows" itself through images. Popular Internet entertainments like online quizzes and tests like alllooksame.com encourage an interrogation of the visuality of race online. Postmillennial science fiction films and advertising campaigns like Apple's iPod commercials and print ads are uniquely responsive to issues regarding the representation of interfaces in cinema but represent people of color as its objects rather than its subjects, in many cases. And online petitions to protest retail and media racism in the offline world use digital visual means to critique offline visual cultures.

The Internet is the world's largest and most extensive vector for still and streaming networked popular media images. Indeed, it possesses its own popular culture, which exists in parallel to, and inevitably intersects with, non-media-based cultural forms such as youth culture, car culture, consumer culture, domestic culture, activist culture, and women's culture. In this book I offer a method for use in analyzing the Internet's visual culture in relation not only to older media forms—a method that has become the standard for analyzing new media—but also to a matrix of lived cultural practices, identities, geopolitics, and postcolonial, racial, and political positions. These positions are expressed through and within other offline vectors as well; they exist within other nonmedia visual cultures.[6] Indeed, as Steve Jones's anthologies of the same name attest, we do live in a "cybersociety"; however, it is defined by its ever-more-frenetic consumption and deployment of digital images of identity by a less-experienced, radically stratified, and broad base of users as well as by the pursuit of unlimited personal freedom and mobility for a small technological elite.[7] In 1998, the year that *Cyber-Society 2.0* was published, most Americans did not yet live in a "cybersociety," but since then the Internet has become a mass visual form.

People of color and women are not as well represented in biennials, the world of zines, independent film, and other expressive forums, much less in mainstream film and media. And all told, their cultural production on the Internet is far from dominant. However, a key difference between the Internet and other media forms is the production of a visual culture expressive of racial and ethnic identity that is potentially available to a much broader group of people. We should celebrate the creative interventions of teenage Muslim girls, pregnant women, and other users who have appropriated the Internet to create visual images that represent themselves in their bodily particularities such as chadors, pregnant bellies, and ultrasound photographs. Yet this encouraging use of the Internet for nonnormative bodies to be displayed, circulated, and modified, to be made to signify racial and gender identities that exceed or resist already-existing templates, must be understood within the larger frame of early-twenty-first-century cultural politics and industrial imperatives. A sea change within the realm of cyberculture and media culture occurred in 2000. The newfound enthusiasm for a more profitable, stable, and visual Internet—Web 2.0—after the earlier disastrous Internet crash tempered utopian sentiments about the Internet's power to transform users' lives and produced new, more modestly framed notions of the self online. The precrash discourse that posed virtual reality as an alter-native to real life was replaced by one that cannily envisions identity online as a set of profiles, preferences, settings, and other protocols rather than a bona fide and understandably creepy "second self." Cautions of Internet addiction have gone by the wayside since Web 2.0, for there is relatively little affective investment in online life posited here; tales of users getting mar-ried or living their "real" lives in online social spaces have withered away, casualties of a postmillennial acculturation to a new concept of virtual com-munity that is less intensely focused on the Internet as a replacement for "real life." Users no longer speak of VR and RL because they no longer feel as closely connected to their overtly fictional identities online. They just don't identify with, or care about, their avatars as much as they once did.

Yet at the same time, people of color and women care *greatly* about how they are visualized on the Internet. They care enough to sign protests about media racism, and when they don't like what they see, they care enough to sign online petitions and perhaps even to sit down and create new some templates, new images of themselves, new databodies that talk back to the dominant. However, the tone I wish to take is cautiously optimistic and tells a story that is necessarily as much about social, economic, and technological constraint as it is about triumphant self-definition and self-determination. In a sense, the evolution of a pervasive graphical practice and culture on the Internet has come to resemble the visual culture of other media; finally there are enough producers of color and of colorful images on the Internet that one can legitimately speak of "black new media" just as one can speak of "black film," "black art," and "black theater." In a sense, however, this merely signifies a repetition of the issues that plague the study of minority discourse in *all* visual cultures. Brave young Arab American women hacking their AIM buddies in their bedrooms are a sentimentally attractive image that fits into a classic narrative of rebellion and resistance against dominant new media cultures. The issue of a basically unthreatened material base for participation, unchanged technological protocols, unchallenged economic systems—in short, the pesky problem of protest within a system that one is nonetheless employing to frame the protest—continues to haunt the study of minority new media cultures. While avatars wearing chadors and DKNY sweaters certainly look different from more mainstream images of American femininity, and in fact contain a wealth of fascinating information that scholars and fans of hybrid cultures will greatly enjoy, they contain exactly the same number of pixels, are formatted in the same file type, and occupy the same amount of space in an IM screen as do all the others. Any deviation from this strict industrial norm simply does not work within the program owing to the file protocols of Instant Messenger, protocols that are immutably exacting and resistant to modification owing to technological lock-in and are the direct result of a mature Internet economy and broad user base. Any change to this platform for communication would require the cooperation and blessing of several different media conglomerates at this point. The changes that are possible using the culture-jamming or hacking model of new media resistance and critique are necessarily constrained and limited by the form or "system" that enables them. The continuing monetization of the Internet's forms and technological apparatuses practically guarantees that this issue will remain a thorny one.

The cases that I examine in this volume exemplify the efforts of previously new and previously unexpressive groups of users who are using the Internet to actively visualize themselves despite and within these constraints, their differing races, their complicated genders, their generative and bereft bodies. Yet at the same time, they are performing this cultural work while living in a post-neoliberal age in which race "doesn't matter"; and it has become profoundly unfashionable to be one thing or another, and actively dangerous to signify race or ethnicity in the public sphere. The American judiciary system is leaning away from protecting citizens who are victimized on the basis of race; however, this trend merely reflects, rather than drives, the culture's profound disenchantment with antiracist discourse altogether. As the Yale legal scholar Kenji Yoshino writes: "Americans are already sick to death of identity politics; the courts are merely following suit."[8] While surveys of Internet usage work to reify the notion of racial groups as traditionally conceived—fast or furious, slow or tepid, as far as they are concerned every single person who can pick up a phone or boot up a computer belongs to a group called "Asian American," "African American," "Hispanic," or "white"—Web sites like alllooksame.com work to remind users that these categories are national, quasi-biological, visual, political, and above all unanchored in facticity and intensely subjective. While these usage or "penetration" surveys are vitally important objects of study by both humanists and social scientists because they are often used to inform public policy regarding education and computer access, they are only part of the story. Though Internet use by racial minorities is indeed increasing, this is not in itself reason to be optimistic about the medium's ability to enfranchise minorities in a realm of friction-free digital production and self-expression. In the true spirit of neoliberalism, being permitted to exist is not the same as equal representation. Digital visual capital is a commodity that is not freely given to all; as has always been the case with capital of any kind, it must be negotiated and at times actively seized by those to whom it would otherwise not be given.

The racio-visual logic of the graphical Internet allows race to be *seen* more than ever before, yet the conditions of its visualization are such that users of color and women from the everyday world are only now forming a nascent digital imaging practice that refuses to "cover" itself, one that exists within a matrix of practices that do. As Susan Courtney wonders: "What makes a culture, in a century marked by intense waves of racial and ethnic immigration and migration, mixing and contestation, form and sustain the belief that 'race' is something we know when we see?... We have much to learn in this regard from cinema, a medium that profoundly contributes to the ascension of the visual as a dominant location and guarantee of racial meaning in the twentieth century."[9] The development of the Internet has been such that visuality has become a form of representation widely available to users as producers only relatively recently. The paradox of digital visuality, a "feature" of the type of broadband infrastructure that we have chosen to develop, is that like cinema it can work to reinstate an understanding of race as always visible and available to the naked eye, a quality to be determined and epistemologically locked down by a viewer rather than understood as contested and contingent. As Courtney contends, the movies assert that the truth of race is a truth that can be known by looking. Yet the other side of this paradox, as my examples illustrate, is that the graphical Internet makes covering less *compulsory*. The Internet is not at all like cinema in this sense; users have the option to perform their identities in ways that are not possible elsewhere. On the Internet, users *do* as well as *are* their race; this networked racial positioning broadcasts this doing in ways that explicitly un-"cover" race. As Yoshino writes: "We see an assimilation model of civil rights formally ceding to an accommodation model.... The assimilation model protects *being* a member of a group, but not *doing* things associated with the group. Under this model, courts protect skin color but not language, chromosomes but not pregnancy, and same-sex desire but not same-sex marriage."[10] Thus is racial and gender inequity perpetuated. The social and legal compulsion to cover, or to "minimize the race-salient traits that distinguish [one] from the white mainstream," is founded on the assumption that a marked racial position is a stigma that the individual has the right and indeed the obligation to hide. And until lately, the structure of the Internet has been such that it has greatly facilitated covering; early utopians especially lauded and adored the Internet's ability to hide or anonymize race as its best and most socially valuable feature. The Internet was just as much a machine for not-seeing as it was a machine of vision, at least in terms of race and gender identity. However, the promiscuous visualization of race by new users of color and women in the postmillennial age claims the right to *do* as well as *be*. All this while myriad other social institutions such as the law, education, medicine, and the culture at large work to un-matter race, to make it cease to mean.

By examining a range of new digital production practices by creators of minority popular visual cultures on the Internet, I have hoped to give a sense of how this group of users *sees*, rather than merely how they *are seen* or represented, what they are making as well as what they are using, what they are doing as well as what they are being. The results are encouraging. However, as the popular *Matrix* sequels and other millennial science fiction films demonstrate, the massification of the Internet has not damaged the market for traditionally racialized representations of people of color as primitive and sexual if black, and machinic and inherently technological if Asian. White people are still depicted as the users that matter in these narratives that are so influential among popular audiences, especially young audiences. It is in some sense a cause for mourning that *The Matrix* films are so popular with youth of color in particular. The profound formal influence of digital visual interface styles and logics on the current language of film, especially science fiction film, reminds us that the visual culture of the Internet bears watching in several media, not just on the laptop screen.

For as Morpheus intones portentously at several points in these films, "It's all connected." The way that the Internet looks is the way that film, television, cell phones, and the ubiquitous screens that surround us look or will come to look. And who is to have root control over this converged media space, this universe of screens? The time during which the Internet could reasonably be viewed as a possible alternative space where egalitarian utopias might be constructed by plucky resistance fighters of any age or gender is long over. In its place we have a situation that is much more complicated, yet far from disheartening. The instances where users *refuse* to cover, the spaces and bodies that they claim, modify, and disseminate on the Internet, display a racio-visual logic of new media identity. This logic dictates that anyone who can take a picture can upload a file and can create visual images of race or commentaries on its visualization that stand in defiance of a neoliberal stance that tries to disappear race. In short, despite its numerous shortcomings, the Internet allows "common" users to represent their bodies and deploy these bodies in social, visual, and aesthetic transactions. This is not the case in film culture, literary culture, or art culture; indeed, the influence of the Internet on these media forms has changed them permanently, creating a new culture of shared participation and popular collaboration, one that continues to profoundly transfigure the way that media industries work.[11]

However, not all has changed. The racio-visual logic of the Internet works as a series of paradoxes. Digital systems such as facial recognition software operationalize and instrumentalize race just as the Human Genome Project tells us precisely which locations on the human gene set "contain" race. The resurgence of scientism, in particular the privileging of the biotechnological sciences, has been powerfully documented and critiqued by scholars such as Donna Haraway, Anne Fausto-Sterling, and Maria Fernandez. This high-cultural valuation of science as a way of understanding identity, behavior, and the self as social actor continues to erode humanistically based notions of the subject as socially constructed. This backlash against social constructivism continues apace in myriad spheres of life and not incidentally undermines the notion of race and gender as socially constituted forms that merit and demand active alteration and negotiation for the better. Yet at the same time, the Internet itself continually offers new opportunities that are taken up by all sorts of users for precisely these types of negotiations to occur at the visual level, a level that is deeply appealing and compelling to a broad range of people. The official public discourse prevalent in educational, political, and other knowledge-creating institutions continues to trumpet the message that we are all the same underneath the skin, triumphantly individual and self-efficacious at all times, and that if we are not, it is our own fault. Yet still, that skin continues to digitally articulate itself in its difference, perhaps for the first time in a public forum that is as yet much less regulated than other media spaces for visual representation. In defiance of public discourse that says that race doesn't exist and doesn't matter, either scientifically or practically, users continue to make avatars, Web sites, quizzes, moving image sequences, and petitions that say that it does, and it does. Despite uneven forms of access to Internet technology, there are burgeoning visual cultures of race on the Internet authored by people of color and women. These cultures flourish in the out-of-the-way spaces of the popular Internet, in the online communities for mothers, teens, disgruntled consumers, and everyday interactions. Really seeing them means looking more closely at the Internet and looking differently.

Notes

Introduction

1. Shaviro, *Connected*, 88.
2. Omi and Winant, *Racial Formation in the United States*, 151.
3. Stratton, "Cyberspace and the Globalization of Culture," 726.
4. Prashad, *Everybody Was Kung Fu Fighting*, 38.
5. Oliver, *Witnessing*, 166.
6. Robert G. Lee, *Orientals*, 160.
7. Boliek, "Powell Leaves Mixed Legacy as FCC Chair."
8. It is important to note that computers became associated with forms of liberation as a result of the work of journalists like Howard Rheingold and impresarios such as Stewart Brand of the Whole Earth Catalog, who advocated the technology as a way of defying mainstream culture. See Frederick Turner's fascinating work on this history in *From Counterculture to Cyberculture: Stewart Brand, the Whole Earth Network, and the Rise of Digital Utopianism*.
9. Omi and Winant, *Racial Formation in the United States*, 46.
10. All citations are from the *October* questionnaire.
11. Sterne's work in *The Audible Past* on digital sound emphasizes the ways that the digital exceeds the purely visual. This concern that visual studies leaves out considerations of sound is shared by Mieke Bal, who cautions in his essay "Visual Essentialism and the Object of Visual Culture" that visual culture studies needs to expand its objects of study by examining extravisual elements and their relation to visuality.
12. Cartright, "Film and the Digital in Visual Studies," 420.
13. Bolter, Grusin, and NetLibrary Inc., *Remediation*; Persson, "Cinema and Computers."

14. This is not to say that communication studies neglects the visual entirely: visual communication studies is an exciting new field that has yet to devote itself to new media. For a fine example of this new scholarship, see Finnegan, *Picturing Poverty*.

15. Gajjala, *Cyber Selves*; Mitra, "Virtual Commonality."

16. The Annenberg Digital Future report shows that time taken out of television use is put into Internet use, rather than detracting from other activities.

17. Mirzoeff, *The Visual Culture Reader*, 3.

18. Hall, "Introduction," 2.

19. Foster, *The Souls of Cyberfolk*, 6.

20. See Nakamura, *Cybertypes*.

21. Eglash, *Appropriating Technology*; Nelson, Tu, and Hines, *Technicolor*; Tal, *The Unbearable Whiteness of Being*.

22. McPherson, "Reload," 468.

23. Parks, "Satellite and Cyber Visualities."

24. Ibid., 284 (italics mine).

25. Berger, *Ways of Seeing*, 46.

26. Manovich, *The Language of New Media*, 61.

27. On the topic of stars, see Dyer and MacDonald, *Stars*; and DeAngelis, *Gay Fandom and Crossover Stardom*.

28. Winant and Omi, "Racial Formation," 124.

29. See Hargittai, "Digital Inequality"; and Hargittai, "Internet Access and Use in Context."

30. Thomas Csordas, cited in Scheper-Hughes, "The Global Traffic in Human Organs."

31. Sandoval, *Methodology of the Oppressed*, 176.

32. Stone, *The War of Desire*.

33. See scholarship on Virtual Valerie for an account of nonnetworked virtual pornography. Media convergence brought about by the Internet demonstrates the ways that this video offers the same view that television does; however, television has become more sexualized since the early nineties, while the Internet is a relatively decentralized many-to-many medium that has always distributed pornography.

34. Banet Weiser, "Consuming Race on Nickelodeon."

35. Shaviro, *Connected*, 77.

36. See Chow, *Ethics after Idealism*, for a discussion of the power of "ethnic film" to authenticate difference via visual depictions of a exotic ethnic past.

37. See Mary Beltrán's work on Jennifer Lopez's transformations across different racial identities.

38. See Johnson, *Interface Culture*; Landow, *Hypertext 2.0*; and Turkle, *Life on the Screen*.

39. Eglash, *Appropriating Technology*, vii.

40. See Wakeford, "Networking Women and Grrls"; and Squires, "Fabulous Feminist Futures."

41. Phelan, *Unmarked*.

42. Amelia Jones, *The Feminism and Visual Culture Reader*, 471.

43. Wright, "Finding a Place in Cyberspace," 53.

1. "Ramadan Is Almoast Here!"

1. Rodowick, *Reading the Figural*, 216.

2. T. L. Taylor has researched the dissatisfactions that female gamers express with the range of female avatars available to them: "Unfortunately, what I have continually found is that women in *Everquest* often struggle with the conflicting meanings around their avatars, feeling that they have to 'bracket' or ignore how they look." Because "avatars are central to both immersion and the construction of community in virtual spaces . . . they are mediators between personal identity and social life," and thus the narrow range of female body types available to players constricts the variety of materials that they have to "work with" in MMORPGs (massively multiplayer online role-playing games). Taylor, "Multiple Pleasures," 35.

3. Bolter, Grusin, and NetLibrary Inc., *Remediation*, 262.

4. Persson, "Cinema and Computers," 51.

5. Most popular Instant Messenger software, like AOL Instant Messenger (AIM), MSN Messenger, and Yahoo! Messenger, allows and encourages users to customize their screen windows with buddy icons. I use the term "AIM buddy" as it is used colloquially, to signify buddy icons used by all IM software applications, not just America Online.

6. See chapter 2 of Nakamura, *Cybertypes*; and Kendall, *Hanging Out in the Virtual Pub*.

7. Davé, "Apu's Brown Voice."

8. While many gaming consoles, such as Xbox online, support networked games over TCP/IP, several of the blockbuster games that generate most of the industry's profits—for example, *Grand Theft Auto*—are still either stand-alone or multiplayer, requiring players to occupy the same physical space. Computer games are more commonly networked, but almost all require membership fees: there.com and secondlife .com are notable exceptions in that they offer free trial periods. In addition, MMORPGs such as *Everquest* and *World of Warcraft* tend to structure gameplay around accomplishing missions and engaging in battle rather than around unstructured socializing and interpersonal communication, unlike IM.

9. For a fascinating scholarly account of ASCII art, see Danet, *Cyberpl@y*.

10. Rehak, "Playing at Being."

11. Silver, "Shop Online," 265. In this chapter Silver provides other useful pieces of information taken from the Pew "Teenage Life Online" 2001 report that confirm the popularity of IM among young people while noting the differences between genders when it comes to use: though both girls and boys are heavy users, "78% of girls online reported using IM compared with 71% of boys who did so. In addition to using IM more than do boys, girls send or receive e-mail more than do boys, with 95% of girls reporting such use compared with 89% of boys" (159).

12. Gans, *Popular Culture and High Culture*.

13. Hall, "Introduction: Who Needs 'Identity'?" 2.

14. Ibid.

15. Crenshaw, "Mapping the Margins."

16. See in particular Alexander R. Galloway's excellent *Gaming: Essays on Algorithmic Culture*.

17. A QuickTime file of the eBay "Clocks" advertisement can be found at "Duncan's TV Ad Land," http://www.duncans.tv/2005/ebay-clocks, along with a commentary by Duncan McLeod.

18. Probot Productions, the creators of this Alien series, has continued to make films using this method, and I thank them for sharing their work with me so generously.

19. Filiciak, "Hyperidentities," 91.

20. Manovich, The Language of New Media, 128.

21. See Barthes, Music/Image/Text; and Foucault, "What Is an Author?"

22. Manovich, The Language of New Media, 30.

23. For examples of this scholarship, see Bolter, Grusin, and NetLibrary Inc., Remediation; and Darley, Visual Digital Culture.

24. Persson, "Cinema and Computers."

25. Ibid., 42.

26. Rebecca Solnit notes the historical connections forged between two of California's biggest industries—computers and motion pictures—by Muybridge's motion studies, which were commissioned by Leland Stanford, founder of Stanford University, a major site of technological innovation in the realm of information systems. "Hollywood and Silicon Valley became, long after these men died, the two industries California is most identified with, the two that changed the world. They changed it, are changing it, from a world of places and materials to a world of representations and imagination, a world of vastly greater reach and less solid grounding." Solnit, River of Shadows, 6.

27. For another example of a technologically mediated type of viewing of the female body in digital culture, see the essays in Flanagan and Booth, Reload, on the Visible Woman. The Visible Woman project produced cross sections of a cryogenically prepared female body for viewing and insertion in a database.

28. Mary Flanagan, "The Bride Stripped Bare," 170.

29. Barthes, Mythologies, 84.

30. Barthes, S/Z, 113–14.

31. Persson, "Cinema and Computers," 41.

32. Stewart, On Longing, 48.

33. See Sterne, "Digital Media and Disciplinarity"; and Silver, Critical Cyberculture Studies. In particular see Nakamura, "Cultural Difference, Theory, and Cyberculture Studies."

2. Alllooksame? Mediating Visual Cultures of Race on the Web

1. See http://cogsci.ucsd.edu/~asaygin/tt/ttest.html for a Web site that details the history of the Turing Test. See also Hofstadter and Dennett, The Mind's I. See as well Stephenson, Cryptonomicon, for a fictionalized but extremely detailed and thoughtful treatment of the role of encryption in the development of modern computing culture and surveillant societies.

2. Codetalkers served in both Korea and Vietnam, and their contributions were evaluated by Major Howard Conner, signal officer of the Fifth Marine Division, as follows: "Were it not for the Navajo code talkers, the Marines never would have taken Iwo Jima." Quoted in Aaseng, Navajo Code Talkers, 99.

3. Cruz, "From Farce to Tragedy," 26.

4. Ibid., 27.

5. Omi, "Racialization in the Post–Civil Rights Era."

6. Robert G. Lee, *Orientals*, 217.

7. Omi, "Racialization in the Post–Civil Rights Era."

8. This depiction of cyberspace as a world of brightly colored, often geometric icon-images was very common in films of the 1990s that depicted navigation from computer networks. *Hackers*, *The Lawnmower Man*, and *Johnny Mnemonic* represent Internet use as a form of three-dimensional flight simulation through abstracted polygonal visual icons, a mode of interface use that resonates far more with video games than with actual computer use or programming today. The problem of representing a fundamentally immobile and reflective or cerebral activity in a visually striking and telegenic fashion has dogged cinematic treatments of cyberspace: the more recent *Swordfish* attempted to address this problem by depicting a computer hacker emoting violently while viewing several computer screens at once, a rare situation for actual computer professionals.

9. Gibson, *Neuromancer*, 170.

10. Ibid., 88.

11. Gibson's *Pattern Recognition* (2003), a novel written almost twenty years after *Neuromancer*, amplifies the notion of networked societies as defined by postliteracy by focusing on the centrality of corporate logos and moving images, or "footage," as information commodities in the near-future world. The emphasis is far less on computers as posthuman entities and far more on the notion of nontextual human vision as constituting a new type of capital and commodity: the novel's protagonist Cayce, a play on the name of Gibson's original protagonist in *Neuromancer*, makes her living "coolhunting" or identifying successful products and logos, and her obsession with locating the creators of a set of streaming video files propels the plot. See as well Jameson, "Fear and Loathing in Globalization," for a discussion of the ways that *Pattern Recognition*'s focus on what he dubs "postmodern nominalism," or a central interest in style, taste, and the importance of branding or naming, creates "global cyberpunk," in which "eBay is certainly the right word for our current collective unconscious" (108).

12. Michaels, *Bad Aboriginal Art*, 82.

13. See Warschauer, "Language, Identity, and the Internet."

14. The Chiapas Web site at http://chiapas.indymedia.org is a good example of this.

15. See Darrell Y. Hamamoto, "White and Wong," for a discussion of "Mr. Wong," a comedic site that engages in ruthless racial stereotyping.

16. Bird, *The Audience in Everyday Life*, 16.

17. On August 24, 2001, "Oaken Din" writes: "I am a Chinese guy living in the Los Angeles area. I see Chinese ppl all the time. I'll see Koreans and Japanese ppl here and there when I am out and about in the LA area. There are a lot of Vietnamese, Indonesian, Mongolian, etc. that I bump into. When it comes to telling them apart, I seem to get it right for the most part between Chinese, Korean, and Japanese. But I scored measurably on your test. I got a four. That tells me how much I know. I suck and am forever changed. Thnx for the eye opener."

18. Original spelling, grammar, and formatting are reproduced from the original post as faithfully as possible.

19. In an article titled "Testing Out My A-Dar," Harry Mok remarks that when he first started the test, he thought, "This was going to be easy. No problem, I'm Chinese. I can spot Chinese people a mile away. I have the Asian sixth sense, an A-dar." After remarking that he failed miserably, he includes Suematsu's comment that "a lot of time just to be polite or politically correct, people go to a difficult long way to find out (what ethnicity or race you are)," Suematsu said. "It's almost like a whether-you're-gay-or-straight kind of thing."

20. Ang, On Not Speaking Chinese, 54.

21. Ibid., 69.

22. Robert G. Lee, Orientals, 147.

23. Ibid., 148.

24. See Palumbo-Liu's discussion in Asian/American of the face as a privileged signifier of Asian identity, in which he writes that the Asian "face is elaborated as the site of racial negotiations and the transformation of racial identity," and that "it is this 'face,' then, not (only) in its phenotypology but (also) in animation, that demarcates essential differences between groups" (87–88).

25. Robert G. Lee, Orientals, 148.

26. See the film Europa, Europa for a comic critique of this same theme of phenotypic racial identification in terms of German visual cultures of identity regarding Jews.

27. Nam, Yell-Oh Girls, 143.

28. Cheng, Inauthentic, 147.

29. Chuh, Imagine Otherwise, 13. Cheng agrees with this, claiming that "what we call 'Asian American' identity is a category that could be more fruitfully thought of, in functional terms, as a 'mixed' racial or ethnic category" (Inauthentic, 125).

30. Chuh, Imagine Otherwise, 145.

31. Spooner, Asian-Americans and the Internet.

32. See Everett, "Click This," as well as past programs and mission statements from the Afro-Geeks conference, http://omni.ucsb.edu/cbs/projects/05agcfp.html (accessed July 2005).

33. See http://eugene.whong.org/hapatest.htm (accessed July 2005).

34. Ginsburg, "Screen Memories and Entangled Technologies," 79.

35. Sardar, "Alt.civilizations.faq."

36. Michaels, Bad Aboriginal Art, 42.

37. Sarai makes all its excellent publications and readers available on the Internet under creative commons licenses. See http://www.sarai.net. This Web site also contains bulletin boards such as the "Cybermohalla," a discussion site designed to mimic a dense urban space such as that hosting the collective itself, as well as outstanding new media criticism by a range of artists, activists, and scholars from a global perspective.

38. Quoted in Lovink, Dark Fiber, 212.

39. Ngugi, Moving the Centre, 30.

40. Ibid., 31.

41. Gloria Anzaldúa tells a similar story that identifies academic institutions as

places where minority cultures and bodies are subjugated by enforced use of the imperial tongue, that is, English. Her chapter is titled "How to Tame a Wild Tongue," in Borderlands/La Frontera. Indeed, American minority narratives having to do with "foreign" language use being punished in institutional contexts are often framed in terms of trauma to bodies and to cultural identities. For additional examples, see Maxine Hong Kingston, The Woman Warrior; and Richard Rodriguez, Hunger of Memory.

42. See Lockard, "Resisting Cyber-English," for a discussion of the ways that linguistic imperialism contributes to widening "digital divides." Lockard writes: "English monopolization cuts deeply into the Internet's potential for social empowerment, as a linguistic prior condition for access ensures that Anglophone technology controls the contents of subaltern mouths. Ngugi argues that 'a specific culture is not transmitted through language in its universality but in its particularity as the language of a specific community with a specific history.' Cyber-English acts as a cultural filter from this perspective, a filter that sifts out cultural particularisms and standardizes expressive experience" (n.p.).

43. Rushdie, "Damme," 50.

44. Ibid., 54.

45. Ibid., 56.

46. In "The New Empire within Britain," Rushdie does discuss racism as a central problem characteristic of Britain's postcolonial period; he calls it "a crisis of the whole culture, of the society's entire sense of itself." See Rushdie, Imaginary Homelands, 129. In his introduction to that collection, he remarks how he was "accused by both Geoffrey Howe and Norman Tebbit of having equated Britain with Nazi Germany" when they first read the piece, while no other negative response seems to have come from any of the others (5). It seems that Rushdie's position as a public intellectual in Great Britain is much more secure when he leaves the discussion of race and racism out of the picture.

47. This debate is not a productive one, yet its persistence is truly remarkable. It has been mirrored in several disciplines, including women's studies. In addition, if we equate language purity with cultural purity, if cultural authenticity and identity reside in the written as well as spoken language, there are already large numbers of people who are missing a vital component of their culture: the poor. This analog divide is a significant factor that was often neglected in early digital-divide rhetoric. Literacy in a "native" language and cultural authenticity are thus conflated, which is somewhat ironic considering the valorization of "primitive" preliterate peoples as somehow the most pure and authentic (though the most underprivileged) of all.

48. Ginsburg, "Screen Memories and Entangled Technologies," 78.

49. Ibid.

50. Jenkins, "Quentin Tarantino's Star Wars."

51. Michaels, Bad Aboriginal Art, 81.

3. The Social Optics of Race and Networked Interfaces in The Matrix Trilogy and Minority Report

1. Thacker, Biomedia, 8.

2. Patricia J. Williams, The Rooster's Egg, 232.

3. Haraway, Modest_Witness, 259. For another excellent reading of SimEve vis-à-vis the alterations that digital imaging has wrought on concepts of visualizing race, see Hammonds, "New Technologies of Race."

4. Haraway, Modest_Witness, 219.

5. See McPherson, "I'll Take My Stand in Dixie-Net," for an outstanding exception.

6. Dyer, White, 9.

7. Ibid., 80.

8. Pisters, The Matrix of Visual Culture, 11.

9. This could be seen as a commentary on the political economy of the Internet. While the networking technology companies that drove the 1990s boom seemed to identify themselves with youth rather than age, in the end that identification was discarded as part of the backlash against utopian cyberculture; while its engineers and programmers may have been young in the early nineties, its captains of industry are no longer distinguished in that way. David Silver's work on "Theglobe.com" is a good example of this.

10. See Nelson, "Introduction: Future Texts," for an excellent description of Afro-futurism.

11. Ebert, "The Matrix Reloaded."

12. Scott, "The Matrix: Revolutions."

13. See Flanagan, "Mobile Identities," for a further discussion. See also the film Simone (2002) for a vivid example of a "synthespian."

14. Shaviro, Connected, 13.

15. Dyer, White, 10.

16. Manovich, The Language of New Media, 49.

17. See Bahng, "Queering the Matrix." Bahng writes that the "final fight scene culminates in Neo and Smith becoming one, in a moment that focuses in on an intimate exchange of internal processes. Neo does not explode Smith as he did at the end of the first Matrix. Instead, he learns Smith's power of viral replication, which has served as a foil to heteronormative reproduction throughout the entire film" (n.p.).

18. Baudrillard, Simulacra and Simulation, 1.

19. West, Race Matters, 38.

20. Ibid., 39.

21. Kuhn, "Introduction: Cultural Theory and Science Fiction Cinema," 10.

22. See Chun's discussion of interfaces and race in Control and Freedom.

23. Haraway, Simians, Cyborgs, and Women, 174.

24. Ibid.

25. Fusco and Wallis, Only Skin Deep, 16.

26. Gilman, "Black Bodies, White Bodies," 224.

27. Ibid., 228.

28. See Parrenas, Servants of Globalization, on the racialized and gendered division of labor in late capitalism.

29. Dyer, White, 80.

30. The Apple iPod advertisements were created by Chiat/Day. The photoshop-support.com Web site features a tutorial that instructs users how to use the application

to create their own iPod-style images. The article, titled "I See Ipod People: The Photoshop Silhouette," explains that "if you're crazy about those ipod ads and want to make one yourself, it's actually pretty easy." See http://www.photoshopsupport .com/tutorials/jennifer/ipod.html.

31. Manovich, *The Language of New Media*, 77.

32. Springer, "Playing It Cool in the Matrix," 91; Alexander, "Cool like Me," 49.

33. Stross, "After 20 Years, Finally Capitalizing on Cool." See also Liu, *The Laws of Cool*, on the intimate association of "cool" with digital networked technologies: "Cool is (and is not) an ethos, style, feeling and politics of information" (179).

34. I wish to thank the artist for permission to reprint "iPod Ghraib," which he has described as "Internet based." See Trek Thunder Kelly's Web site at http://www.trekkelly.com/garage/ipod-ghraib/ for this and other examples of digitally created images from his "Super-Pop" series. His "rebrands," "crossbrands," "real art," and "celebrity rebrands" superimpose corporate iconography from brands such as Prada and Calvin Klein on photographic and painted images of Sitting Bull and Frida Kahlo, blending the languages of modern advertising and art. The "iPod Ghraib" images are one of a series of "rebrands" along with "Target© Iraq," "Microsoft Soup," and "Xerox Windex." The artist's Web site explains: "*Re-branding* substitutes familiar brands in an effort to expose their embedded meanings by bringing them out of context."

35. Sontag, "Regarding the Torture of Others."

36. See Shaviro, *Connected*, and Pisters, *The Matrix of Visual Culture*, for examples of this type of critique.

37. Gilroy, *Against Race*, 23.

38. Ansen, "Murder on the Spielberg Express."

39. Elmer, *Profiling Machines*, 73 (italics mine).

40. See Matrix, *Cyberpop*, for an incisive reading on the ways in which *Gattaca* comments on racial identity in relation to biometrics, passing, and genetic engineering.

41. Mark Williams, "Closely Belated?"

42. Oliver, *Witnessing*, 151.

43. Palumbo-Liu, *Asian/American*, 93.

44. Gilroy, *Against Race*, 19.

45. Scheper-Hughes, "The Global Traffic in Human Organs," 193. Fears that traffic in human organs will reflect geopolitical power imbalances and perpetuate racism have been evident in literature such as the work of the Ghanaian novelist and theorist Ama Ata Aidoo since the 1970s. In *Our Sister Killjoy*, Aidoo confronts techno-utopians by writing: "Anyway, the Christian Doctor has himself said that in his glorious country, niggerhearts are so easy to come by. . . . Yet she had to confess she still had not managed to come round to seeing Kunle's point: that cleaning the Baas's chest of its rotten heart and plugging in a brand-new, palpitatingly warm kaffirheart, is the surest way to usher in the Kaffirmillennium" (100–101).

46. See Sassen, *Globalization and Its Discontents*.

47. Castells, *End of Millennium*, 68.

48. Ibid.

49. Wood, "The Metaphysical Fabric That Binds Us," 11.

50. Foster, "The Transparency of the Interface," 70.

51. Gunning, "Tracing the Individual Body," 29.

52. Wood, "The Metaphysical Fabric That Binds Us," 9.

53. Silverman, "Back to the Future," 111.

54. Advanced reproductive technology (ART), in vitro fertilization (IVF), and the Human Genome Project (HGP). The pencil test and the paper bag test both employ everyday household objects to classify people based on phenotype. In the American South, an African American with a skin tone lighter than a brown paper grocery bag was considered "light" enough to participate in privileged social groups and activities, and in South Africa, the admixture of "black blood" was judged partially by whether a person's hair would cling to a pencil if wound around it or would spring away from it. Haraway is seldom cited as a critic on the topic of race despite her long-standing and very public discussion of such matters in the "The Cyborg Manifesto," a foundational text for cyberculture studies, and in Modest_Witness, which contains a whole chapter on race and technoscience. Conversely, Gilroy is rarely noted as a commentator on cyberculture and network society despite his intense interest in it as a driving force behind the crisis in raciology.

55. Chinn, Technology and the Logic of American Racism, 90.

56. Ibid., 146.

57. Hosein, "An Open Letter to the ICAO."

58. Lowe, Immigrant Acts. I am grateful to Grace Hong for this insight.

59. Eglash, "Race, Sex, and Nerds," 57.

60. Cited in Chinn, Technology and the Logic of American Racism, 134.

61. Anderson, Imagined Communities, 13.

62. See Manovich, The Language of New Media, 46; and also see Manovich, "Image after The Matrix," for a longer discussion of the ways that digital film production, as exemplified by techniques used in the Matrix films, is built on a radically different "base" from analog film; while its "surface" appears photographic in the same way that viewers are used to, the structure of the image itself is coded and informationally formatted for optimal modularity and compositing, rather than being all of a piece or continuous like an analog image.

63. Oliver, Witnessing, 153.

4. Avatars and the Visual Culture of Reproduction on the Web

1. "The Silence," aired July 18, 2005.

2. There is an actual Web site called "maternitytoday.com" (accessed July 2005), but it looks nothing like the site featured on Six Feet Under, whose producers created a fictitious home page just for this scene. In an ironic twist, the real maternitytoday.com focuses on publicizing "maternity homes" for young girls and women who wish to bear children but are unable to keep them. The site also features ads by NARAL, exhorting women to "protect choice: don't let Bush replace O'Connor with an anti-choice Justice," as well as advertisements for $1 "pro life wristbands" and an offer of a $250 grocery card in exchange for taking a "women's rights survey" administered by www.consumerrewards.com. The creation of fictional Web sites for use in feature films is becoming increasingly common, as I discuss in the introduction to this book, both as a means of circumventing copyright problems and as a way

to legitimate the "realness" of the narrative. The Internet has become an increasingly ubiquitous aspect of everyday life, partly due to wireless home networking and laptop computers, both technologies that Brenda is shown using in this scene, and devoting screen time to the Web sites that people use within the diegesis helps to guarantee its sense of realness.

3. Georges and Mitchell, "Baby Talk," 184.

4. Ibid.

5. See Koerber, "Postmodernism, Resistance, and Cyberspace," for an exceptional empirical analysis of feminist mothering Web sites that are part of the "Feminist Mothers and AlternaMomsUnite! Webrings." Koerber notes: "A recurring theme in all the sites I examined is the idea that parents know better than experts how to raise their children. Notably absent from all these Web sites in the kind of impossible-to-live-up-to advice that feminist scholars have critiqued in mainstream parenting advice literature" (229). She concludes that cyberspace does indeed offer a way for mothers to combat prevailing cultural norms about "parenting" but limits her analysis to textual postings made by women and does not discuss the visual culture of these sites.

6. See Cartright, "Film and the Digital in Visual Studies," for an insightful analysis of the way that endoscopy, like ultrasound, goes "beyond the visual to include other sensory registers" (429). Virtual endoscopy, a tool that enables doctors in training to practice surgical procedures on virtual models of human organs, engenders a "new sort of gaze, a relationship with the visual representation that propels the viewing subject into the realm of full sensory experience, and full bodily perception, but with his sense disintegrated and misrouted" (431). Ultrasound as well provides a compromised and partial experience of the body, the main difference being that almost all fetal ultrasounds that are viewed depict either the viewer's or a close friend's own fetus rather than a generic or anonymous model, thus creating different stakes in the act of viewing.

7. Phelan, *Unmarked*, 133.

8. Rodowick, *Reading the Figural*, 212.

9. Nakamura, *Cybertypes*. See chapter 2 for an extended discussion of cross-racial passing in LambdaMOO and the dynamic of identity tourism.

10. Foster, *The Souls of Cyberfolk*, 6.

11. The name of this Web site has been changed to protect the privacy of its members.

12. Brenda Danet writes that "no full-fledged, systematic history of [ASCII art] exists in print" partly because of its ephemeral nature. Her chapter titled "ASCII Art and Its Antecedents" traces the history of "text-based art—pictures or visual images created with letters, numbers, and other typographic symbols on the computer keyboard" as a category of computer play. In chapter 2, she discusses the use of signature files as spaces for play, particularly among people whose professional identities are not at stake when writing or receiving e-mail. See Danet, *Cyberpl@y*, 195.

13. Flanagan, "Mobile Identities, Digital Stars, and Post Cinematic Selves."

14. Flanagan, "The Bride Stripped Bare," 154.

15. Gans, *Popular Culture and High Culture*, 95.

16. Weil, "The Modernist Nursery?" 75.

17. Rob Walker, "Sophisticated Baby," 20.

18. Sparke, *As Long As It's Pink,* 74.

19. See Bowlby, *Carried Away* and *Just Looking.*

20. John A. Walker, "Hyperreality Hobbying."

21. Kapsalis, "Making Babies the American Girl Way," 224.

22. See websitesthatsuck.com for some of the principles of "good" Web site design.

23. Star, "From Hestia to Homepage," 638.

24. Gans, *Popular Culture and High Culture,* 146.

25. Pinney and Peterson, *Photography's Other Histories,* 219.

26. Images used in this chapter have had identifying details removed to protect the privacy of the poster.

27. Sprague, "Yoruba Photography," 252.

28. See http://www.freewebs.com/prettyprinsess and http://www.over-the-moon.org/dollz for some examples of popular avatar construction sites, the first of which caters explicitly to users wanting to creating pregnant avatars. These sites assume a female user; some feature only female "dollz," are notably hospitable to amateurs, and usually assume no prior knowledge of computer graphics, in contrast to the tone evident in many software-oriented sites that cater primarily to men. As Don Slater notes in "Domestic Photography and Digital Culture," this characteristically technologically oriented gendering obtains as well in the photographic industry, which has marketed cameras to women based on "ease of use" and marketed darkroom equipment and high-end cameras to men based on their superior performance. Many of the creators of these dolls request that permission be given before download, and that credit be given in a byline before the user displays an image on the Web. Thus this "gift economy" of avatars comes with some caveats that imply ownership.

29. Quoted in Squires, "Fabulous Feminist Futures," 365.

30. Wakeford, "Networking Women," 356.

31. Stabile, *Feminism and the Technological Fix,* 84.

32. Ibid.

33. See Doyle and O'Riordan, "Virtually Visibile," for further discussion of d'Agoty.

34. Cartright, *Screening the Body,* 30.

35. Ibid.

36. Mirzoeff, *The Visual Culture Reader,* 18.

37. Haraway, "The Persistence of Vision," 677.

38. Hansen, *New Philosophy for New Media.* See as well Manovich, *The Language of New Media,* for an account of the "dynamic screen."

39. Burnett and Marshall, *Web Theory,* 18.

40. Phelan, *Unmarked,* 133.

41. Currier, "Assembling Bodies in Cyberspace," 552.

42. See Doyle, *Wetwares.*

43. New media criticism by Jennifer Gonzalez and Doyle and O'Riordan has showcased the site as an example of these possibilities. See Gonzalez, "The Appended Subject"; and Doyle and O'Riordan, "Virtually Visible."

44. Mirzoeff, *The Visual Culture Reader,* 6.

45. Farred, *What's My Name?,* 7.

46. Cartright, "Film and the Digital in Visual Studies," 424.
47. Druckrey, *Ars Electronica*; and Hansen, *New Philosophy for New Media*.
48. Cartright, "Film and the Digital in Visual Studies," 424.
49. Manovich, *The Language of New Media*.
50. Currier, "Assembling Bodies in Cyberspace," 526.
51. Slater, "Domestic Photography and Digital Culture," 145.
52. Ibid., 134.
53. Nakamura, *Cybertypes*, 131.
54. Elkins, *Pictures of the Body*, 276.
55. Ibid., 277.
56. See Lesy and Van Schaick, *Wisconsin Death Trip*.
57. Ibid., n.p.
58. Sontag, *Regarding the Pain of Others*, 24.
59. Rodowick, *Reading the Figural*, 221.
60. Mirzoeff, "Invisible Empire."
61. Cited in Rodowick, *Reading the Figural*, 212.
62. Ibid., 217.
63. Johnson, *Interface Culture*, 148. For an insightful discussion of the connections between contemporary cooking Web sites like epicurious.com and the ways that they intersect with this history of gender and early computing, see Brown, "Cooking and Computers."
64. And no images at all of children or babies in most cases: fantasy games like *Everquest* and *Ultima Online* are adult-only. *The Sims*, an extremely popular digital game that simulates domestic activities like cleaning, taking out the trash, and working, is a notable exception in that it encourages players to build families. It is also exceptional in that at least half its users are women.
65. Rodowick, *Reading the Figural*, 216.

5. Measuring Race on the Internet

1. Rodowick, *Reading the Figural*, 215.
2. Chun, *Control and Freedom*; Lee and Wong, *Asian America.net*; Palumbo-Liu, *Asian/American*; Nakamura, *Cybertypes*.
3. Robert G. Lee, *Orientals*, 189.
4. U.S. Census, "Census 2000 Sf3 Sample Data, Table Pct63d."
5. See Hamamoto, "White and Wong."
6. See the extensive literature on the topic of racial stereotyping and media, particularly television, such as Gray, *Watching "Race"*; Hamamoto, *Monitored Peril*; Morrison, *Playing in the Dark*; Noriega, *Shot in America*; and Torres, *Living Color*.
7. McChesney, Wood, and Foster, *Capitalism and the Information Age*, 24.
8. Gans, *Popular Culture*, 207.
9. Beacham, quoted in McChesney, Wood, and Foster, *Capitalism and the Information Age*, 24.
10. Spooner and Rainie, *African-Americans and the Internet*.
11. Spooner and Rainie, *Hispanics and the Internet*.
12. Castells, *The Rise of the Network Society*, 374.

13. Alkalimat represents an entirely different perspective. He is the founder and promoter of "eBlack," described as the technological successor to black studies. See Alkalimat, "Eblack: A 21st Century Challenge." Its manifesto states that "eBlack, the virtualization of the Black experience, is the basis for the next stage of our academic discipline," and that "eBlack depends upon everyone having access to and becoming active users of cybertechology." But Alkalimat is not at all interested in black expressive culture on the Internet although this is how most people of color online are using it. He affirms that the Internet must be used for educational purposes and that education is where the Internet's value lies. In this way he is a classic digital dividist, meaning that he has an unreflectively positive opinion of the Internet's "educational" value to people of color.

14. Hester-Williams, "The Reification of Race in Cyberspace."

15. Ang, *Living Room Wars*, 12.

16. For more writing on the impossibility of defining media audiences, see Bird, *The Audience in Everyday Life*; and Ang, *Living Room Wars*.

17. Ang, *Living Room Wars*, 8.

18. See Bolter, Grusin, and NetLibrary Inc., *Remediation*.

19. Hoffman and Novak, "Bridging the Racial Divide on the Internet."

20. Robert G. Lee, *Orientals*, 189.

21. Chun, *Control and Freedom*.

22. Nakamura, *Cybertypes*, 9.

23. Lee and Wong, *Asian America.net*, ix.

24. Ibid., xvi.

25. See Silver, "Looking Backwards, Looking Forwards," for his formulation of the three stages of Internet scholarship. He describes these as "popular cyberculture," characterized by a journalist bent and utopian tone, "cyberculture studies," and "critical cyberculture studies." Barlow's proclamation belongs to the first group.

26. Spooner and Rainie, *Hispanics and the Internet*.

27. Spooner, *Asian-Americans and the Internet*.

28. Spooner and Rainie, *African-Americans and the Internet*.

29. Lee and Wong, *Asian America.net*, xiv.

30. The "Young and the Connected" report states in footnote 2 that "the figures for whites, African-Americans, and Hispanics come from our survey work in August and September 2001. However, we did not have enough Asian-Americans in those samples to draw statistically significant conclusions." In some cases there were fewer than a hundred respondents for some questions about Internet use, casting doubt on the validity of these findings.

31. See Warschauer, "Reconceptualizing the Digital Divide," which argues that "the concept provides a poor framework for either analysis or policy, and suggests an alternate concept of technology for social inclusion." See as well Warschauer, *Technology and Social Inclusion*.

32. Nelson, "Introduction: Future Texts," 5.

33. Spooner and Rainie, *Hispanics and the Internet*.

34. Spooner, *Asian-Americans and the Internet*.

35. This needs to be more fully addressed in cyberculture scholarship. See McLaine, "Ethnic Online Communities."

36. See Mark Poster, *What's the Matter with the Internet,* for a nuanced critical-theory approach that identifies and analyzes sites of resistance on the Internet.

37. Gray, *Watching "Race,"* 151.

38. Kelley, *Yo Mama's Disfunktional,* 46.

39. See *Giant Robot,* an Asian American youth zine with a national circulation, as well as its spin-off Web site, giantrobot.com, for an example of a nascent Asian American youth movement expressed in print media. *Giant Robot,* which is based in Los Angeles' Japantown, is a pan-Asian group that has also opened a restaurant and a retail store. Its founders Eric Nakamura and Martin Wong often give presentations at universities about the independent media movement.

40. Tu, "Good Politics, Great Porn," 274.

41. Ibid., 277.

42. Nakamura, *Cybertypes,* 133.

43. See Robert G. Lee, *Orientals,* and Palumbo-Liu, *Asian/American,* on the model minority myth and how the often-false characterization of Asian Americans as non-political has served to cement their status as at least partially assimilable.

44. See McLaine, "Ethnic Online Communities."

45. Aoyagi, "Buddhists Decry Use of Bodhisattva Images on Swimwear."

46. Chang, in Jenkins et al., *Ego Trip's Big Book of Racism,* 216.

47. *Cyberactivism* is inconclusive on this point but does suggest that online petitions are important sites of study for social researchers.

48. Aoyagi, "Asian or Gay?"

49. This issue's cover features a photograph of a young man wearing a fur coat, jewelry, and leather pants, next to the caption "Nick Lachey: American's Number One Husband Bares It All." The magazine's flirtation with gay style is always delicately balanced with its heteronormativity: to be a "husband" is definitively to be heterosexual, yet to be cast as the adjunct to a more powerful woman, in this case Lachey's then-wife Jessica Simpson, an "A list" media celebrity in contrast to Lachey's "B list" status, is emasculating if not outright queer.

50. Lowe, *Immigrant Acts,* 11–12.

51. Hamamoto, "White and Wong," 256.

52. Galloway, *Protocol,* 113.

53. See http://www.petitiononline.com/details4/petition.html (accessed July 14, 2004).

54. Fusco and Wallis, *Only Skin Deep,* 23.

55. McCaughey and Ayers, *Cyberactivism,* 5.

56. See Golub, "History Died for Our Sins," on the uses of whiteness in the context of civil rights docudramas of the nineties.

57. In *Monitored Peril,* Hamamoto notes that Asians with advanced computer skills have functioned in this country as "intellectual coolie labor": "The advanced technical skills immigrants bring to the imperial core society are vital to the dynamism of postindustrial capitalism, yet once in the United States they run headfirst into the history of anti-Asian racism" (249).

58. Wright, "Finding a Place in Cyberspace," 49.

59. Ibid., 57. Thomas and Wyatt support and expand on this claim in their article "Access Is Not the Only Problem."

Epilogue

1. Poster, "Visual Studies as Media Studies," 67.
2. Ibid., 68.
3. See Sterne, "The Computer Race Goes to Class."
4. Mirzoeff, *The Visual Culture Reader*, 6.
5. Ibid., 3.
6. See Bolter, Grusin, and NetLibrary Inc., *Remediation*, for an example of new media criticism and theory that stresses the foundations of new media in old media practices, concepts, and vocabularies.
7. Steve Jones, *Cybersociety 2.0*.
8. Yoshino, *Covering*, 183.
9. Courtney, *Hollywood Fantasies of Miscegenation*, 113.
10. Yoshino, *Covering*, 173.
11. The wide popularity of YouTube, blogs, and digital zines attest to the ways that cinema and the literary and journalistic arts have come to include amateur or nonprofessional content, thus transforming the notion of the media professional.

Bibliography

Aaseng, Nathan. *Navajo Code Talkers*. New York: Walker, 1992.

Aidoo, Ama Ata. *Our Sister Killjoy*. Essex: Longman, 1977.

Alexander, Donnell. "Cool like Me: Are Black People Cooler than White People?" In *Shiny Adidas Tracksuits and the Death of Camp*, ed. *Might* magazine. New York: Berkley Boulevard, 1988.

Alkalimat, Abdul. "Eblack: A 21st Century Challenge." *Mots Pluriels* 19 (2001).

Anderson, Benedict. *Imagined Communities*. London: Verso, 1991.

Ang, Ien. *Living Room Wars: Rethinking Media Audiences for a Postmodern World*. New York: Routledge, 1996.

———. *On Not Speaking Chinese: Living between Asia and the West*. London: Routledge, 2001.

Ansen, David. "Murder on the Spielberg Express." *Newsweek*, July 1, 2002. http://www.mscnb.com/news/841231.asp#BODY (accessed February 5, 2003).

Anzaldúa, Gloria. *Borderlands/La Frontera*. 2nd ed. San Francisco: Aunt Lute Books, 1999.

Aoyagi, Caroline. "'Asian or Gay?' Piece in 'Details' Magazine Angers AA Community." *Pacific Citizen*, April 2–15, 2004, 1, 4.

———. "Buddhists Decry Use of Bodhisattva Images on Swimwear." *Pacific Citizen*, May 21–June 3, 2004.

Bahng, Aimee. "Queering the Matrix: When Survival Is at Stake." Paper presented at "Qgrad: A Graduate Student Conference on Sexuality and Gender," UCLA, Los Angeles, Calif., 2003.

Bal, Mieke. "Visual Essentialism and the Object of Visual Culture." *Journal of Visual Culture* 2 (2003): 5–32.

Banet Weiser, Sarah. "Consuming Race on Nickelodeon." Unpublished manuscript. 2005.

Barlow, John Perry. "A Declaration of the Independence of Cyberspace." http://homes.eff.org/~barlow/Declaration-Final.html.

Barthes, Roland, and Stephen Heath. *Music/Image/Text*. New York: Hill and Wang, 1977.

———. *Mythologies*. New York: Hill and Wang, 1972.

———. *S/Z*. New York: Hill and Wang, 1974.

Baudrillard, Jean. *Simulacra and Simulation*. Ann Arbor: University of Michigan Press, 1994.

Beltrán, Mary. "The Hollywood Latina Body as Site of Social Struggle: Media Constructions of Stardom and Jennifer Lopez's 'Cross-Over Butt.'" *Quarterly Review of Film and Video* 19, no. 1 (2002): 71–86.

Berger, John. *Ways of Seeing*. London: British Broadcasting Corporation, 1972.

Bird, S. Elizabeth. *The Audience in Everyday Life: Living in a Media World*. New York: Routledge, 2003.

Boliek, Bruce. "Powell Leaves Mixed Legacy as FCC Chair." *Hollywood Reporter*, January 22, 2005.

Bolter, J. David, Richard Grusin, and NetLibrary Inc. *Remediation: Understanding New Media*. Cambridge: MIT Press, 1999.

Bowlby, Rachel. *Carried Away: The Invention of Modern Shopping*. New York: Columbia University Press, 2001.

———. *Just Looking: Consumer Culture in Dreiser, Gissing, and Zola*. New York: Methuen, 1985.

Brown, Tamar. "Cooking and Computers: Reconsidering New Media Forms." Paper presented at the Media and Cultural Studies Colloquium, University of Wisconsin, Madison, 2003.

Bukatman, Scott. *Terminal Identity: The Virtual Subject in Postmodern Science Fiction*. Durham, N.C.: Duke University Press, 1993.

Burnett, Robert, and P. David Marshall. *Web Theory: An Introduction*. New York: Routledge, 2003.

Cartright, Lisa. "Film and the Digital in Visual Studies: Film Studies in the Era of Convergence." In *The Visual Culture Reader*, ed. Nicholas Mirzoeff, 2002.

———. *Screening the Body: Tracing Medicine's Visual Culture*. Minneapolis: University of Minnesota Press, 1995.

Cassell, Justine, and Henry Jenkins. *From Barbie to Mortal Kombat: Gender and Computer Games*. Cambridge: MIT Press, 1998.

Castells, Manuel. *End of Millennium*. 2nd ed. Malden, Mass.: Blackwell, 2000.

———. *The Rise of the Network Society*. 2nd ed. Malden, Mass.: Blackwell, 2000.

Cheng, Vincent John. *Inauthentic: The Anxiety over Culture and Identity*. New Brunswick, N.J.: Rutgers University Press, 2004.

Chinn, Sarah E. *Technology and the Logic of American Racism: A Cultural History of the Body as Evidence*. Critical Research in Material Culture. New York: Continuum, 2000.

Chow, Rey. *Ethics after Idealism: Theory, Culture, Ethnicity, Reading*. Theories of Contemporary Culture, vol. 20. Bloomington: Indiana University Press, 1998.

Chuh, Kandice. *Imagine Otherwise: On Asian Americanist Critique*. Durham, N.C.: Duke University Press, 2003.

Chun, Wendy. *Control and Freedom: Power and Paranoia in the Age of Fiber Optics.* Cambridge: MIT Press, 2005.

Courtney, Susan. *Hollywood Fantasies of Miscegenation: Spectacular Narratives of Gender and Race, 1903–1967.* Princeton, N.J.: Princeton University Press, 2005.

Crenshaw, Kimberle Williams. "Mapping the Margins: Intersectionality, Identity Politics, and Violence against Women of Color." In *Critical Race Theory: The Key Writings That Formed the Movement,* ed. Kimberle Crenshaw, Neil Gotanda, Gary Peller, and Kendall Thomas, 357–83. New York: New Press, 1995.

Cruz, Jon. "From Farce to Tragedy: Reflections on the Reification of Race at Century's End." In *Mapping Multiculturalism,* ed. Avery Gordon and Christopher Newfield, 19–39. Minneapolis: University of Minnesota Press, 1996.

Currier, Dianne. "Assembling Bodies in Cyberspace: Technologies, Bodies, and Sexual Difference." In *Reload: Rethinking Women + Cyberculture,* ed. Mary Flanagan and Austin Booth. Cambridge: MIT Press, 2002.

Danet, Brenda. *Cyberpl@y: Communicating Online.* New Technologies/New Cultures. Oxford: Berg, 2001.

Darley, Andrew. *Visual Digital Culture: Surface Play and Spectacle in New Media Genres.* Edited by Roger Silverstone et al. Sussex Studies in Culture and Communication. New York: Routledge, 2000.

Davé, Shilpa. "Apu's Brown Voice: Cultural Inflection and South Asian Accents." In *East Main Street: Asian American Popular Culture,* ed. Shilpa Davé, Leilani Nishime, and Tasha Oren. New York: New York University Press, 2005.

DeAngelis, Michael. *Gay Fandom and Crossover Stardom: James Dean, Mel Gibson, and Keanu Reeves.* Durham, N.C.: Duke University Press, 2001.

Doyle, Julie, and Kate O'Riordan. "Virtually Visible: Female Cyberbodies and the Medical Imagination." In *Reload: Rethinking Women + Cyberculture,* ed. Mary Flanagan and Austin Booth. Cambridge: MIT Press, 2002.

Doyle, Richard. *Wetwares: Experiments in Postvital Living.* Minneapolis: University of Minnesota Press, 2003.

Druckrey, Timothy. *Ars Electronica: Facing the Future; A Survey of Two Decades.* Electronic Culture: History, Theory, Practice. Cambridge: MIT Press, 1999.

Dyer, Richard. *White.* London: Routledge, 1997.

Dyer, Richard, and Paul MacDonald. *Stars.* New ed. London: BFI Publishing, 1998.

Ebert, Roger. "*The Matrix Reloaded.*" *Chicago Sun-Times,* May 14, 2003.

Eglash, Ron. *Appropriating Technology: Vernacular Science and Social Power.* Minneapolis: University of Minnesota Press, 2004.

———. "Race, Sex, and Nerds: From Black Geeks to Asian American Hipsters." *Social Text* 20, no. 2 (2002): 49–64.

Elkins, James. *Pictures of the Body: Pain and Metamorphosis.* Stanford, Calif.: Stanford University Press, 1999.

Elmer, Greg. *Profiling Machines: Mapping the Personal Information Economy.* Cambridge: MIT Press, 2004.

Evans, Jessica, and Stuart Hall. *Visual Culture: The Reader.* Thousand Oaks, Calif.: Sage, 1999.

Everett, Anna. "Click This: From Analog Dreams to Digital Realities." *Cinema Journal* 43, no. 3 (2004): 93–98.

Farred, Grant. *What's My Name? Black Vernacular Intellectuals*. Minneapolis: University of Minnesota Press, 2003.

Filiciak, Miroslaw. "Hyperidentities: Postmodern Identity Patterns in Massively Multiplayer Online Role-Playing Games." In *The Video Game Theory Reader*, ed. Mark J. P. Wolf and Bernard Perro, 87–102. New York: Routledge, 2003.

Finnegan, Cara A. *Picturing Poverty: Print Culture and FSA Photographs*. Washington, D.C.: Smithsonian Books, 2003.

Fiske, John. *Reading the Popular*. New York: Routledge, 1989.

Flanagan, Mary. "The Bride Stripped Bare to Her Data: Information Flow and Digibodies." In *Data Made Flesh: Embodying Information*, ed. Robert Mitchell and Phillip Thurtle. New York: Routledge, 2004.

———. "Mobile Identities, Digital Stars, and Post Cinematic Selves." *Wide Angle* 21, no. 1 (1999): 77–93.

Flanagan, Mary, and Austin Booth, eds. *Reload: Rethinking Women + Cyberculture*. Cambridge: MIT Press, 2002.

Foster, Tom. *The Souls of Cyberfolk: Posthumanism as Vernacular Theory*. Minneapolis: University of Minnesota Press, 2005.

———. "The Transparency of the Interface: Reality Hacking and Fantasies of Resistance." In *The Matrix Trilogy: Cyberpunk Reloaded*, ed. Stacy Gillis. London: Wallflower Press, 2005.

Foucault, Michel. "What Is an Author?" In *The Foucault Reader*, ed. Paul Rabinow, 101–20. New York: Pantheon, 1984.

Fusco, Coco. *The Bodies That Were Not Ours and Other Writings*. New York: Routledge, 2001.

Fusco, Coco, and Brian Wallis. *Only Skin Deep: Changing Visions of the American Self*. New York: Harry N. Abrams, 2003.

Gajjala, Radhika. *Cyber Selves: Feminist Ethnographies of South Asian Women*. Walnut Creek, Calif.: AltaMira Press, 2004.

Galloway, Alexander R. *Gaming: Essays on Algorithmic Culture*. Minneapolis: University of Minnesota Press, 2006.

———. *Protocol: How Control Exists after Decentralization*. Cambridge: MIT Press, 2004.

Gans, Herbert J. *Popular Culture and High Culture: An Analysis and Evaluation of Taste*. New York: Basic Books, 1999.

Georges, Eugenia, and Lisa M. Mitchell. "Baby Talk: The Rhetorical Production of Maternal and Fetal Selves." In *Body Talk: Rhetoric, Technology, Reproduction*, ed. Mary M. Lay, Laura J. Gurak, Clare Gravon, and Cynthia Myntti, 184–203. Madison: University of Wisconsin Press, 2000.

Ghosh, Rishab Aiyer, ed. *Code: Collaborative Ownership and the Digital Economy*. Cambridge: MIT Press, 2005.

Gibson, William. *Neuromancer*. New York: Ace Science Fiction Books, 1984.

———. *Pattern Recognition*. New York: G. P. Putnam's Sons, 2003.

Gilman, Sander. "Black Bodies, White Bodies: Toward an Iconography of Female Sexuality in Late Nineteenth-Century Art, Medicine, and Literature." In *Race, Writing, and Difference*, ed. Henry Louis Gates, 223–61. Chicago: University of Chicago Press, 1985.

Gilroy, Paul. *Against Race: Imagining Political Culture beyond the Color Line*. Cambridge: Belknap Press, 2000.

Ginsburg, Faye. "Screen Memories and Entangled Technologies: Resignifying Indigenous Lives." In *Multiculturalism, Postcoloniality, and Transnational Media*, ed. Ella Shohat and Robert Stam, 77–98. New Brunswick, N.J.: Rutgers University Press, 2003.

Golub, Mark. "History Died for Our Sins: Guilt and Responsibility in Hollywood Redemption Histories." *Journal of American Culture* 21, no. 3 (1998): 29–41.

Gonzalez, Jennifer. "The Appended Subject: Race and Identity as Digital Assemblage." In *Race in Cyberspace*, ed. Beth Kolko, Lisa Nakamura, and Gil Rodman. New York: Routledge, 2000.

Gray, Herman. *Watching "Race": Television and the Struggle for Blackness*. Minneapolis: University of Minnesota Press, 1995.

Gunning, Tom. "Tracing the Individual Body: Photography, Detectives, and Early Cinema." In *Cinema and the Invention of Modern Life*, ed. Leo Charney and Vanessa R. Schwartz, 15–45. Berkeley: University of California Press, 1995.

Hall, Stuart. "Introduction: Who Needs 'Identity'?" In *Questions of Cultural Identity*, ed. Stuart Hall and Paul du Gay, 1–17. London: Sage, 1996.

Hamamoto, Darrell Y. *Monitored Peril: Asian Americans and the Politics of TV Representation*. Minneapolis: University of Minnesota Press, 1994.

———. "White and Wong: Race, Porn, and the World Wide Web." In *Image Ethics in the Digital Age*, ed. Larry P. Gross, John Stuart Katz, and Jay Ruby, 247–67. Minneapolis: University of Minnesota Press, 2003.

Hammonds, Evelyn. "New Technologies of Race." In *Processed Lives: Gender and Technology in Everyday Life*, ed. Jennifer Terry, 108–21. New York: Routledge, 1997.

Hansen, Mark B. N. *New Philosophy for New Media*. Cambridge: MIT Press, 2004.

Haraway, Donna. *Modest_Witness@Second_Millennium.FemaleMan©_Meets_Onco-Mouse™: Feminism and Technoscience*. New York: Routledge, 1997.

———. "The Persistence of Vision." In *The Visual Culture Reader*, ed. Nick Mirzoeff, 677–84. New York: Routledge, 2001.

———. *Simians, Cyborgs, and Women: The Reinvention of Nature*. New York: Routledge, 1991.

Hargittai, Eszter. "Digital Inequality: From Unequal Access to Differentiated Use." In *Social Inequality*, ed. Kathryn Neckerman. New York: Russell Sage Foundation, 2004.

———. "Internet Access and Use in Context." *New Media and Society* 6, no. 1 (2004): 137–43.

Hayles, Katherine. *How We Became Posthuman: Virtual Bodies in Cybernetics, Literature, and Informatics*. Chicago: University of Chicago Press, 1999.

Hester-Williams, Kim. "The Reification of Race in Cyberspace: African American Expressive Culture, FUBU and a Search for Beloved Community on the Net." *Mots Pluriels* 19 (2001). http://motspluriels.arts.uwa.edu.au/MP1901khw.html (accessed January 3, 2002).

Hoffman, Donna L., and Thomas P. Novak. "Bridging the Racial Divide on the Internet." *Science* 280, no. 5362 (1998): 390–91.

Hofstadter, Douglas R., and Daniel Clement Dennett. *The Mind's I: Fantasies and Reflections on Self and Soul*. New York: Bantam, 1982.

Hosein, Ian. "An Open Letter to the ICAO: A Second Report on 'Towards an International Infrastructure for Surveillance of Movement.'" 2004.

Jameson, Fredric. "Fear and Loathing in Globalization." *New Left Review* 23 (2003): 105–14.

Jenkins, Henry. "Quentin Tarantino's Star Wars? Digital Cinema, Media Convergence, and Participatory Culture." In *Rethinking Media Change: The Aesthetics of Transition*, ed. David Thorburn, Henry Jenkins, and Brad Seawell. Cambridge: MIT Press, 2003.

Jenkins, Sacha, Elliott Wilson, Chairman Jefferson Mao, Gabriel Alvarez, and Brent Rollins. *Ego Trip's Big Book of Racism*. New York: Harper Collins, 2002.

Johnson, Steven. *Interface Culture*. New York: Basic Books, 1997.

Jones, Amelia. *The Feminism and Visual Culture Reader*. In Sight. New York: Routledge, 2003.

Jones, Steve. *Cybersociety 2.0: Revisiting Computer-Mediated Communication and Community*. New Media Cultures. Thousand Oaks, Calif.: Sage Publications, 1998.

Kapsalis, Terry. "Making Babies the American Girl Way." In *Domain Errors! Cyberfeminist Practices*, ed. Maria Fernandez, Faith Wilding, and Michelle M. Wright, 223–34. New York: Autonomedia, 2002.

Kelley, Robin D. G. *Yo Mama's Disfunktional! Fighting the Culture Wars in Urban America*. Boston: Beach Press, 1997.

Kendall, Lori. *Hanging Out in the Virtual Pub: Masculinities and Relationships Online*. Berkeley: University of California Press, 2002.

Kingston, Maxine Hong. *The Woman Warrior: Memoirs of a Girlhood among Ghosts*. Vintage International ed. New York: Vintage Books, 1989.

Koerber, Amy. "Postmodernism, Resistance, and Cyberspace: Making Rhetorical Spaces for Feminist Mothers on the Web." *Women's Studies in Communication* 24, no. 2 (2001): 218–40.

Kuhn, Annette. "Introduction: Cultural Theory and Science Fiction Cinema." In *Alien Zone: Cultural Theory and Contemporary Science Fiction Cinema*, ed. Annette Kuhn, 1–12. London: Verso, 1990.

Landow, George P. *Hypertext 2.0*. Rev. and amplified ed. Baltimore, Md.: Johns Hopkins University Press, 1997.

Lee, Rachel C., and Sau-ling Cynthia Wong. *Asian America.net: Ethnicity, Nationalism, and Cyberspace*. New York: Routledge, 2003.

Lee, Robert G. *Orientals: Asian Americans in Popular Culture*. Philadelphia: Temple University Press, 1999.

Lesy, Michael, and Charles Van Schaick. *Wisconsin Death Trip*. New York: Anchor Books, 1991.

Liu, Alan. *The Laws of Cool: Knowledge Work and the Culture of Information*. Chicago: University of Chicago Press, 2004.

Lockard, Joe. "Resisting Cyber-English." *Bad Subjects: Political Education for Everyday Life*, no. 24 (1996). http://eserver.org/bs/24/lockard.html (accessed June 12, 2007).

Lovink, Geert. *Dark Fiber: Tracking Critical Internet Culture*. Electronic Culture: History, Theory, Practice. Cambridge: MIT Press, 2002.

Lowe, Lisa. *Immigrant Acts: On Asian American Cultural Politics*. Durham, N.C.: Duke University Press, 1996.

Manovich, Lev. "Image after *The Matrix*." http://www.manovich.net (accessed July 5, 2005).

———. *The Language of New Media*. Cambridge: MIT Press, 2001.

Matrix, Sidney Eve. *Cyberpop: Digital Lifestyles and Commodity Culture*. New York: Routledge, 2006.

McCaughey, Martha, and Michael D. Ayers, eds. *Cyberactivism: Online Activism in Theory and Practice*. New York: Routledge, 2003.

McChesney, Robert W., with Ellen Meiksins Wood and John Bellamy Foster. *Capitalism and the Information Age: The Political Economy of the Global Communication Revolution*. New York: Monthly Review Press, 1998.

McLaine, Steven. "Ethnic Online Communities: Between Profit and Purpose." In *Cyberactivism: Online Activism in Theory and Practice*, ed. Martha McCaughey and Michael D. Ayers. New York: Routledge, 2003.

McPherson, Tara. "I'll Take My Stand in Dixie-Net." In *Race in Cyberspace*, ed. Beth Kolko, Lisa Nakamura, and Gil Rodman, 117–31. New York: Routledge, 2000.

———. "Reload: Liveness, Mobility, and the Web." In *The Visual Culture Reader*, ed. Nicholas Mirzoeff, 458–70. New York: Routledge, 2002.

Michaels, Eric. *Bad Aboriginal Art: Tradition, Media, and Technological Horizons*. Theory Out of Bounds, vol. 3. Minneapolis: University of Minnesota Press, 1994.

Mirzoeff, Nicholas. "Invisible Empire: Embodied Spectacle and Abu Ghraib." *Radical History Review*, no. 95 (2005): 21–44.

———. *The Visual Culture Reader*. 2nd ed. New York: Routledge, 2002.

Mitra, Ananda. "Virtual Commonality: Looking for India on the Internet." In *The Cybercultures Reader*, ed. David Bell and Barbara M. Kennedy, 676–94. New York: Routledge, 2000.

Mok, Harry. *Testing Out My A-Dar: Trying to Pick Out Who Is What*. http://www.inthefray.com/200203/imagine/same12/same12.html.

Morrison, Toni. *Playing in the Dark: Blackness and the American Literary Imagination*. New York: Vintage, 1992.

Nakamura, Lisa. "Cultural Difference, Theory, and Cyberculture Studies: A Case of Mutual Repulsion." In *Critical Cyberculture Studies: Current Terrains, Future Directions*, ed. David Silver. New York: New York University Press, 2006.

———. *Cybertypes: Race, Identity, and Ethnicity on the Internet*. New York: Routledge, 2002.

Nam, Victoria. *Yell-Oh Girls! Emerging Voices Explore Culture, Identity, and Growing Up Asian American*. New York: Quill, 2001.

Nelson, Alondra. "Introduction: Future Texts." *Social Text* 20, no. 2 (2002): 1–15.

Nelson, Alondra, with Tuy Tu and Alicia Hines. *Technicolor: Race, Technology, and Everyday Life*. New York: New York University Press, 2001.

Ngugi wa Thiongo. *Moving the Centre: The Struggle for Cultural Freedoms*. Portsmouth: James Currey/Heinemann, 1993.

Noriega, Chon A. *Shot in America: Television, the State, and the Rise of Chicano Cinema*. Minneapolis: University of Minnesota Press, 2000.

Oliver, Kelly. *Witnessing: Beyond Recognition*. Minneapolis: University of Minnesota Press, 2001.

Omi, Michael. "Racialization in the Post–Civil Rights Era." In *Mapping Multiculturalism*, ed. Avery Gordon and Christopher Newfield, 178–86. Minneapolis: University of Minnesota Press, 1996.

Omi, Michael, and Howard Winant. "Racial Formation." In *Race Critical Theories: Text and Context*, ed. Philomena Essed and David Theo Goldberg, 123–45. Malden, Mass.: Blackwell Publishers, 2002.

———. *Racial Formation in the United States: From the 1960s to the 1990s*. 2nd ed. New York: Routledge, 1994.

Palumbo-Liu, David. *Asian/American: Historical Crossings of a Racial Frontier*. Stanford, Calif.: Stanford University Press, 1999.

Parks, Lisa. "Satellite and Cyber Visualities: Analyzing 'Digital Earth.'" In *The Visual Culture Reader*, ed. Nicholas Mirzoeff, 279–92. New York: Routledge, 2002.

Parrenas, Rhacel. *Servants of Globalization*. Stanford, Calif.: Stanford University Press, 2001.

Persson, Per. "Cinema and Computers: Spatial Practices within Emergent Visual Technologies." In *Technospaces: Inside the New Media*, ed. Sally Munt, 38–55. New York: Continuum, 2001.

Petchesky, Rosalind Pollack. "Fetal Images: The Power of Visual Culture in the Politics of Reproduction." In *Reproductive Technologies*, ed. Michelle Stanworth. Minneapolis: University of Minnesota Press, 1987.

Phelan, Peggy. *Unmarked: The Politics of Performance*. New York: Routledge, 1993.

Pinney, Christopher, and Nicolas Peterson. *Photography's Other Histories*. Objects/Histories. Durham, N.C.: Duke University Press, 2003.

Pisters, Patricia. *The Matrix of Visual Culture: Working with Deleuze in Film Theory*. Cultural Memory in the Present. Stanford, Calif.: Stanford University Press, 2003.

Poster, Mark. "Visual Studies as Media Studies." *Journal of Visual Culture* 1, no. 1 (2002): 67–70.

———. *What's the Matter with the Internet?* Minneapolis: University of Minnesota Press, 2001.

Prashad, Vijay. *Everybody Was Kung Fu Fighting: Afro-Asian Connections and the Myth of Cultural Purity*. Boston: Beacon Press, 2001.

Rehak, Bob. "Playing at Being: Psychoanalysis and the Avatar." In *The Video Game Theory Reader*, ed. Mark J. P. Wolf and Bernard Perron, 103–27. New York: Routledge, 2003.

Rodowick, David Norman. *Reading the Figural; or, Philosophy after the New Media*. Post-contemporary Interventions. Durham, N.C.: Duke University Press, 2001.

Rodriguez, Richard. *Hunger of Memory: The Education of Richard Rodriguez; An Autobiography*. New York: Bantam Books, 1983.

Rushdie, Salman. "Damme, This Is the Oriental Scene for You!" *New Yorker*, June 23 and 30, 1997, 50–61.

———. *Imaginary Homelands*. London: Penguin, 1991.

Sandoval, Chela. *Methodology of the Oppressed*. Theory Out of Bounds, vol. 18. Minneapolis: University of Minnesota Press, 2000.

Sardar, Ziauddin. "Alt.civilizations.faq: Cyberspace as the Darker Side of the West." In *The Cybercultures Reader*, ed. David Bell and Barbara M. Kennedy, 732–52. New York: Routledge, 2000.

Sassen, Saskia. *Globalization and Its Discontents: Essays on the New Mobility of People and Money*. New York: New Press, 1998.

Scheper-Hughes, Nancy. "The Global Traffic in Human Organs." *Current Anthropology* 41, no. 2 (2000): 191–221.

Scott, A. O. "*The Matrix: Revolutions*." *New York Times*, November 5, 2003.

Shaviro, Steven. *Connected; or, What It Means to Live in the Network Society*. Electronic Mediations, vol. 9. Minneapolis: University of Minnesota Press, 2003.

Silver, David, ed. *Critical Cyberculture Studies: Current Terrains, Future Directions*. New York: New York University Press, 2006.

———. "Looking Backwards, Looking Forwards: Cybercultures Studies, 1990–2000." In *Web.studies: Rewiring Media Studies for the Digital Age*, ed. David Gauntlett, 19–30. London: Arnold, 2000.

———. "'Shop Online!': Advertising Female Teen Cyberculture." In *Society Online: The Internet in Context*, ed. Philip E. Howard and Steve Jones, 157–71. Thousand Oaks, Calif.: Sage, 2004.

———. "Theglobe.com: Image, Anti-image, and the Shifting Languages of New Media." Paper presented at the American Studies Association Conference, Houston, Texas, 2002.

Silverman, Kaja. "Back to the Future." *Camera Obscura*, no. 27 (September 1991): 109–32.

Slater, Don. "Domestic Photography and Digital Culture." In *The Photographic Image in Digital Culture*, ed. Martin Lister, 129–46. New York: Routledge, 1995.

Solnit, Rebecca. *River of Shadows: Eadweard Muybridge and the Technological Wild West*. New York: Viking, 2003.

Sontag, Susan. *Regarding the Pain of Others*. New York: Farrar, Straus and Giroux, 2003.

———. "Regarding the Torture of Others." *New York Times Magazine*, May 23, 2004.

Sparke, Penny. *As Long As It's Pink: The Sexual Politics of Taste*. San Francisco: Pandora, 1995.

Spooner, Tom. *Asian-Americans and the Internet: The Young and the Connected*. Pew Internet and American Life Project, http://www.pewinternet.org.

Spooner, Tom, and Lee Rainie. *African-Americans and the Internet*. www.pewinternet.org.

———. *Hispanics and the Internet*. Pew Internet and American Life Project, http://www.pewinternet.org.

Sprague, Stephen F. "Yoruba Photography: How the Yoruba See Themselves." In *Photography's Other Histories*, ed. Christopher Pinney and Nicolas Peterson. Durham, N.C.: Duke University Press, 2003.

Springer, Claudia. "Playing It Cool in the Matrix." In *The Matrix Trilogy: Cyberpunk Reloaded*, ed. Stacy Gillis, 89–100. London: Wallflower Press, 2005.

Squires, Judith. "Fabulous Feminist Futures and the Lure of Cyberspace." In *The Cybercultures Reader*, ed. David Bell and Barbara M. Kennedy, 360–73. London: Routledge, 2000.

Stabile, Carol A. *Feminism and the Technological Fix*. New York: St. Martin's Press, 1994.

Star, Susan Leigh. "From Hestia to Homepage: Feminism and the Concept of Home in Cyberspace." In *The Cybercultures Reader*, ed. David Bell and Barbara M. Kennedy, 632–43. New York: Routledge, 2000.

Stephenson, Neal. *Cryptonomicon*. New York: Avon Press, 2002.

Sterne, Jonathan. *The Audible Past: Cultural Origins of Sound Reproduction*. Durham, N.C.: Duke University Press, 2003.

———. "The Computer Race Goes to Class: How Computers in Schools Helped Shape the Racial Topography of the Internet." In *Race in Cyberspace*, ed. Beth Kolko, Lisa Nakamura, and Gil Rodman, 191–212. New York: Routledge, 2000.

———. "Digital Media and Disciplinarity." *Information Society* 21, no. 5 (Fall 2005): 249–60.

Stewart, Susan. *On Longing: Narratives of the Miniature, the Gigantic, the Souvenir, the Collection*. Durham: Duke University Press, 1993.

Stone, Allucquère Rosanne. *The War of Desire and Technology at the Close of the Mechanical Age*. Cambridge: MIT Press, 1995.

Stratton, Jon. "Cyberspace and the Globalization of Culture." In *The Cybercultures Reader*, ed. David Bell and Barbara M. Kennedy, 721–31. New York: Routledge, 2000.

Stross, Randall. "After 20 Years, Finally Capitalizing on Cool." *New York Times*, January 16, 2005, B5.

Tal, Kali. *The Unbearable Whiteness of Being: African American Critical Theory and Cyberculture*. http://www.gse.buffalo.edu/FAS/Bromley/classes/socprac/readings/Kali-Tal-unbearable.htm (accessed February 9, 2005).

Taylor, T. L. "Multiple Pleasures: Women and Online Gaming." *Convergence* 9, no. 1 (2003): 21–46.

Thacker, Eugene. *Biomedia*. Minneapolis: University of Minnesota Press, 2004.

Thomas, Graham, and Sally Wyatt. "Access Is Not the Only Problem: Using and Controlling the Internet." In *Technology and In/Equality: Questioning the Information Society*, ed. Sally Wyatt, 21–45. New York: Routledge, 2000.

Torres, Sasha. *Living Color: Race and Television in the United States*. Console-ing Passions. Durham, N.C.: Duke University Press, 1998.

Tu, Thuy Linh Nguyen. "Good Politics, Great Porn: Untangling Race, Sex, and Technology in Asian American Cultural Production." In *Asian America.net: Ethnicity, Nationalism, and Cyberspace*, ed. Rachel C. Lee and Sau-ling Wong, 267–80. New York: Routledge, 2003.

Turkle, Sherry. *Life on the Screen: Identity in the Age of the Internet*. New York: Simon and Schuster, 1995.

Turner, Fred. *From Counterculture to Cyberculture: Stewart Brand, the Whole Earth Network, and the Rise of Digital Utopianism*. Chicago: University of Chicago Press, 2006.

U.S. Census. "Census 2000 Sf3 Sample Data, Table Pct63d." 2000.

Wakeford, Nina. "Networking Women and Grrls with Information/Communication Technology." In *The Cybercultures Reader*, ed. David Bell and Barbara M. Kennedy. London: Routledge, 2000.

Walker, John A., and Sarah Chaplin. *Visual Culture: An Introduction*. New York: St. Martin's Press, 1997.

Walker, Rob. "Hyperreality Hobbying." *New York Times Magazine*, February 20, 2005, 22.

———. "Sophisticated Baby." *New York Times Magazine*, July 24, 2005, 20.

Warschauer, Mark. "Language, Identity, and the Internet." In *Race in Cyberspace*, ed. Beth Kolko, Lisa Nakamura, and Gil Rodman, 151–70. New York: Routledge, 2000.

———. "Reconceptualizing the Digital Divide." *First Monday*. http://www.firstmonday.org/issues/issue7.7/warschauer/index.html (accessed July 2005).

———. *Technology and Social Inclusion: Rethinking the Digital Divide*. Cambridge: MIT Press, 2003.

Weil, Elizabeth. "The Modernist Nursery." *New York Times Magazine*, November 26, 2004, 71–75.

West, Cornel. *Race Matters*. Boston: Beacon Press, 1993.

Williams, Mark. "Closely Belated? Thoughts on Real-Time Media Publics and *Minority Report*." Paper presented at the Futures of American Studies Institute, Dartmouth College, 2004.

Williams, Patricia J. *The Rooster's Egg*. Cambridge: Harvard University Press, 1995.

Wood, Aylish. "'The Metaphysical Fabric That Binds Us': Proprioceptive Coherence and Performative Space in *Minority Report*." *New Review of Film and Television Studies* 2, no. 1 (2004): 1–18.

Wright, Michelle. "Finding a Place in Cyberspace: Black Women, Technology, and Identity." *Frontiers: A Journal of Women Studies* 26, no. 1 (2005): 48–59.

Yoshino, Kenji. *Covering: The Hidden Assault on Our Civil Rights*. New York: Random House, 2006.

Publication History

Earlier versions of chapter 2 were previously published as "Alllooksame? Mediating Asian American Visual Cultures of Race on the Web," in *East Main Street: Asian American Popular Culture,* ed. Shilpa Davé, Leilani Nishime, and Tasha Oren (New York: New York University Press, 2005); and "Alllooksame? Mediating Visual Cultures of Race on the Web," *Iowa Journal of Cultural Studies* (2002): 73–84. Reprinted with permission.

Portions of chapter 3 were previously published as "The Multiplication of Difference in Post Millennial Cyberpunk Film: The Visual Culture of Race in the Matrix Trilogy," in *The Matrix Trilogy: Cyberpunk Reloaded,* ed. Stacy Gillis (London: Wallflower Press, 2005), 126–37; and "Interview with Lisa Nakamura," by Tom Leeser, in *Viralnet,* an online publication of the Center for Integrated Media at the California Institute of the Arts, Valencia, California, 2004. Reprinted with permission.

Portions of chapter 5 were previously published as "Interrogating the Digital Divide: The Political Economy of Race and Commerce in New Media," in *Society Online: The Internet in Context,* ed. Phil Howard and Steve Jones (London: Sage Press, 2003), 7–83. Reprinted with permission.

Electronic Mediations

Katherine Hayles, Mark Poster, and Samuel Weber, series editors

Index

Abercrombie and Fitch controversy, 186–87, 194, 199
Abu Ghraib photographs, 115–16, 167–68
Achebe, Chinua, 87, 90
acronyms, 153
Active Worlds (3-D space), 39
addiction, Internet, 205
advanced reproductive technologies (ART), 140
African Americans: and computer use, 97–98; as cool, 100, 103, 112–13, 116, 128; in film, 98–100, 103; in gaming, 18–19; and Internet, 175, 179, 181–84, 200, 224n13; in literature, 108
Aidoo, Ama Ata, 90
AIM buddies: defined, 42; ethnic, 53, 69; and identity, 30–31, 56, 63; as liminal, 45; loading time, 43–44; purpose, 42, 44; and self-representation, 52; as tacky, 68–69; term, 213n5; types, 42–43
Alexander, Donnell, 112

Alkalimat, Abdul, 224n13
alllooksame.com, 31, 70–94, 206; home page, 79; popularity of, 82–83, 94; postings on, 80–82; and race, 80, 82; responses to, 78–80; test questions, 79, 81, 83, 86–87
American Girl dolls, 139–41
Anderson, Benedict, 129
Ang, Ien, 77, 83, 177
Ansen, David, 119
Anzaldúa, Gloria, 90, 125, 216–17n41
AOL Instant Messenger. See AIM buddies
Aoyogi, Caroline, 186
APIHR (Asian Pacific Islanders for Human Rights), 191
Apple iPod. See iPod commercials
Apter, Emily, 6–8
Armstrong, Carol, 6–8
ART (advanced reproductive technologies), 140
art history: and visual culture studies, 6–8, 11
ASCII art, 43, 221n12

Lisa Nakamura is associate professor in the Institute of Communication Research with a joint appointment in Asian American studies at the University of Illinois, Urbana-Champaign. She is author of *Cybertypes: Race, Ethnicity, and Identity on the Internet* and coeditor of *Race in Cyberspace*.